WEST

LIKE

LIGHTNING

WEST

LIKE

LIGHTNING

THE BRIEF, LEGENDARY RIDE OF THE
PONY EXPRESS

JIM DeFELICE

WM

WILLIAM MORROW
An Imprint of HarperCollins *Publishers*

HarperCollins books may be purchased for educational, business, or sales promotional use. For information, please email the Special Markets Department at SPsales@harpercollins.com.

A hardcover edition of this book was published in 2018 by William Morrow, an imprint of HarperCollins Publishers.

FIRST WILLIAM MORROW PAPERBACK EDITION PUBLISHED 2019.

Designed by Leah Carlson-Stanisic

Library of Congress Cataloging-in-Publication Data has been applied for.

ISBN 978-0-06-249678-2

19 20 21 22 23   LSC   10 9 8 7 6 5 4 3 2 1

TO ALL THE RIDERS, PAST, PRESENT, AND TO COME.
AND FOR CHRIS, WHO WOULD HAVE LOVED IT.

CONTENTS

GO!

FORT KEARNY, NEBRASKA TERRITORY

November 7, 1860, 1:10 a.m.[1]—A young man stomps back and forth on the porch of a building at the edge of the fort, nibbling on a cookie and waiting impatiently for a dispatch from St. Louis. A cold, bitter wind whips across the parade ground nearby, pelting him with bits of sod and grit picked off the plain that stretches forever around the camp, the earth as flat and endless here as any spot in the vast interior of the United States. There's a romance to that space, and to the darkness as well, but it's for others to feel. He's here to do a job; his main sensation is adrenaline, and a little bit of fear, mixed with anxious anticipation and a keen desire to get *moving*.

Any other night of the year, the short, sinewy frontier kid pacing in jeans and buckskin jacket would be tucked into bed in his flannels, and dreaming of horses and pretty girls. Officially, anyway. More likely, he'd be at the local saloon—a hovel with a fireplace and ready booze—whooping it up, toasted by eastern tenderfoot travelers and sharing stories of the mountain men he'd met. But any nocturnal doings had to stay quiet, given his employer strictly forbade the consumption of intoxicating liquors and went so far as to ban *cursing*. Most dangerously, the young man's employer—Alexander Majors, one of three partners in the master enterprise—had a habit of showing up on the frontier unexpectedly.

But there'd be no time for carousing this evening. This was election night, with the country's future on the line; would it be Lincoln and disunion? The young man's job was to take the answer west, across the great American desert, for he was a proud employee of the Central Overland California & Pikes Peak Express Company, aka the Pony Express.

Or simply, "the Pony." Already a legend in its own time.

ALEXANDER MAJORS, TOO, WAS A LEGEND, AT LEAST OUT HERE, A LIT-eral whip-cracker, one of the best ox men in the business. As religious as he was hardy, Majors was the third partner of a storied triumvirate: Russell, Majors & Waddell, a company on the brink of becoming a western freighting and delivery empire. Central Overland was a subsidiary of sorts, the brainchild of William H. Russell—the visionary of the team, a raconteur adept at backslapping and political maneuvering, a sometime wizard at finance, and an unabashed booster of the future. "Napoleon of the West" some called him, meaning it a deep compliment. If Russell and Majors were yin and yang, their third partner, William B. Waddell, was an organizer, thinker, and bean counter, a man more comfortable in the office than among the herds, but a critical spot of glue between the partners and the operation.

The young man looked across the porch at his horse, impatient to be going. You couldn't blame him. Kearny was a fort in name only; the word bestowed on it a martial air that didn't fit the reality. Perched at the edge of civilization near the Platte River, Kearny was a four-acre parade ground fenced off by hastily built wooden structures on each side; even the guardhouse was less than imposing.

What made Kearny important was its location, dead in the middle of the path taken by emigrants to Oregon . . . Salt Lake City . . . California . . . the silver and gold fields of Pikes Peak and the Sierra foothills—in fact, Fort Kearny stood in the way of just about any place you wanted to go west of the Missouri. It was a frontier supercenter where nearly anything you needed to continue along the trail—flour, wagon wheels, a nip or two—could be obtained at the fort or the nearby village. You might find a doctor, or at least someone who called himself one; if the local Indians were on the warpath, the soldiers could be roused to protect you.

But its most important offering tonight was the metal device clicking inside the building the Pony rider was pacing around: a telegraph.

A TELEGRAPH?

Pony Express?

Didn't the former kill the latter?

Not exactly.

The *real* story of the Pony Express, like the history of the Old West and America in general, is far more complicated and nuanced than most of us learned in school. The Pony—legendary conqueror of space and time, harbinger of progress—existed on the cusp of great change, partook of that revolution, and both affected and was consumed by it.

The service did one thing: deliver mail and assorted telegraph messages, mostly in connection with the postal service, though the Pony itself was a private concern. And it did it very well and very quickly: ten days from Missouri to Sacramento, a time so quick that grown men practically wept at the idea.

They cheered and hosanna'd and generally loved the notion, even though most wouldn't spend the five bucks it cost to send a letter that whole distance. It was the idea that counted. Debuting in April 1860, the Pony got faster and cheaper as time went on; men applauded even more, but still were reluctant to pay. The *idea* of speed was the intoxicating thing.

America in the fall of 1860—the high point of the Pony, and about midway through its brief eighteen-month existence—was itself a mélange of contradictions. On the brink of Civil War, the country was a heap of technological change: steam power, electricity, flush toilets, and modern sewers—the nation was transforming itself at a pace even faster than in our own time. Bold, rugged, and innovative, the Pony Express was of its time, an almost perfect embodiment of 1860 America. In the end, it succeeded in breaking out of that time, becoming a touchstone not just of the past but equally of the endlessly promising future suggested by speed, information, and distance.

We tend to think of the "Pony" as a narrow, straight line, a clean flash across two-thirds of the country. But the service was more like the multistrand filaments of a lightning storm. There was a main shaft—the bolt of riders relaying across the country from home station to home station at what was then warp speed. At the same time, there were branches and one-offs, occasional detours and even retreats.

The Pony was always part of a larger communication system, with branches and roots that spread out from the main line. Much of the information the Pony carried was meant to be shared, and it was, quickly, with all means available—telegraph, the printing press, word of mouth. Legends and tall tales crisscrossed it all, meandering across the plains and over the mountains, following in the dust of the pony's hoofbeats from first to last. The Pony rider may never have detoured, but the stories often did—and that remains a good part of its charm.

Those of us who have lived through the late twentieth and early twenty-first centuries may think we invented the idea that information is a commodity. The Pony reminds us that not only was information a prized commodity in the nineteenth century, but that it has always been, one prized so highly that humans will drop old habits of gathering or sharing it quite readily if some new method promises more speed or efficiency.

Communication, rapid and sure, was the Pony's original mission. But something else was born with the service, something far less ephemeral than a whisper, more potent than lightning. The Pony became legend embodied even before the first riders set off from St. Joseph, Missouri, and Sacramento, California; the successful arrival of the mail packets at their respective destinations cemented that status.

And the ultimate irony: the Pony was never meant as an end in itself, but rather as a means to another goal. It was only one of several steps toward an empire transporting goods as well as information. It was conceived as a bold venture, but also an ephemeral one.

But lest we get too philosophical and lose the essential thread, not to mention the actual romance of the enterprise, let's return to that impatient kid outside the telegram shack, stomping his feet in a forlorn effort to warm his five-four, one-hundred-and-ten-pound frame as the wind kicked up, and wondering when the hell he can get on with his ride.

EAGER TO BE IN THE SADDLE, THE PONY RIDER—HE WAS MOST LIKELY Richard Cleve, a twenty-one-year-old local boy—went into the office and stood by the soldier handling the telegraph. While the telegraph services on the eastern and western ends of the Pony trail were not technically part of the company, the Pony had a close relationship with them, sharing an office in Sacramento with one and regularly taking messages from lines at or near their stations. These were typically delivered on special cards, carried to places on the route or to offshoots where the lines did not stretch.

Cleve rode this route more than a hundred times, but the November 7 run was special, arranged to bring bulletins about the presidential election held the day before across the prairie and mountains to Fort Churchill (east of present-day Carson City), where another telegraph station would transmit the message to California. To speed things up, additional stations and relays had been placed along the route; where normally horses would be changed every ten miles or so, in most places on this run they would be swapped at five.

Russell had conceived of the run some weeks before, initially thinking they'd give the election results free of charge to every newspaper along the route. He changed his mind about that when his paid customers raised hell. Still, money wasn't the aim of this trip, and at least the basics of the information—i.e., who won—would get out at each stop, if only because the riders weren't good at keeping secrets. Russell wasn't being particularly civic minded when he put the trip together, nor was he rallying for the First Amendment and freedom of the press. His motives were far more practical: any dispatch with the results would announce "Via the Pony Express" or an equivalent phrase, reinforcing the primacy not just of the Pony but of the company that ran it.

Everyone in the country knew this was a momentous election, easily the most important since George Washington's, and far more contested. America had split between sectional and political poles, with slavery as the fault line. There were four candidates: Stephen Douglas, John Breckinridge, Abraham Lincoln, John Bell.

Douglas and Breckinridge were both Democrats; only two years before, Douglas had faced off for the US Senate against Lincoln in Illinois when the latter ran under the banner of the newly formed Republican Party, which had risen from the ashes of the Whigs. Douglas was a moderate Democrat. Popular in Missouri, he favored continued compromise on the issue of slavery—a stance that earned him roughly 30 percent of the vote and 12 of the 303 electoral votes cast. His interparty rival, Breckinridge, was the favorite of Southern Democrats, who wanted slavery extended to all territories, a stance that won him about 18 percent of the vote and 72 electoral votes, thanks to solid majorities in every state of the South.

These days, John Bell is mostly forgotten, but he fared better than Douglas in terms of electoral votes. The Tennessee native had a résumé as thick as an encyclopedia, having served as a congressman, secretary of war, and senator. He had the wisdom to decline the offer of being made Speaker of the House, but lest you think too highly of him, he was the author of the Indian Removal Act, passed in 1830, which set the notorious Trail of Tears in motion. (Because of the act, Cherokee and other eastern tribes were forcibly "relocated" west to present-day Oklahoma, where in time they came into conflict with other tribes and, more disastrously, whites looking for fresh land.)

Bell was considered the compromise version of the old Whig side, advocating the Union "as it is," and the Constitution "as it is"—a sort of distorted mirror image of Douglas. A slave owner, which Douglas was not, he was considered a moderate at a time when radicals were in demand.

Lincoln and his party were on the other side of the divide. They were antislavery, some passionately so. *Banishing the evil from the New World soil*—their words—was a popular sentiment among Republicans, though in that context Lincoln himself was a moderate, never publicly in favor of abolition before or during the campaign. (In fact, it took two-plus years of war to get him to that point, and even then he was cautious about it.)

The South, though, called Lincoln a radical and by the time of the election had decided that anything short of a win by Breckinridge would doom slavery and end the world as they knew it. They had a solution: leave the Union, by force if necessary.

THE KEY ON THE DESK BEGAN TO CLICK. CLEVE DUCKED INTO THE OF-fice, watching the clerk's fingers dance, first to acknowledge that he hadn't fallen asleep, then to scrawl the message on the cards the Pony rider was to carry.

Lincoln.

Lincoln!

"Here!" shouted the soldier to the rider as the key fell silent. "Go!"

LINCOLN AND HIS COUNTRY

The subject of the message had just gone to bed in Springfield, Illinois, some five hundred miles away as the eagle flies. He'd waited past midnight in the state courthouse, sitting with allies, reporters, and acquaintances for the results, both local and countrywide. Even given the extreme turnout—just over 81 percent of the electorate voted, the second-highest turnout of all time (the 1876 election saw a slightly higher percentage)—the results were delivered expeditiously, and Lincoln knew when he walked the half-dozen blocks to his house that he would take on the most difficult job of his life in four months.

Like many of the men who rode for the Pony, Abraham Lincoln had been born on the frontier and moved west to stay with it. In some respects his childhood was similar to that of many; his father was a carpenter and farmer, and young Abe learned as much in the fields as he did from books until he was out on his own. As an adult, he was skinnier, taller, and uglier than most people, let alone the Pony's riders. He educated himself to the point of becoming an accomplished lawyer, albeit one often looked down upon by big-city rivals, to their detriment. By the time of the Pony Express, he had served as a congressman (elected as a Whig, he opposed the Mexican-American War), become a hit on the judicial circuit as a clever attorney, and most famously, run for the US Senate against Douglas in 1858.

Lincoln had launched that campaign with a speech at the state-house that declared a nation divided against itself could not stand. Now he was about to face the test of that proposition.

America in 1860 was split north and south, but also east and west. For the Pony, both of those divisions were important—north and south for political reasons, east and west for practical. Oregon, ad-mitted as a state in February 1859, had just joined California (1850) as America's farthest-west state. A thousand miles separated them from the rest. Surrounding them were five large territories—Washington, Nebraska, Utah, Kansas, and New Mexico—with a few swaths of no-(white)-man's-lands in between.[2]

Of the thirty-four states in the Union, nineteen outlawed slavery. The shift represented a trend that had recently accelerated: when the Constitution was adopted, "slave states" outnumbered "free" eight to five. (Some of these "free" states still had slavery but had relatively small populations of slaves and were in the process of eliminating it.) A period of parity characterized by the Missouri Compromise in 1820 lasted until 1854, when the Kansas-Nebraska Act left the matter to state voters, initiating open warfare in Kansas as partisans jockeyed for power. The political conflict was at a rough standstill in 1860, with neither side able to muster enough support in the US Senate to win ad-mission, despite having organized three different state constitutions.

While slavery was the key issue of the 1860 presidential campaign and the proximate cause of tremendous grief, it was only one aspect of the country. Wracked by a depression in 1857 (called a "panic" at the time, in many ways a more appropriate term), the country was slowly recovering. The boom caused by the 1849 California gold rush had leveled off; smaller gold and silver rushes in Nevada near Virginia City and Caspar as well as Colorado near Pikes Peak provided a fresh impetus for fortune seekers.

Invention was the country's lifeblood. Commercial steam engines had been perfected in Europe during the previous century; their arrival in the United States made many things possible. One of the most important was, like the Pony, a conqueror of space and time: the steam locomotive, which in 1860 had only recently reached as far as the eastern bank of the Missouri River.

It was at St. Joseph's that the Pony and railroad came together. It was here where all full westward runs of the service began, and all full eastward runs ended. The city, hunkered on the eastern shore of the Missouri, was the jumping-off point for the frontier, and its end.

ST. JOE'S

With a population just under ten thousand, St. Joe's punched far above its weight in the regional economy. Part of this was geography—it had a favorable spot on the river, easy to dock at, safe to cross, with the train terminus not far from the ferry. Part of this was its history—it had been established as a trading post more than two decades before by Joseph Robidoux, a legendary fur trader. Robidoux's profession is too poorly appreciated today; the words conjure images of thick-bearded, backwoods ruffians with smoking muskets in one hand and rusted leg traps in the other. But trappers like Robidoux were astute businessmen as well as daring explorers. Dealing furs was a serious, moneymaking business in the eighteenth and nineteenth centuries. Consider: the foundation of the Astor family fortune—the richest family in America before the Civil War, by most accounts—was built on a foundation of fur trading. John Jacob Astor IV might still have gone down bravely with the *Titanic* when it hit the iceberg in 1912, but he would have been in steerage and most likely unremarked if his grandfather hadn't developed rapacious affinity for fur-bearing mammals shortly after the Revolutionary War.

Robidoux was cut from the same pelt. Born in 1783 in St. Louis—French at the time—he was the third Robidoux to be named after Jesus's father, and like those forebears he traded fur. Kicked out of what became Chicago by other traders who didn't want the competition, he prospered on the Mississippi and at Council Bluffs (across from the future Omaha). He did so well that John Jacob Astor's company eventually bought him out, making him a very rich man.

Restless, Robidoux found his way to a bend in the Missouri River south of his old haunts. After the land around his trading post was added to Missouri via the Platte Purchase, he rejected an offer from speculators to buy it outright and instead hired two men to draw up rival street plans for the property's development.

One came up with a layout that would have won an A+ in any urban planning course: symmetrical boulevards, large parks, grand promenades.

The other sliced and diced the geography for maximum profit.

Robidoux went for the bucks.

That was 1843. By 1860, St. Joe's was a bustling fulcrum point between west and east. Stores supplied goods travelers needed, and at a relative bargain: you could pick up a wagon for as little as $65, compared with $100 at Independence, Missouri, farther downriver; a good mule might be had for $30 to $60, compared with Independence's $60. There was a competitive entrepreneurial spirit in the city, demonstrated not only by its role in bringing a railroad in, but also in convincing Russell, Majors, and Waddell to locate the Pony Express there.

In 1859, putting the service together over a route they already ran stagecoaches on, Russell et al. looked for a suitable place to use as the eastern terminus. They already had offices in Lexington and across the river in Leavenworth, Kansas; either could have served the company, as could several other towns on both sides of the river. But even though it wasn't yet in service, the promise of the Pony excited people. St. Joe's, in particular, desired the prestige that would come from having the express company's headquarters inside its limits. The mayor and leading businessmen came together and offered the company an extremely favorable contract, deeding ten lots to the firm as well as making other concessions that would lower the business's costs, such as allowing employees to travel free on the Hannibal & St. Joseph Railroad.

FROM MISSOURI, NOVEMBER 8

The land granted to the Pony Express was on the south side of town, near the railroad terminus and the envisioned train yards. A stable for the stage and the Pony were located on the hill above the railroad and the river on Penn Street, just below the Patee House, a four-story luxury hotel in which in the spring of 1860 the Pony opened an office on the ground floor.

The Patee House was constructed by John Patee in 1858 for the staggering cost of $200,000; it had over a hundred rooms and a large, fancy ballroom on the second floor. Patee envisioned the brick building as the centerpiece of a booming area that would extend the city south, away from the already overcrowded business district. Locating the Pony offices there affirmed his vision—as did the reports from celebrities who seem to have preferred it to not only St. Joe's other hotel but also establishments in St. Louis and beyond.

The Pony was as big or bigger than any of the politicians, businessmen, and lecturers who filled its hallways. Speed made it famous: those ten days. Ten days to connect Missouri to California. Toss in another two and change to make the trip from New York or Washington, and the time seemed unworldly in an age when weeks, if not months, were the norm for coast-to-coast communication.

LAUNCHED AS A ONCE-A-WEEK SERVICE IN APRIL 1860, THE PONY WAS running from St. Joe's twice a week by Lincoln's election, every Thursday and Sunday. Following up the earlier telegraphed dispatches, correspondents at St. Joe's prepared letters with fuller details on November 8, destined for editors at various locations west.

Some had the headline on the outside of the envelope: ELECTION NEWS: LINCOLN ELECTED!

The rider waiting to take the mail from St. Joe's was a twenty-year-old Kentucky implant named Johnny Fry. Slim and on the short side, he was typical of Pony riders. Johnny and his brushed-back hair would pass unnoticed on any city street even in his Sunday best; overcoat rumpled, vest slightly askew, tie hopelessly off-kilter, he could fuss up for the photographer and still come off plain.

Put the boy on a horse, though, and he became something godlike. It wasn't just speed, though his sleek, lightweight frame and low profile on the hoof were augmented by an unworldly sense of how to extract the best from his beasts. Just twenty—an age more mature in 1860 than today, but still considered young—Johnny had acquired the aura of a celebrity around town. All the Pony riders had it. Pony riders were athletes, able (and required) to ride fast for hours on end, in any weather, through often hostile terrain and occasionally life-threatening conditions.

Though usually armed with a pistol, the riders relied on speed as their first order of defense against an enemy. For in the stretches beyond St. Joe's they were far from any help; using a gun even from the saddle meant giving an enemy that much better a chance at overtaking you.

Stopping for any reason was forbidden. There was a strict time schedule governing your progress as a rider. You barely halted to change horses every ten or fifteen miles; you did that, on average, in three minutes, maybe five or six or seven times in the course of your run. (It depended on the stretch of the route.) When you got off the horse at a home station to let the next rider take the mail, your legs were shaky, and your arms and neck ached, to say nothing of your backside—but if anyone asked, you were ready and happy and eager to go again, because you were a Pony man.

Johnny Fry, especially.

MOST OF THE CROWD MILLING AROUND THE PATEE HOUSE DISCUSSING the election as Johnny waited for the clerk to hand over the mail were

Democrats. They had split their votes between Douglas and Breckinridge, according to whether they thought Missouri should stay in (Douglas) or leave (Breckinridge) the Union. Lincoln, who'd passed through St. Joe's a year before, was as unpopular there as he was in the rest of the state.[3] The divisions were sharp and sentiment high. Johnny Fry probably kept his mouth shut, as he leaned Union—a stand that would get him killed three years later by a unit only slightly less famous than the Pony in those parts, Quantrill's Raiders.

Fry has one further claim to historical fame—he is said by many to be *probably* the man who inaugurated the Pony Express, the first rider to take the mailbag as the service launched from St. Joe's.

Probably. Because like almost everything connected to the Pony Express, there is no gospel record of the event. In fact, there's no way to be absolutely certain he did *any* run, though there is plenty of testimony to that effect. The records of the parent company were lost to history, leaving historians to sort through scraps of evidence.

RUNNING INTO HISTORY

The one fact firmly known about the first run is that it was late—because of a train.

The launch of the Pony Express on April 3, 1860, was a grand affair in St. Joe. The riders had been the toast of the town the night before, with a ball in the Patee House's expansive second-floor ballroom. A crowd gathered to see the horse and rider off at 4:00 P.M. They were so boisterous they spooked the horse; the rider had to take him down the street to the Pony stables to get away from the crowd. More than one onlooker filched a hair from the poor pony's tail as a souvenir.

Speeches were made; the mayor predicted great things, for the service, for the country, and most especially the city. The crowd cheered. All was ready.

The only problem: the mail wasn't ready. And the Pony couldn't leave until it was.

A small stack of mail for California was due to come on the train

from Hannibal, but the mail had been delayed at Detroit. Despite
speed that had even veteran passengers closing their eyes and hanging on around curves, the train was two and a half hours late. Scheduled to leave at four, the rider didn't get off until a quarter past seven.

Fry—or whoever the first rider was—beat his time allotment; between him and the men who followed, they managed to make up
enough time to get the mail across country on schedule. It was not
the last time that man and beast would be called on to compensate
for the shortcomings of machines, nor would it be the only irony involved in the Pony's history.

ABOUT THAT FIRST RIDER: MOST HISTORIANS HAVE SETTLED ON FRY,
citing the memories of St. Joe residents, which were recorded years
after the fact.

But Alex Carlyle is another strong candidate, and one I prefer.[4] The
best testimony in his favor is a letter from Jack Keetley, another rider
for the line. Keetley, in a letter dated August 21, 1907, from Salt Lake
City talked about the first ride, with a mixture of details correct and
less so. He noted that Carlyle was the nephew of Ben Ficklin, the company's superintendent; if Ficklin had any say on who would have the
honor of riding out of St. Joe—and he had all the say—it would be
hard to imagine him passing over his nephew.

Keetley notes that the first runs were to Guittard's; the line was
subsequently shortened to Seneca. He says that Carlyle lasted only
about two months, leaving because he had consumption; Fry took his
place. Keetley, who was riding on another section at the start of the
service, eventually came east to replace him, with Gus Cliff the very
last rider on that leg of the route.

The biggest knock on Keetley's testimony is that it was printed
in the very first book on the Pony, written by William Lightfoot
Visscher. Visscher, described by one historian as an alcoholic who
liked to give temperance lectures—quite a few did—was not a stickler
for accuracy, and much of what he writes in the book can be sourced
to his imagination.

Admittedly, the account was written long after the fact. And historians who have questioned Keetley's veracity point out that he gets the time wrong for the start of the first ride. But what he reports was the time when it was *supposed* to start, something a rider elsewhere on the line would have known. He boasts that he had the longest ride—a claim common to authentic Pony riders. He mentions Fry as the next rider in line, and he had nothing to gain or lose by giving Carlyle credit. He also has many details about the Pony correct, most especially the fact that it was seen by its owners as a money loser from the start.

There are other candidates—Johnson William Richardson, who was mentioned in a St. Joe's newspaper that week, would be the next best, and one accepted by the most thorough historians of the service, Raymond and Mary Settle.[5] But that's part of the lore of the Pony—you never know anything for 100 percent certain.

GETTING OFF

The first ride was distant past now, seven months and what seemed like a lifetime gone. Johnny didn't have to worry about his horse being spooked or pinched by souvenir seekers. His only concern was to get across the river while the ferry was still running, then ride out to the next station in Kansas. Much of that ride would be at night, in the cold, and he was anxious to get going. He eyed the letters arranged on the clerk's counter in the Pony's corner of the large room, more than ready to scoop them up himself.

Mostly written on tissue-thin paper, the letters were thin and the messages brief, the Facebook updates of their time. The cost of transmission was pegged to weight; that November it was down to $2.50 a quarter ounce, a concession on the minimum price, which had started at $5 for up to a half ounce. Every so often, though, correspondents went overboard; one supervisor remembered a letter practically bursting at the seams, for which the writer was charged twenty-five dollars.[6]

Today's pile of mail was on the high side, perhaps due to the election, greater than the usual forty-nine or so pieces Johnny had been taking from St. Joe to Sacramento or San Francisco these past weeks.[7] A good number of other letters were carried and dropped along the way. Though the total per trip varied hugely—from a dozen to ten times—it was all the same to Johnny. Get 'em there, fast; no need to count.

The clerk took the letters and packed them into a special mail carrier called a "mochila." (*Mochila* is a Spanish word that in modern usage means "backpack.") The mochila had four nearly square pouches attached to a leather blanket that draped over the rider's saddle, with openings for the horn and cantle. Sewn two to a side, the pouches could be locked against thieves and the elements. They were rather small, about the size of a standard hardcover book. Letters and cards were bundled inside oilskin—thin fabric treated with oil or wax to make it waterproof; in the days before Gore-Tex, it was the go-to rain protector—before being placed inside. Three of the four were customarily secured, used for material going to the end of the line; a fourth, unlocked, held letters and telegraph cards picked up or distributed along the way.

The pouches were positioned fore and aft of where the rider's legs would reach down to the stirrups. The mochila was cut to fit easily over the special saddles used by the Pony, which were smaller and lighter than most models used elsewhere at the time. Everything was designed to keep things light and quick—the mochila would go from saddled horse to saddled horse in a matter of moments and weigh as little as possible.

Frank Root, who worked as a clerk (and nearly everything else) for Russell et al., remembers as many as seven hundred letters being taken west per week,[8] though most historians estimate that the Express moved no more than one hundred on average.

Among the last letters to be added to Johnny's pack that day was a hastily written dispatch from a correspondent for the *Rocky Mountain News* in Denver; it was to be delivered to the Pony station in

Julesburg, and from there taken by stage to Denver. On the outside cover to underline its importance he wrote "Election news/ Lincoln elected."[9] The Pony clerk packed it in the "way pocket," along with a slip that would be used to record the time the mochila arrived at each home station. Ahead or behind, the next rider would be expected to stay on schedule or make up for any tardiness.

Mochila finally full, Johnny seized it and headed out. His relief was waiting at the Smith Hotel in Seneca, Kansas, a bit over seventy miles away. With a whistle and a cheer, he was off, hurling himself down the hill toward the center of town, nestled on the banks of the Missouri.

Thin and supple, the mochila's leather wrapped tightly around the saddle and flanks of the horse, barely noticed by the rider. Johnny thought only of where he was going. Galloping down the street, he passed the Pony stable and headed for the ferry, waiting a few blocks away. He was going west, toward Bloody Kansas, South Pass, the Great Divide, California . . . riding in the direction of gold, Indian wars, and the future. On the trail ahead were legends like Pony Bob, the notorious Jack Slade, Wild Bill Hickok, the irrepressible Buffalo Bill Cody, and a hundred or more other men just as brave, crazy, and cutthroat.

The men Johnny passed as he neared the water walked about as if in a daze, murmuring among themselves. For once they didn't wave; their conversation was not about the bold figure of rider and horse, but of the future of their country.

MONEY, AMBITION, AND OTHER COMPLICATIONS

MEANWHILE, BACK EAST

While Johnny and his horse were biding their time on the ferry across the Missouri, the man who had brought the Pony Express to life was leaving his office a thousand miles away. Though a native of Missouri, William H. Russell had not been there in months, and by all appearances had come to prefer the grand life of Washington and New York, especially. There was power in the eastern cities, and money, and most of all, vision.

Russell's New York City office was on Pine Street, one block over from Wall Street. The Continental Bank Building on Nassau Street was freshly built, a five-story building featuring massive arched windows and the latest building technology.[1] It was the world's first fireproof building, no mean selling point in a city whose business district had been wiped out in a spectacular winter fire some twenty-five years before. New York was the financial and creative epicenter of the country, outstripping Boston and Philadelphia, to say nothing of sleepy Washington. Southern cities like Charleston weren't even in the discussion.

And Russell had put himself at the city's epicenter. One end of Pine Street led to the East River waterfront, a bustling center of commerce, filled with high-masted ships and, lately, steamers. At the other, up the hill, was the churchyard of Trinity Episcopal Church, whose towering spires shaded the graves of some of the most distinguished members of the generation that had built the city and led the Revolution. The streets between the cemetery and the wharves held the offices of countless merchants and speculators, financiers and bankers.

Russell knew many of them very well. While he had spent much of his life on the frontier, his home and his company's future was among them.

RUSSELL

William Hepburn Russell was born in Burlington, Vermont, on January 31, 1812, six months before the start of the war against Britain. Among his ancestors was a man who plotted against the British king Charles II only to get cold feet, though not soon enough to avoid losing his head in what is now known as the Rye House plot. After his descendants moved to America, they retained no fondness for the royal house; Russell's father, William Eaton Russell, fought against the British in the War of 1812, in which according to some, he had commanded forces in the Battle of Lake Champlain.[2] The elder Russell died in 1814; William's mother remarried and the family moved to western Missouri soon after.

As a young man, William Russell worked for merchant companies in Liberty, Missouri. He married the daughter of a prominent preacher, Harriet Elliot Warder; she died early in their marriage, leaving him with five children.[3] Russell went into business with some friends as a merchant and store owner. Despite a business failure in 1845, he amassed property and wealth, speculating in property and branching out into the transportation business. He delivered military supplies to Santa Fe and did well enough to build a twenty-room mansion in Lexington, Missouri, at the time an up-and-coming city on the edge of the frontier, a jumping-off place for pioneers and other fortune seekers.

Russell was a slave owner, and, sorry to say, a rather avid supporter of the "institution": when Congress overturned the Missouri Compromise by granting new states the right to vote yea or nay on whether to allow men to own other men, Russell became treasurer of the Lafayette County Emigration Society—a group dedicated to helping pro-slavery emigrants to that Kansas county. He was a supporter of Senator David R. Atchison and the pro-slavery Law and Order Party.

In 1850, Russell helped start the Lexington Mutual Fire and Marine Insurance Company and was also on a committee formed to bring a railroad to Leavenworth. He was active in the local Baptist church and helped organize a college for young women. The following year, he joined with another ardent Baptist and neighbor named William B. Waddell, a wholesaler and store owner, to ship freight for the army. The two men knew each other well, in church and out; they'd worked together to help form the town's fire company. Waddell, too, was an investor, though on a smaller scale than Russell. While not considered a "plunger"—the era's name for speculators who liked to take chances—Waddell did have a bit of the gambler in him; during the gold rush he financed a speculative trip to the California gold fields, hoping to reap some of the profits.

It was a bust.

The partnership between Waddell and Russell was on much firmer grounds. Russell was the visionary; Waddell was more the administrative type, attending to organizational details and overseeing the books. They operated several ventures, all connected—shipping goods to the army at Fort Leavenworth was their main business, but they also had a store and eventually engaged in real estate speculation. Both men had interests beyond their partnership, Russell especially—he continued to cart supplies to Fort Leavenworth under a separate contract with another business partner even while working with Waddell.

Freighting was potentially a highly lucrative business, especially when dealing with the government, but there were downsides. You made a large capital outlay in the beginning of the year to buy your oxen and whatever else you needed, usually using credit, then prayed you avoided disaster and were paid on time when you delivered.

Army contracts were only good for a year, which made it difficult to plan or build your company.

In 1854, the army changed the way it did business. Rather than giving several companies one-year contracts, it rolled everything together and offered a two-year contract. A single bidder would transport supplies from Leavenworth to Fort Union, New Mexico, and Salt Lake City in Utah, along with any other installation or camp in between.

It was a huge opportunity, potentially worth millions, at a time when millions were real money. But the job was so big that one company, not even Russell and Wardell's, could handle it all.

And so they hooked up with another Missourian, a man very much unlike themselves, Alexander Majors.

MAJORS

Russell was a promotor who shone at handshaking and backslapping; he was the sort who could walk into a room and chat up anyone, especially if he had business or political connections. More likely than not, he'd have people seeing the world his way when he left, and it was a rosy world to boot.

Majors was a fellow who rolled up his sleeves and got down in the dirt to get things done. If there was a whip that needed cracking, all the better. Born in Kentucky in 1814, Majors moved to Missouri at age five. He remembered that wagon ride well into his old age, recalling details like the pile of furs he saw in St. Louis before settling farther north. He lost his mother when he was only six and counted that loss as his greatest heartbreak in life. And that was saying something.

Surviving an Indian attack and later tornadoes, Majors was a child of the frontier, raised in a log cabin at a time when a good portion of western Missouri was still covered with thick-trunked trees. After he married, he found it difficult to make a living as a farmer and started working in the freighting business. He had a way with animals and the men who handled them, able to coax the most from both. In August 1848, he set out with six wagons and teams to supply an army unit at Santa Fe; within a few years he was commanding five times as many wagons.

Unlike Russell or Waddell, Majors knew the Great Plains and how to move goods through them from hard experience. Wagons on the frontier were generally driven by teams of six oxen on trails that might completely vanish from sight in bad weather. An expedition could take months—his first trip to Santa Fe was considered a record setter at "only" ninety-two days.

He made $650 a wagon his first trip, and with six wagons his profit neared $4,000—a tidy sum for a failed farmer at a time when laborers generally might make $2 a day.

Not that freighting was easy work, even for a trail boss. You walked all day, slept in the cold and damp, built fires out of buffalo chips. As boss on the trail—and Majors loved being on the trail, even when he was so successful he could have stayed home—you commanded animals and men given to complaining loudly and proclaiming that they would rather be somewhere else, under anyone else's command.

Bullwhackers kept their oxen going anyway they could—their name suggests the preferred method. It was a physical job, and while you didn't need to have massive muscles, those didn't hurt. Intelligence, on the other hand, was considered optional. Teamsters (the more socially acceptable name than bullwhacker or ox driver) were generally seen by polite society as a step above imbeciles. Their appearance did their reputation no favors—walk alongside six big-butt, castrated bulls in the hot sun for twelve hours a day, months on end, and no one's calling you a fashion plate.

(Oxen, castrated male cows bred for their ability to move heavy stuff long distances, had several advantages over horses or mules for pulling wagon. Cost was most important, but there was also the fact that they were reasonably tasty compared to mules or horses if things went south along the way.)

Majors had a more benevolent, even enlightened attitude. He cared about his employees and tried to take care of them, or at least their Christian souls. Majors put his beliefs into practice with an enthusiasm few others in his profession did, whether as investor or bullwhacker in chief. It was common for trains of wagons to travel on Sundays. Majors's did not; he pulled up Saturday afternoons and wouldn't move out again until Monday, observing the Sabbath, giving men and beasts a much-needed rest. He gave wagon masters Bibles, on which they swore out an oath:

> While I am in the employ of A. Majors, I agree not to use profane language, not to get drunk, not to gamble, not to treat animals cruelly, and not to do anything else that is incompatible with the conduct of a gentleman. And I agree, if I violate any of the above conditions, to accept my discharge without any pay for my services.[4]

There's plenty of evidence that the rules—especially those covering cursing and drinking—were observed in the breach when Majors was not around to enforce them. But he was exceedingly proud of those rules, and in his autobiography declared that he had never found it necessary to fire anyone because they had been broken. "My employees seemed to understand in the beginning of their term of service that their good behavior was part of the recompense they gave me for the money I paid them."[5]

The oath, or something like it, became a staple of every company Majors was part of.

BIG BUCKS AND GRAND VISION

From the beginning, the partnership between the three men was complicated and entangling. Their company straddled the Missouri, going by different names on each side of the river. In Lexington, Missouri, where Russell and Waddell already had an office and a store, it was known as Waddell, Russell & Co. On the other side of the river, it was called Majors & Russell.[6] There was no legal difference between the two, and as time went on the entire enterprise was generally known as Russell, Majors & Waddell. The three men were equal partners; each put in a third of the capital, which came to $60,000.[7]

They had other interests besides delivering the army's supplies. They sold goods, groceries, hardware, both at town stores and to soldiers on the trail. The trio dabbled in Kansas real estate near Leavenworth, where the fort was. And they continued their own operations on the side, Russell especially: he was on the board of a railroad company in Leavenworth and helped establish a Kansas bank, serving as its president. (He even had his picture printed on a bank note, a custom of the time.[8])

But freighting for the army was the main engine driving not only their partnership, but also their other ventures. How much money could the trio make moving stuff? Plenty, if things went well, and they did, at first.

The 1854 army contract called for payment on a one-hundred-pound per one-hundred-mile basis, depending on the location and date, with as little as $1.14 charged; rates rose to $2.20, with a price bump programmed in based on performance. The contract called for a minimum of 50,000 pounds, but the maximum—2.5 million—was a far more reasonable expectation. Payment was capped at $2.5 million, but there was every reason to believe the contract was worth near that.

In today's money, that computes to over $68 million.

They did have significant expenses. Waddell supervised the purchase of some 7,500 oxen that first year, which Majors assembled into teams of 325 under the supervision of a wagon master. All told, the company was employing some seventeen hundred people by the time the wagons were ready to roll.

Their wagons were mostly state of the art. These were "prairie schooners," the iconic wagons with rounded tops and a gently curved, almost-boatlike body. They were large rigs, the tractor trailers of the day, able to carry between five and seven thousand pounds, with reinforced wheels and wide iron tires. (Rubber would have worn off quickly, and been far too expensive. The iron tires were taken off and adjusted as the wheels shrank, the wood drying out.)

The wagons cost $190. The company bought five hundred of them the first year. Add in the cost of warehouses and incidentals like straps and whips, and so on—not incidental at this scale—and the investment must have been over half a million dollars before the first bag of goods was loaded.

Then there were the labor costs: wagon masters were highly paid—$125 a month for the privilege of bossing around some thirty or so men. You got food with that, but no guff—anyone who dared disobey the trail boss could be fired on the spot, which meant walking home without pay. A teamster earned from $25 to $30, considerably more than they could make as farm laborers.[9] That took labor costs for Russell, Waddell, and Majors well over half a million dollars. Still, those were acceptable costs, potentially yielding more than 100 percent profit, and providing a basis for other revenue streams—some of those wagons could be used for other purposes, ditto the men and everything else.

In Russell's vision, the government contract would do more than provide a hunk of revenue; it would finance the construction of a transportation network over much of the West. With that established, they could crowd out competitors, helping create an empire that had a veritable monopoly over delivery in an area they expected to boom in population. Railroads would come—possible routes for a transcontinental railroad had already been studied—but that was not only in the future but another opportunity: someone had to pick up goods from the stations and distribute them.

The company did extremely well in its first two years. Majors recalled later that they showed a profit free and clear of $150,000 in each of those years, and they were just getting started.

Success fired Russell's imagination. For William H. Russell didn't just want to own a freight company. He saw the outfit as part of a larger empire, something that partook of the country's vast potential.

The future was all around him—the telegraph, the train, steamboats, factories—and he was part of it all.

There was only one thing he didn't count on: armies have a tendency to get involved in wars.

THE UTAH WAR

The area covered by the freight contract included the Utah Territory, today not only the state of Utah but Nevada and chunks of Colorado and Wyoming as well. By far the largest white population in the territory was clustered near the Great Salt Lake, populated almost entirely by Mormon pioneers who'd fled persecution in 1847, establishing what they eventually hoped would be the capital of the state of Deseret.

Deseret would have extended into California and Idaho, Oregon, and Arizona. The powers that be back in Washington didn't think that was a particularly good idea for a number of reasons. The slavery question—would the state be pro or con—and the sheer size of the territory were critical points against Deseret, but hostile attitudes toward Mormons were an important reason as well. The area was split up into smaller sections, with Brigham Young appointed governor of the Utah Territory in 1851.

Relations between Washington and Utah were not friendly. Seeking to exert more control over the territory, President James Buchanan decided to replace Young with Alfred Cumming in 1857. Realizing there would be conflict, army units were ordered to Salt Lake; Russell, Majors & Waddell were directed to supply the soldiers, who embarked on one of the most inept campaigns of all time.

The exact requirements of both the government and the transport company became a matter of great debate. But there's no disputing this: the transport trains were devastated by Mormon attacks, and the company lost over $300,000 worth of equipment. On top of that, they were owed about the same for the supplies lost with the wagons, so that by the end of 1857 the company figured it was owed $642,242.45.

The government didn't want to pay. Or more precisely, Congress wouldn't allocate money to cover the bills. In theory, this was a quarrel between the War Department and Congress, which hadn't allotted any money for the war, let alone the losses. But the people who weren't paid were Russell, Majors, and Waddell.

That was a serious financial hole, especially since most of the costs had been financed, the usual practice. The strain was compounded by the army's need to transport more material in 1858 under a new contract. At exactly the time they needed credit to finance the coming year's activities, Russell, Majors, and Waddell had to borrow to pay off past liabilities. It was like carrying two mortgages at once.

Russell went to Washington to see what he could do about getting paid. He met with senators, congressmen, and the president. Most especially, he met with the secretary of war, John B. Floyd, who was in charge of the army.

Floyd, like everyone else Russell spoke to, couldn't do anything about Congress. Nor did he have any funds—the budget was already shot. So Russell suggested that he give the company what were called "acceptances"—notes that said the War Department was going to pay Russell, Majors & Waddell money at some point in the future. Technically, these were time drafts, promises to pay an amount at a certain time, similar to notes issued by banks and used as credit in trade.

Similar, but not the same: Floyd had no authority to issue them, which meant they were not legal obligations, though no one seems to have questioned that at the time. Floyd appears to have felt he had no choice but to help Russell's company, and the papers he issued did just that—Russell took a total of $400,000 in acceptances in March 1858 and used them as collateral to raise other financing.

So far, so good.

For such valuable pieces of paper, the acceptances were rather plain looking and simply put; they had the date of issue, the date they would mature, and a reference to the contract that underlay the payment. Here's a later one, in its entirety:

$15,000 Washington, September 11, 1860

Eight months after date pay to our own order, at the Bank of the Republic of New York City, fifteen thousand dollars, for value received, and charge to account of transportation contract of the 12th day of April, 1860

Russell, Majors & Waddell

Hon J. B. Floyd

(No. 78)

Accepted.[10]

Another man—say, Majors or Waddell—might have taken the trouble over financing and getting paid as a sign to pull back. Russell, however, was not the sort to let difficulties get him down. On the contrary, his conversations in Washington that winter and early spring only fed his ambition.

From his point of view, everything looked great. He and his firm had a monopoly on army transport. The next step was all transport, civilian and government. A mail contract would be part of the mix.

That, too, was lucrative—a million dollars to take mail from the Missouri to California.

There was a roadblock: the mail contract was held by a company affiliated with a group that dominated transport in the United States. But Russell knew how to wrestle it away: start the Pony Express.

BLEEDING KANSAS, BLEEDING MEN

TIES AND TALES

As soon as the ferry hit the western shore of the Missouri at Elwood, Kansas, Johnny Fry hit the ground running, galloping off the landing along a rock road at full speed. The terrain was flat, the settlements sparse; Johnny could make good time.

Of all the tales that ride along with the Pony riders, the best ones involve affairs of the heart, and the finest of those are attached to Johnny. Aboard his horse he was a stud, a bona fide heartthrob who had women lining up to give him cakes and cookies as he passed. One legend gives him, or rather a suitor, credit for the invention of the round donut: supposedly a winsome lass noticed that after grabbing her cruller, Johnny had trouble holding it in his hand while riding. She took the ordinarily straight piece of dough, joined it together at the ends, and had a solution.

Great story, even if there are numerous other claimants to the invention, both in the US and abroad.

In *The Story of the Pony Express* (1955), Raymond and Mary Settle tell a story about Fry and his adventures with another girl on the route. According to the Settles, the young lady wanted Johnny to donate his red kerchief or necktie for a log cabin quilt she was sewing. The quilts—patchwork jobs with bright colors and various shapes—were popular at the time, with meanings obvious and hidden: a quilt hung at the front of a house with a black patch at the center supposedly signaled a safe haven on the Underground Railroad.

In this case, red was a signal that she wanted him to court her. Johnny apparently was of a different opinion and didn't honor her request, or slow down, when she appeared one day. So the next time he was due to arrive, the girl mounted her horse and gave chase.

Despite the fact that Johnny would have been riding one of the fastest horses in the county and was, himself, one of the fastest horsemen around, the girl caught up to him. He still refused to give over the kerchief. The girl grabbed for it, and missed—but came away with part of his shirt, if not his heart.

HORSE SENSE

The girl was nowhere to be seen that night. Shirt and spirit intact, Johnny and the election letter continued westward, treading down a favorite shortcut as he headed to a small stable and inn in Troy, Kansas, his first exchange. He was well known at the stop, for he often had breakfast there—when coming the other way, after delivering to St. Joe's.[1] Trading horses, he took a new shortcut northwest and fording the Muddy Creek, which at this time of year without rain was barely that, and rode on up to the memorably named town of Log Chain for a fresh horse.

The mechanism for changing horses was simple, and pretty much the same along the entire route. A man, or often a middling-young boy, would wait with a fresh mount around the rider's expected time. Generally, there were two or three horses at each transfer station, with a few more at the home stations. The horse would already be watered and saddled. The rider was equipped with a horn, which he could sound to alert the station as he approached; most often this wasn't necessary, and many historians seem to think it was abandoned after the early rides.

The rider would slide off the horse, lift the mochila, and put it on the new mount. Then he'd be off again, thundering onward for another ten or fifteen miles. Not all the run would be made at full gallop; in fact, a full-out gallop, which might be made at 25 or 30 miles an hour, was rare; this wasn't the Kentucky Derby, and the roads, even in Kansas, were rarely smooth. The bulk of the ten or fifteen miles would be covered in a good trot or a canter, with eight to ten miles an hour usually considered the average.

While it's possible that some of the horses were thoroughbreds that had found their way west where Waddell's horse buyers spotted them, the farrier in Seneca who knew his horse flesh reported that most of them were ponies, half or mostly wild when bought.

Or as he put it, "the worst imps of Satan in the business."[2] He remembers needing two men to help him wrestle them into submission long enough to nail their shoes to their hooves. "We used to say that the company had bought up every mean, bucking, kicking horse that could be found," Pony rider William Campbell told historian Arthur Chapman years after the Pony faded into memory. "But they were good stock and could outrun anything on the trail."[3]

The company advertised for two hundred gray mares in the Leavenworth area alone as they geared up; others were bought in each of the main sections of the trail. There were roughly one hundred and sixty stations, each with at least two or three horses, and more at the larger home stations where the riders were relieved as well as the mounts. The exact number dedicated to the service isn't known, but between four and five hundred is a reliable estimate. Figuring changes every ten miles or so, it would have taken between a hundred and fifty and two hundred for the entire route per trip.

CONTINUING ON, FRY REACHED SENECA—NOT YET INCORPORATED AS A town, but already well known by stagecoach passengers because of the Smith Hotel, a largish wooden house built by John Smith[4] two years before.[5]

Smith's was a home station; here another rider took over and Fry could go to bed, resting until it was time to take the eastbound dispatches back east to St. Joe's. Fry lived in Kansas, and it's possible that depending on the work schedule he could go home to his farm when he was done. But more likely he would have slept in the hotel if there were empty beds. Otherwise, he bunked in the stable around the corner.

This stretch had one great variable: the ferry across the river. Often riders going east arrived so late at night that they had to leave their horse for the night, boarding a waiting rowboat that took them across to the city, where presumably they hoofed the mile or so uphill to the Patee House with the mochila. The horse would be retrieved the next day, returned to the stable a few blocks from the hotel.

"ORPHANS PREFERRED"

Riding for the Pony was a strenuous affair, even in the relatively civilized sections of Kansas where Johnny and the occasional substitute rode. What you needed was not so much physical strength—you were riding on the horse, not the other way around—but endurance. Lasting in a saddle for hours on end, in hot and cold, was a special kind of skill. With some notable exceptions—like Johnny—riders burned out quickly. Nearly all were short and lightweight, which helped the horses go faster, but meant less padding and resistance to the aches and pains of the trail.

They were well paid—different riders remembered from $40 to $100 per month, with the average usually given around $50, plus food and board at the stations.

Home stations, mostly chosen from existing stagecoach stops, featured food that ranged from mediocre to horrible. Bacon was a staple, along with dried fruit and beans. As was coffee. Sausage was fatty, but a treat if present. The bread was usually cooked at the station and might be a highlight; it might also knock a few teeth out.

Fresh meat?

Surprisingly, not so much, not even in Kansas and Nebraska where farming was a going concern. Most of the edible cooking was done by the wives of the station keepers, though the gender of the chef was not necessarily an indication of quality. Out in the deserts of the Utah Territory—which included present-day Nevada—not only was fresh meat an impossible dream, but even getting water to a few of the transfer stations was an operation in itself. Hay and grain had to be hauled in there as well.

There was no Department of Labor monitoring lunch breaks in 1860, but with riders in the saddle for six or eight or even more hours, they had to eat during their ride. With the exception of Johnny Fry's pies and donuts, the record is mum about trail lunches. Buckets and thick cloth were the lunch boxes of the day, but it's easier to imagine a rider grabbing a hunk of bread or maybe a turnover-style pie while changing horses at one of the larger exchanges, then eating on the run.

Board occasionally meant a nice bed at a hotel or inn, but more often it was blanket in an attic or a place in the hay. Most riders didn't do fancy; on the whole they were local kids who not only knew the area but were used to the conditions of the frontier where they worked.

Rider Elijah Nicholas Wilson, who rode out in the western Utah and Nevada area, remembered that riders were charged for the saddle they used, with the money coming from their wages; the service would also sell them a revolver if they didn't have one, advancing the gun and taking payment from their wages. The job paid far more than the eighteen-year-old had ever earned (and more than many would later on), but Wilson still thought it too low. "Our pay was too small for the hard work and the dangers we went through," he'd remember years later.[6]

One measure of what the job was like is an advertisement for riders allegedly posted as the service geared up:

Wanted: Young, skinny, wiry fellows not over eighteen. Must be expert riders, willing to risk death daily. Orphans preferred.

It's a famous ad, included in countless tellings of the Pony, often done up in old-style typography with appropriate illustrations and anxious exclamation marks.

Unfortunately, like many mementos of the Pony, it appears to be bogus, concocted years after the last Pony rider had shaken the dust from his jeans and gone off into the sunset. But it does capture the *spirit* of the riders, who while they may not have faced death at least twice or four times a week, were nonetheless expected to be hardy, adventurous souls, willing to push themselves and their mounts to the limit.

THE MANAGERS

History came to treat the riders like superstars, so much so that many would claim to have ridden for the Pony without having come close to one of its stables. But the unsung heroes of the Pony were the stationmasters and the supervisors who formed the company's backbone. Without those middle managers, the mail wouldn't have gone through at all.

The Pony's infrastructure was built largely around the stagecoach line from Leavenworth to Denver that Russell had started with John S. Jones the year before. The route was divided into five different sections, with a superintendent in charge of each area, mustering the home stations and answering to Benjamin F. Ficklin, a stockholder and supervisor whom Russell at first trusted but quickly came to despise.

A mustachioed thirtysomething in 1860, Ficklin had been kicked out of the Virginia Military Institute (VMI) as a teenager for being a poor student and general cutup. He's said to have painted the superintendent's horse to look like a zebra and buried the poor man's boots under the snow, but it wasn't until he fired a howitzer without authorization that he got expelled.

Ficklin's father was a well-known merchant in Charlottesville, which may have been a factor in Ficklin's getting back into VMI's good graces a few years later, although a more popular story is that he claimed to have been gravely wounded in the Mexican War and won the sympathy of the administration. Whatever the reason, Ficklin was readmitted. He repaid their confidence by graduating fourth-from-last in his class.

This didn't stop him from becoming a teacher; when that didn't work out, he went West, where he found work as a freighter and then a surveyor, became a US marshal, joined the army in time for the Mormon War, and eventually joined Russell's stagecoach company. By then, he had tamed his wilder side, and his management abilities came to the fore. Whatever Russell's eventual opinion of him, he was by all accounts an excellent manager, and a sizable portion of the credit for establishing the Pony must go to him.

California senator William M. Gwin—a good friend of Russell's—credited Ficklin with the idea of the Pony Express; supposedly the men discussed it during a stagecoach ride some years before Russell proposed it. It was the sort of claim often associated with the Pony—enticing, possible, almost plausible, and completely unprovable.

But there was no doubt about Ficklin's ability to round organizations into shape. Ficklin, with a great deal of help and muscle from an ornery assistant named Joseph A. "Jack" Slade, cleaned up problems on the stage line after Russell and Jones bought out a competitor and his lucrative mail contract and changed the route. Said problems included horse theft and disappearing stock as well as unreliable service; putting things right turned around what could have been a disastrous expansion.

The following year, with the Pony line built over the skeleton of the stagecoach line, Ficklin supervised the entire operation. With the partners busy, he was the hands-on manager of the service.

Maybe the credit Ficklin took for this rubbed Russell the wrong way. Maybe Ficklin's the-hell-with-authority attitude resurfaced. Finally after a blowup over how often the Pony should run, Russell in the summer of 1860 told Majors and Waddell that it was either Ficklin or him. When they put him off, Russell threatened to resign as president and told them they could buy out his interests for half a million dollars.

Waddell and Majors tried to make nice and convinced Ficklin to apologize.

It didn't take. Ficklin saw no other option but to tender his resignation, which was promptly accepted.

He headed east, where he tried to get his own mail contract and hooked up with the Pacific Telegraph Company, which aimed at connecting east and west by a transcontinental telegraph. His involvement was short-circuited by the Civil War. Loyal to his state rather than the Union, the Virginia boy was commissioned a major, specializing in blockade running. He even was suspected as an accomplice in Booth's assassination of Lincoln. Released, he eventually set up a stagecoach operation in Texas, only to die during a visit to Washington in 1871. He'd swallowed a fishbone while eating; trying to remove it, the doctor cut an artery and he bled to death.

BLEEDING KANSAS

The bucolic, gently rolling hills and flat farmland Johnny and the other riders passed through in eastern Kansas was peaceful only when viewed from the distance. At any point in the night, flames might erupt at a church or a farm known—or thought—to harbor an abolitionist. Escaped slaves made their way in the darkness to safer ground. Fanatics like John Brown plotted attacks on prominent slaveholders.

It had been this way for six years, ever since Congress blew up the Missouri Compromise and threw the question of slavery to the people in states-to-be.

Had the Missouri Compromise been followed, Kansas and Nebraska would have been nonslaveholding states. Nebraska, sparsely settled, with a tougher climate for agriculture (it was then thought), wasn't considered particularly amendable to slavery. But Kansas, bordered on two sides by slaveholding states, was.

Something similar had been tried in California in 1850; the state constitution had outlawed slavery. Proslavery forces remained powerful in the state, but there had been no violence to speak of over the issue.

Kansas was different. With the balance of power in Congress tipping, the South felt threatened; many saw the abolition of slavery as an inevitable numbers game: give the North more votes, and it would be outlawed everywhere. Slave interests—including all of the Pony's principals, not just Russell—put their money to work, encouraging settlers from Southern states already comfortable with slavery and muscling pro-slavery politicians into power. Abolitionists in the North encouraged followers to migrate, creating a minor boom. The fight was on for supremacy.

A territorial census in 1855 counted under 10,000 people. Some 107,000 people lived in the state according to the 1860 census.[7] Kansans couldn't vote for president in 1860, but their future was very much on the line, as were their passions. Lincoln had passed through on a speaking tour the year before, stopping not only in Leavenworth on the Missouri River but also in Elwood and Troy, both part of the Pony route.

His themes would be fleshed out a year later in a famous speech at Cooper Union in New York City. Not yet an official candidate for president—that was several months away—Lincoln built on his fame in the debates against Stephen Douglas in the Illinois senate campaign of 1858, but also incorporated arguments against the radicalism of John Brown, who was infamous in Kansas for guerrilla attacks against proslavery interests and civilians he believed favored slavery. (Lincoln happened to be in Leavenworth the day John Brown was hanged.)

In his talks, Lincoln characteristically tried to walk a line between opposing slavery and radicalism, condemning Brown's actions while at the same time condemning the "institution." He argued as a lawyer did, calling on precedent:

> No great while after the adoption of the original Constitution, North Carolina ceded to the Federal Government the country now constituting the State of Tennessee; and a few years later Georgia ceded that which now constitutes the States of Mississippi and Alabama. In both deeds of cession it was made a condition by the ceding States that the Federal Government should not prohibit slavery in the ceded terri-

tory. Besides this, slavery was then actually in the ceded country. Under these circumstances, Congress, on taking charge of these countries, did not absolutely prohibit slavery within them. But they did interfere with it—take control of it—even there, to a certain extent. In 1798, Congress organized the Territory of Mississippi. In the act of organization, they prohibited the bringing of slaves into the Territory, from any place without the United States, by fine, and giving freedom to slaves so bought. This act passed both branches of Congress without yeas and nays. In that Congress were three of the "thirty-nine" who framed the original Constitution. They were John Langdon, George Read and Abraham Baldwin. They all, probably, voted for it. Certainly they would have placed their opposition to it upon record, if, in their understanding, any line dividing local from federal authority, or anything in the Constitution, properly forbade the Federal Government to control as to slavery in federal territory.[8]

He argued from that precedent that slavery not be abolished, but rather confined:

But enough! Let all who believe that "our fathers, who framed the Government under which we live, understood this question just as well, and even better, than we do now," speak as they spoke, and act as they acted upon it. This is all Republicans ask—all Republicans desire—in relation to slavery. As those fathers marked it, so let it be again marked, as an evil not to be extended, but to be tolerated and protected only because of and so far as its actual presence among us makes that toleration and protection a necessity. Let all the guarantees those fathers gave it, be, not grudgingly, but fully and fairly, maintained. For this Republicans contend, and with this, so far as I know or believe, they will be content.

He claimed that Republicans were not radicals, saying Brown was not a Republican:

You charge that we stir up insurrections among your slaves. We deny it; and what is your proof? Harper's Ferry! John Brown!! John Brown was no Republican; and you have failed to implicate a single Republican in his Harper's Ferry enterprise. If any member of our party is guilty in that matter, you know it or you do not know it. If you do know it, you are inexcusable for not designating the man and proving the fact. If you do not know it, you are inexcusable for asserting it, and especially for persisting in the assertion after you have tried and failed to make the proof. You need to be told that persisting in a charge which one does not know to be true, is simply malicious slander.

Lincoln told Republicans that they should not attempt to overthrow slavery in the states where it was already a fact of life, but fight against it in the new territories:

Wrong as we think slavery is, we can yet afford to let it alone where it is, because that much is due to the necessity arising from its actual presence in the nation; but can we, while our votes will prevent it, allow it to spread into the National Territories, and to overrun us here in these Free States? If our sense of duty forbids this, then let us stand by our duty, fearlessly and effectively.

What went unmentioned in Lincoln's speech, and presumably in those he gave in Kansas, was the fear many whites had of a slave revolt. Nor did his words reassure anyone worried about the changing balance of power between the North and South, or which government— his state's or the one far away in Washington, DC, dominated by men who cared not a whit for him—would determine his future.

The undeclared war between interests had resulted in mostly property damage—"only" seventy deaths were directly tied to the issue in the years before the Civil War, and even if the real number was, as some suspect, larger, it was not by later standards a huge percentage. Yet it was still shocking, contrary to what people, even in the East, expected. Indian raids, outlaws, gunfights in the center of town—somehow these didn't rate the alarm that political violence did.

Pony riders were not immune to the passions, but they were not challenged on the routes, at least until the war started the following year. Still, the presence of marauding forces on either side must have added to the pucker factor as they made their way across the divided territory.

BACK ON THE TRAIL

Fresh horse, fresh rider, and maybe a new letter or two inside, the mochila made its way west to Ash Point—remembered now only in a road name—and Guittard, where horses were changed at a year-old two-story, twelve-room inn run by George Guittard. The rider continued to Marysville, a lively town of fiftysome houses where stabbings and gunplay were popular, at least according to newspaper correspondents like Albert Richardson, who always seemed to arrive after the action settled down.

Richardson never got into a fight himself, which he may have considered a stroke of good fortune. If so, his luck gave out during the Civil War, when Richardson was working as a journalist and/or a spy for the North. Taken prisoner, he escaped, only to discover that his wife and young daughter had passed away. He published his first-person spy story in 1865 as *The Secret Service, the Field, the Dungeon, and the Escape*, a minor classic of intrigue and first-person narrative nonfiction. But things went from bad to worse for him: he was shot in New York by his fiancée's divorced husband and died in 1869.[9]

However raucous Marysville may have been, it was substantial enough to contain a stable used by Russell's stage company as well as the Pony. Riders only changed horses there, then splashed across the Big Blue through a valley that took them to Hollenberg, whose namesake owner ran a store, post office, and inn out of a long, one-story house while not farming in the nearby fields. The station was also called Cottonwood, likely after the name of the nearby creek.

Joseph Barney Wintle, age twenty, took the mochila at Hollenberg; he'd been riding from the start of the service. Wintle's trail was mostly along the Little Blue River; flat and straight for much of the way, he could fly. He had some incentive—while Indians were not generally troublesome on this part of the route, Wintle was once chased by a small group who apparently wanted to rob him. Spurring his horse, he quickly outpaced them, but he rode the animal so hard that it died after he made the exchange.

Wintle had a few other Indian run-ins he lived to tell about. Once, he said, he met a rider who'd run away from an ambush, escaping with a hole in his hat rather than his head. Another time, he claimed, he rode straight into an Indian camp.

From Hollenberg the riders going west through Nebraska went to Rock House (also called Otoe). Then came Rock Creek, the station made famous, or infamous, by Wild Bill Hickok.

WILD BILL

The first fact to know about Wild Bill is not complicated: his name wasn't Bill.

Pretty much nobody called him Wild, either, at least not that fall when the Pony and news of Lincoln's election were passing through. Not that he wasn't wild. He was just unknown, an anonymous hand in Russell, Majors, and Waddell's employ. A good worker by most accounts, though at least by reputation he would not seem to have abided much by the oath of sobriety and propriety administered by Majors or on his behalf.

The complications come in when historians try to separate fact from fiction. Most of them end up twisted in knots.

Born in Troy Grove, Illinois, in May 1837, James Butler Hickok was one of seven children—another boy died soon after birth. His father, William, was a frontier farmer who had thought about becoming a minister and had owned a store before his ambitions were narrowed by the Panic of 1837. William became a Quaker and helped escaping slaves find freedom on the Underground Railroad; there was a cellar with a hidden door in the family home said to be used to hide refugees. One of the favorite stories about James's childhood has him clinging to his father's wagon as they escaped lawmen or bounty hunters while on a mission to help slaves one day.

William Hickok died in 1852; James left the family farm by 1854, working on the Illinois and Michigan Canal, a ninety-four-mile ditch that ran from the Chicago River in Bridgeport to LaSalle-Peru, where it hooked up with the Illinois River, making it a highway from the Great Lakes to the Mississippi. If the story can be believed, James Hickok protested when his boss started beating the animal pulling the barge; Hickok's protests were vehement—he tossed the oaf into the canal, marking the end of Hickok's career as a canal man.

The story fits with others told of him besting bullies as a young man and lines up—somewhat—with his better-documented deeds later in life. On the other side of the ledger, his personality was said to be a hard one; friends didn't come easy. And he loved to gamble. A lot. More than anything, really,

His mother didn't approve of him playing cards, nor did she like him (or anyone) drinking. He claimed in a letter home in 1858 that he'd given up both—for the past two years. If so, he found his way back soon after.

By the fall of 1860 he was in Kansas Territory, working for Russell, Majors & Waddell or one of their related companies. He was also, in his spare time, probably riding with the army of General Jim Lane. Lane was Kansas Free-Stater, a hero to abolitionists, a villain to those on the other side. The slang term for Lane and his ilk was "Jayhawker," the term given to anti-slavery militias battling "Border ruffians"—their opposing number on the pro-slavery side. These were not friendly card games: both sides regularly burned out families and stole whatever they wanted from the enemy, and occasionally did the same to people theoretically on their side.

Lane got a more formal command in the war: when not fighting, he represented the state in the US Senate, where his guerrilla tactics may have been even better appreciated. Details of Hickok's career as a Kansas Jayhawker were lost with any houses he may or may not have burned.

There is a story that, at some point that fall, Hickok's more respectable day job took him to northern New Mexico, just below the modern border with Colorado, where he was driving a wagon through Raton Pass. The wooded hills on either side of the trail were capable of holding many surprises: in this case, a large black bear, which ambled out of the brush and demanded a toll.

Black bears are not as aggressive as their grizzly cousins under most circumstances; the normal way of dealing with them is to simply scare them off.

Hickok shouted at the bear, but it remained in his path. The horses Hickok was leading recommended fleeing with noises that strongly suggested panic. Not taking their advice, Hickok grabbed his whip and leaped to the ground.

The bear was not impressed, nor did it reconsider when Hickok pulled his gun and fired off a warning shot.

At some point, two bear cubs appeared on the other side of the wagon, which set the entire affair in a different light for Hickok, who understood deep family ties—he loved his own mom dearly. Before he could inform the bear of this, the animal attacked.

Hickok fared poorly in the fight, being left with a broken arm and marks appropriate to a mauling.

Beside establishing Hickok's bona fides as a tough guy, the story explains what Hickok was doing at Rock Creek the following year, essentially lolling around: he'd been assigned a kind of working non-leave, recuperating from injuries, specifically that broken arm.

Hickok was in the Rock Creek area some months later when a man named David McCanles came to see the stationmaster about rent due. McCanles had settled on the land sometime before. Part of the Oregon Trail, his property included a creek that had to be crossed by anyone trying to go west. The water wasn't much most of the year—you could pretty much leap or splash across. Getting down to it was the rub. Nature had perforated the earth so sharply that getting across took raw muscle and considerable time. Detouring was inconvenient.

McCanles had a solution: he built a bridge.

The toll he charged depended on any number of factors, including his whim. As a general rule, the higher the water, the more desperate the pioneer, and the higher the charge.

Any crossing where the train of travelers would stop also demanded a store, which McCanles built on the eastern side of the creek as part of a small ranch. The toll bridge was a moneymaker, but selling it along with the ranch was apparently more profitable, and McCanles did just that several times, extending credit with terms that allowed him to repossess the bridge when the buyer fell into arears.

A cynic might say that McCanles arranged for sales to be made at high tide on the creek and on the trail, when a prospective buyer would envision a steady flow of money. Only afterward would it become obvious that traffic couldn't quite cover cash flow. This would explain how McCanles managed to sell and repossess the bridge before leasing (or in some accounts, selling) it to the Russell companies around the time Russell and Jones started the stage business.

On July 12, 1861, McCanles took his son and two employees, James Woods and James Gordon, with him to see stationmaster Horace Wellman about money the company owed him. He'd raised the issue before, repeatedly, and recently offered to accept supplies in lieu of cash, only to be turned down.

When am I getting my money? McCanles demanded, in a loud voice and probably a good sprinkling of expletives. At some point, Hickok walked up and asked what the yelling was about.

The two men knew each other well enough for McCanles to tell him that he had no quarrel with him, and that in fact they were friends, a point on which Hickok disagreed but seems not to have pressed. Instead, he went inside the small cabin. McCanles resumed yelling, demanding that that stationmaster come out and settle the matter.

The stationmaster, Horace Wellman, was not inside, but his

wife was. Whatever she told McCanles failed to calm him down. He stormed inside the cabin, to his eternal regret: as he stepped in, Hickok nailed him in the heart with a bullet from a rifle. The bullet threw him back and he stumbled out of the house to the ground, where his son found him faceup, a breath or two from dying.

Woods ran up to the house, where Hickok shot him with a pistol, mortally wounding him. Woods stumbled outside; Mrs. Wellman finished him with a hoe.

Hickok shot at McCanles's other man, Gordon, wounding him as well, but not badly enough to keep him from running toward the creek. Two other employees from the stage company joined Hickok and Mr. Wellman as they chased Gordon. One of the men had a dog; the dog cornered Gordon, who was then shot by someone with a shotgun. The younger McCanles escaped; Hickok grabbed one of the workers at the station and accused him of being an ally of McCanles. The man pleaded innocence and begged for his life; Hickok let him go after smacking him with the barrel of his pistol.

That, at least, was the outline of the tale everyone told the law a few days later when Sheriff E. B. Hendee showed up with a warrant for the arrest of Hickok, Wellman, and Doc Brink, one of the men who'd chased Gordon to the creek. (Brink, who worked later as an Indian scout, may have ridden briefly for the Pony, though this was not listed in his obituary—perhaps because he had tried to distance himself from the murder and Wild Bill during his lifetime.)

The three claimed self-defense, with Mrs. Wellman as their star witness. Young McCanles was not allowed to testify, supposedly because of his age.

If the jury took the time to grab a drink while deliberating, it was a quick one—they acquitted all three in near record time.

THE STORY HAS MANY GAPS. MORE THAN A FEW HAVE THEORIZED that the incident had *something* to do with the hostilities between North and South, though evidence that McCanles was a Confederate guerrilla is lacking. There are also theories that Hickok was romantically involved with Mrs. Wellman, though you'd think in that case Mr. Well-man would have sung a different tune in the courtroom.

But no one disputes that Hickok killed McCanles and at least wounded the other two men. And it's beyond argument that the incident was the start of Hickok's legend. Blown out of recognizable facsimile by an 1867 article in *Harper's New Monthly Magazine*—Hickok was said to have killed ten men single-handedly in the confrontation as he protected the poor woman—the outlines of the tale have thrilled folks for over a hundred and fifty years, even while the holes have baffled them. Hickok was already locally famous by the time the magazine story appeared, both for his prowess as a Union scout and his gunfight with former Confederate Dave Tutt, who was a victim of his legendary quick draw . . . and aim, always important.

HEROES AND LEGENDS

Among the great mysteries regarding Hickok is where his nickname came from. McCanles is often credited with coming up with "Bill," though it was hardly an endearment. In the favored version of the tale, Hickok had worked for McCanles, who took note of his nose and called him "Duck Bill." The other workers thought that was a hoot, and it stuck.

"Wild" is more understandable; at the time it was a common adjective, applied as part of a nickname not just to those of outgoing personalities—which Hickok doesn't seem to have had—but men whose exploits were exceedingly brave—which his service during the war, let alone the shootings, would have given evidence of. It could also apply, justly, to his reputation for being a lousy drunk.

Tradition declares that the first person to have used the nickname was a woman in a crowd at Independence, Missouri, in 1862, when Hickok stepped in and stopped the lynching of a bartender. Impressed by his bravado, she is supposed to have yelled "Ain't he wild," forever branding a hero with a tag easily burned into the national conscious.

Maybe. There's romance in it, at least.

Among the many stories told of Hickok and his life are endearing anecdotes about him reading Kit Carson's life story and meeting the famous trapper/guide/soldier himself on the trail. The stories can't be completely dismissed, even if they are highly improbable—Carson's "autobiography," written by DeWitt C. Peters, wasn't published until 1858, somewhat past the tender years when Hickok is said to have studied it.

From the very first article in *Harper's*, Hickok's story was littered with tropes and literary motifs, patterns of writing (and fabrication) that can be traced back through a thousand years of the printed word. But that doesn't invalidate the thread of truth that is sewn through many of the stories, both of Hickok and other legends. Nor should it obscure the greater truths at play, and the very reasons those tropes and motifs are employed.

Kit Carson—a real person, with real heroics—was a hero to many in the country at the time the first *Harper's* article about Wild Bill was written. By linking Hickok to him, both physically and thematically, the author and later storytellers were not just taking a shortcut in describing his characteristics. They set out a lineage of the frontier, a line of heroes that spoke to their readers. They knew Carson's qualities—independence, courage, a sense of justice, and above all self-reliance; they saw them again in Hickok, and in countless others in the West. These were qualities they understood innately, traits they associated with the West, and more important, their country, and themselves.

Harper's may have been read by frontier hearths and even in the occasional outhouse, but the magazine's real audience was back east. Readers' lives weren't generally as dangerous or physically daunting, but they were cutting new trails as well: in commerce, in science, even in how they lived. The line of "real life" heroes stretching back through Hickok and Kit Carson to the founders of the country connected them to the deeper values that their lives were founded on.

They saw that, too, in the Pony Express.

People were excited about the service, not just because they wanted information as quickly as possible, but because the service and especially its riders embodied or symbolized some of the things they cared about: courage, physical prowess, the willingness to risk all in a race against Nature and Time.

If gunplay figured into it, so much the better, but you didn't have to be literally wild to be celebrated. Being tenacious and undaunted in the face of myriad hardships would do.

OF COLTS AND CRANKS

GUNS

Mention of gunfighters puts one in mind of guns, and the natural question this raises is: What sort of weapons did Pony riders carry?

Many popular books and museum displays claim that Pony riders were outfitted with Spencer repeaters and a pair of Colts. The Spencer repeater was an excellent rifle, a lever action that carried seven bullets, allowing the shooter to get off seven shots before having to stop and reload. Designed by Christopher Miner Spencer, it was one of the weapons that revolutionized warfare, since to that point most practical rifles were muzzle loaded, which even the best-trained soldier found a hassle in combat—and forget about having to do that on horseback.

There's a problem with the story, though—the Spencer wasn't manufactured until the middle of the Civil War, after the Pony's demise.[1] (Lincoln, being truly a hands-on executive, took a few shots with the gun himself before directing a reluctant army to buy it.)

One Pony rider, Henry Tuckett, was said to have carried a slightly earlier repeater, a lever-action Henry. Patented in October 1860, the gun fired sixteen rounds from a tubular magazine before needing to be reloaded; the rounds were self-contained rimfire cartridges, vastly different from the paper cartridge and cap systems common to that point. Tuckett's having it even a few months later—say by late spring, just before the service's demise—seems unlikely, given the very low production rates until 1864 or so. But this is at least theoretically possible. So, too, is the possibility that some member of the company had the slightly earlier Volcanic Repeater—which influenced the Henry's design so much it could be called the Henry 1.0—which was also in the West at the time.

Far more common and likely to be found anywhere in the Old West were Sharps rifles. These were a popular series of long guns; later models were famous as buffalo killers. The single-shot, paper cartridge rifles loaded from the breech, which made loading much quicker than with older weapons. Just as important, they were renowned for their accuracy. Speed and accuracy are relative—the guns used paper cartridges and caps; a calm head and steady hands were essential. There were both full-length and carbine models; the latter were somewhat easier to carry and wield on a horse.

But in reality, not many riders would have carried *any* rifle, be it a newfangled repeater or something far more popular, like a Sharps. Long guns are unwieldy on a horse. Cavalry units—say, the one George Armstrong Custer took charge of at Gettysburg—generally dismounted to use them effectively during the nineteenth century. That was not a good tactic for a single Pony rider, who would be giving up his biggest advantage over an enemy; namely, his horse's feet.

Pistols were more practical, though these, too, would have been weapons mostly of last resort. Colts were extremely popular on the frontier in 1860, and while not the *only* pistol available, they make sense as the weapon of choice for a rider. At twenty-five bucks apiece, they were a serious investment, but they were easier to aim and fire from the saddle. Just as important, a wise pursuer would hesitate after a shot was fired, knowing there were more where that came from; any hesitation would add to the Pony rider's speed advantage.

Pony riders were expected to have their own weapons; if they wanted, they could buy one on time from the company—Russell, Majors & Waddell fronted them the gun, taking a few dollars every payday until it was paid for.

SAMUEL COLT

The revolver has an important place in the history of the West. Technically any gun capable of firing multiple bullets without reloading, thanks to a revolving chamber, revolvers date at least to the sixteenth century but weren't practical until the nineteenth. Practicality required a host of innovations and inventors, but mostly it took one man above all: Samuel Colt. He was so successful, and his guns so good, that his name became synonymous with pistols—much to the chagrin of competitors like Smith & Wesson, who put out a good product themselves.

A Connecticut Yankee, Colt was a questioning sort—biographers say he stripped down guns as a seven-year-old and got in trouble in school for a July Fourth celebration involving explosives that went awry. He's said to have gotten the inspiration for revolving mechanisms by watching the spokes in a ship's wheel.

Given the strange path inspiration takes, there's no reason to doubt the origin story. But it shortchanges the actual creative act.

Pretty much from day zero until Colt, guns were thought of as solid tubes with a hole at one end and a controlled—hopefully—explosion at the other. You might mess with the tube: strengthen it, put a spiral groove inside to make your bullet fly straighter, make it longer, saw it off. You might concentrate on the exploding part, making the boom bigger and faster. What you didn't do, unless you were crazy or Samuel Colt, was hack off the most important part of that long tube and spin it around.

Colt's insight was that the basic design of the weapon could be broken into parts in a way that hadn't been done before. In order to make that practical—to quiet the right side of the brain and its warnings about pending explosions—he had to come up with a mechanism to hold his broken-out part together. It had to be solid enough to withstand an explosion, yet flexible enough to move on to the next round when its time came. It had to lock into place without blocking anything.

The basic ingredients for making the revolver work—springs, le-
vers, latches, and so on—were readily available. Metal making and
gunsmithing were skills that, while greatly improved in the years before Colt, had developed on their own and were available to anyone.
Likewise for the evolution of bullets and the explosions that propelled
them—a procession from flintlocks to percussion caps to metal cartridges was greatly aided by the discovery of mercury fulminate. All
these contributed in subtle ways to Colt's invention; it was his genius
to use them in new ways.

Colt was unique, but this sort of genius was thriving all around him
in eighteenth-century America. People were looking at crowded city
blocks and saying, why not build higher? They saw disconnected rivers and envisioned canals between them. They saw a steam engine—
more controlled explosions, really—and imagined labyrinths of gears
that could propel ships and wagons.

It was the same sort of creative impulse that propelled men to
string a relay of horse stations across deserts and mountains and
prairies.

It's one thing to see those possibilities in your head, and another to
manifest them in the real world. Starting with a wooden model and
drawings, Colt hooked up with a gunsmith named Anson Chase in
Hartford to produce a working model, which blew up in Colt's hands
when he tried it. Undeterred, though slowed by the need to earn
money to eat, Colt eventually produced working prototypes of both
a pistol and a rifle, patenting them in Europe in 1835 and America—
even then the bureaucracy was slow—the following year.

Financial backers were secured and a factory was opened in Paterson, New Jersey. Maybe the idea was too radical, but the guns didn't
sell in the numbers needed to make the venture a financial success;
the company went belly-up, declaring bankruptcy in 1842.

On its own, Colt's revolver was a work of genius and would have
surely inspired others, revolutionizing weaponry. But someone else's
revolver would have won the West if not for Colt's perseverance and
another burst of genius, this time even less obvious.

After the bust of the Paterson factory, Colt went back to blowing big things up, demonstrating his prowess with mines (called torpedoes back then) for Congress and anyone else who liked to see things explode. In the meantime, the United States went to war with Mexico. General Zachary Taylor, then commanding the army in Texas and south, was impressed by the efforts of rangers under Samuel H. Walker; sending him home to recruit another batch, Taylor told the captain to fetch up more of the guns they were using—original five-shot Colts. (Yes, five-shooters. Not six.)

Walker got hold of Colt. Colt had neither a factory nor blueprints for the guns anymore; he'd lost the first and given away the second. But with help from Eli Whitney—more famous today for his cotton gin—Colt built a new factory and produced a new line of revolvers, starting with what today is called the Walker pistol.

The Walker was—still is, if you can get your hands on one—a six-shot, single-action revolver some fifteen and a half inches long, with a nine-inch round barrel and cast brass trigger guard. It fired a .44-caliber bullet. (*Single-action* means that the hammer has to be pulled back manually to fire; your thumb was invented for that satisfying click at the back of the chamber before pressing the trigger. By contrast, a double-action pistol can be fired in one of two ways—using your thumb to pull back the hammer, or simply pressing the trigger, which pulls the hammer back automatically. Single-action came first, double-action later. And while we're detouring: *.44 caliber* means that the bullet was 44 one-hundredths of an inch in diameter. The bullets were propelled by black powder ignited by a percussion cap; the user made his own bullets, poured the powder in the chamber, put a bullet in, then used a lever on the underside of the barrel to tamp everything down. Caps were then placed on the back end of the cylinder; when struck, they ignited the black powder, which in turn sent the bullets flying. By the time of the Pony, paper cartridges had been developed; later guns would use cartridges that put everything into a convenient metal package.)

The Walker was a large and heavy pistol by our standards and had a lot of room for improvement, but it was a revolution in 1847. The army put an order in for a thousand, and Colt was on his way. Beyond the genius of his original idea, he conceived a factory that could manufacture the guns on an assembly line—an innovation nearly as revolutionary as the wheel. To do this successfully, the parts had to be interchangeable, which meant precise measurements, skilled craftsmen, dependable tooling, and plentiful power. Most important, it required creative thinking—looking at the manufacturing process of making one gun at a time, piece by piece, and realizing it could be different.

Two other things helped the Colt become ubiquitous. The first was the government, whose large contracts spurred production and improvements in the design. Last but not least, Colt's outsized success depended on marketing—first word of mouth, then advertising, paid and free.

Samuel Colt died in 1862; his wife, Elizabeth, carried on with the company, which continued to produce excellent weapons after the war and to this very day. The pattern of its success: good design, quality manufacturing, strong brand recognition—and, yes, large contracts from government sources—are as important today as they were then, even for businesses far outside the realm of arms.

THE PONY'S PISTOLS

But the question remains: Assuming the Pony riders were carrying Colts, which is highly likely, which Colt was it?

The successors to the Walker included a series of models known as the Dragoon. Fourteen inches long with a seven-and-a-half-inch barrel, the Dragoon included a sketch of a fight with Indians on its cylinder—not a bad inspiration, perhaps. It, too, was a six-shooter that fired a .44-caliber bullet. It would have been a prized possession of any Pony rider.

Another candidate would have been the Colt 1851 Navy, a slightly smaller six-shooter that used a .36-caliber bullet. And then there are the army models, the pocket pistols.

The Dragoon is mentioned in at least one account. But whether that was meant specifically or as a generic description—the word was used both ways—is unclear.

It's possible that not all riders carried one, let alone the two that many writers claim. Samuel Clemens—a.k.a. Mark Twain—declared that the rider he encountered was unarmed. On the whole, though, it's likely that riders carried a Colt over most of the territory the trail covered.

WHAT THEY WORE

What'd the riders look like?

Young, white—no blacks or Indians are recorded, and only one or two riders are specifically mentioned as being Mexican—generally short and on the lighter side. Images of riders today generally portray them wearing dungarees and a red flannel shirt, but there was no official, company-supplied uniform; what they wore was typical dress for a workingman out west. Blue denim was prized as a durable material and extremely popular, but the mass-produced, sturdy, riveted jeans we associate with the period had yet to be invented; most clothes at this point were still made by hand and even homespun.[2] If you weren't wearing denim, you might be wearing wool, dyed a soft brown—the dye came from butternuts. In the winter, the best coats were made of lined leather or buffalo fur. Buckskin jackets and leggings were a native invention appropriated by whites, especially on the frontier; they were durable and practical. In some cases the clothing was bought from Indians and not merely copied. It's said fringes were not only decorative; they also helped wick water away from the material.

Knitted socks—cotton or maybe wool—were usual; boots were de rigueur. Riding a dusty road—which pretty much describes the entire length of the Pony's trail—you would generally use a cloth bandanna outlaw style to keep some of the dust off your face.

Men's hair usually covered their ears and reached down to the collar at the back; various caps could cover it, from soft felt work caps to wide-brimmed hats. The Stetson cowboy hat and its imitators were still a few years off.

Most men were clean-shaven, though by the time of the Pony beards were becoming a thing. Muttonchops and dundrearies—sideburns—were extended and fashioned, and having a beard on your chin didn't necessitate a mustache on your lip.

If you were one of the owners of the Pony, you dressed far differently, at least when you were in town. Matching pants, vests, and coats had come into style a few years before; these would be made from wool, though the quality would vary partly for the intended use—superfine wool was for the best occasions, medium wool for more run-of-the-mill days. Dress white shirts were made of linen or cotton. The real sign of your station and the literal height of fashion was your top hat, made of silk—the stovepipe, familiar from the photos of Lincoln.

And women?

Dresses, nearly always; one-piece usually on the frontier and two-piece back east or for fancier occasions. Skirts were worn over foundation garments, and a bodice on top of a corset. One-piece dresses looked similar, with the bodice sewn to the skirt. Collars were often separate pieces. Most women on the frontier made their own clothes, sometimes growing their own flax (for linen) or raising sheep for wool that they carded, spun, and wove into homespun cloth. But store-bought calico—inexpensive cloth made from cotton, easily dyed and printed—was the most popular material if you could afford it and had a store handy.

Cotton and imported silk were store-bought, often hand-embroidered. Even out west, many women would consult with some magazine like *Godey's Lady's Book*, which had colored fashion plates of the newest fashions from Europe and back east; they would then use

the pictures as models for their own creations, either from scrat᷎
by altering older dresses.

There was one shocking development in women's fashion around
this time: bloomers. These were trousers gathered at the ankles and
worn under a short skirt. A plainer version, more of a split skirt, was
sometimes worn by western ranch women and frontier women for
riding horses or working in the fields.

Fancy hoop skirts—known usually as crinolines—were a Sunday
church affair on the frontier; they were too difficult to work in, and a
hazard around fireplaces and the like besides.

But the most important piece of a woman's wardrobe may have
been the long apron she wore, which protected the one or two dresses
she might own from sparking embers, flying fat, and greasy hands.
On the frontier, aprons would often be made from flour sacks—little
went to waste.

OVER THE PRAIRIE

Having crossed into Nebraska, the Pony rider and his mail followed
the Little Blue River, heading in the direction of the Platte River and
Fort Kearny. Little Blue was and remains a shallow, meandering
waterway—not lazy, exactly, but not one to overachieve either. This
made it an almost perfect river for travelers in the mid-nineteenth
century, something you could trust as a water source and guide,
while still providing an ample place to ford—assuming the weather
was with you. For that reason, the Little Blue—and its brother Big
Blue, to the east—were popular with travelers on the Oregon Trail.
The Pony route along Little Blue followed that trail for much of its
eastern half, heading to Virginia City and then Big Sandy, a home
station where another rider took over.

Though the path over the plains was generally wide and "easy" ir
Nebraska, there were still potholes and pitfalls. Frank Helvey, an I
diana boy who'd worked his way up from substitute to regular ri
was speeding toward Big Sandy from Kansas one day when his ᷎

broke its leg. Helvey slung the mochila over his shoulder and completed the run on foot.

Two stops beyond Big Sandy, the trail threaded through the Narrows, a gangplank of a route along the river, hemmed in by bluffs. By this time of year, the ground had crumbled into dry sand. Winds picked up bunches, adding grit to the bursts of cold that promised a hard prairie winter. Things were different in spring: the area around the water could be almost lush green, and here and there trees clustered, not yet used as building material or fuel.

Pony riders regularly passed large wagon trains of settlers heading westward, most either for Oregon or Utah. While the migration to both territories had passed its peak, about thirty-one hundred people moved over the trail toward one or the other territories in 1860. But these numbers were dwarfed by the number of travelers heading toward California: nine thousand.[3]

Pioneers would usually group up in Missouri, assembling trains of a dozen or two up to three hundred wagons strong. They would elect captains and often hired guides who'd been across the route before. The trail itself wasn't a specific road; on the plains, a traveler had any number of ruts to follow in the same general direction. Pony riders passing would invariably veer close by, shouting the latest news or gossip they'd heard along the way. Given the length of the journey—on a good day, the train might move twenty miles, but those days were rare—Pony riders were seen often in the spring and early summer.

THUNDERING ACROSS THE PLAIN THAT NOVEMBER, THE RIDER SAW dust billowing on the horizon. It was far too late for a wagon train. Even the most clueless pioneer would know winter was coming on; if it was relatively light there, it would be blizzard-like at the mountain asses.

As the rider closed in, a stagecoach appeared at the head of the furl- nob of grit and dirt; headed to a station it shared with the Pony, d by a prince of the prairie—a stagecoach driver.

The odds were he was a fellow employee of Russell, and in any event worthy of a whoop and hello. But as famous as the Pony rider might be, he was minor royalty compared with the "whip" at the front of the stage. A driver was both pilot and guide, his word absolute on the long stretches between stations.

The best were also impromptu entertainers between stops. Robert Sewell—known for reasons lost to history as "Old Bob Ridley"—was popular along this portion of the line. The owner of the station at Log Chain, he held a day job driving between Kansas and Fort Kearny. Old Bob was a joker and more than a bit of a storyteller, entertaining passengers with tales tall and otherwise. According to Frank A. Root, another driver who held just about every job possible for Russell and his partners, Old Bob loved chewing tobacco but hated paying for it. Old Bob rarely had to: he would ask passengers if he could have a plug. They'd oblige, and he'd cut off a wad with his knife. Then, handing it back, he'd suddenly remember he had a brother who liked to chew and cut off another hunk for him. One of his victims, a congressman from Missouri, saw the result and threw it back to him.

"I guess the whole family chews, and you'd better take the rest."[4]

A number of stage lines, short and long, went through Kansas, Nebraska, and other points west. The most popular coach of the time was the Concord, made by Abbot, Downing & Company of Concord, New Hampshire. With a large set of wheels up front and even bigger ones at the back, the Concord typically carried nine people arranged on three benches, with passengers stacked three across on each. The middle bench was where the door was; the only consolation to being squeezed there was the fact that you were first out at a stop. The carriage was so narrow it was practically mandatory to lean your arm out the open window, assuming you were tall enough to reach it.

Baggage and goods being shipped could be bundled in a compartment at the back or on top—or, often, left on the floor where they competed for room with the passengers' feet. This was especially true of the mail, which consisted of not only sacks of letters but bundles of newspapers, which had been accorded special travel privileges by

Congress. When the going got tough, the newspapers were the first items discarded—even then, the media's popularity was low.

Unlike freighters, stagecoaches were pulled by teams of mules and sometimes horses; both were easier to handle and persuade than oxen, which in the case of the mules says something about the cattle. Stubborn as they could be—hence the old saying—a good team in the hands of an experienced whip could manage six or more miles an hour on a reasonable road and trudge dependably through a washout on a bad one. Horses might go faster, but they needed easier treatment and generally gentler roads. The ability to deal with heat was especially important on the Butterfield route, whose path through El Paso and on to California featured some of the hottest, driest stretches imaginable.

Like the Pony riders, stagecoaches ordinarily didn't make long stops until they came to the end of their line. If you were hungry, you got out at a station and waited until the next stage made its way through, a space often measured in days.

THE CRANK'S CRANK

If Pony riders and stagecoach drivers were a colorful crew, so too were many of their passengers. A few were famous in their time— Horace Greeley, editor of the *New York Tribune*, was a cross between Roger Ailes and Rush Limbaugh, and just as well known. (Except for their politics: Greeley was a liberal Republican.) Others were not yet famous but would be soon—Samuel Clemens, better known as Mark Twain, traveled to Nevada not long after the letter announcing Lincoln's election.

But the most notable stagecoach passenger of all time—at least if you're a historian—was a British traveler named Richard Francis Burton.

Burton—unrelated to the '60s/'70s actor and serial husband of Elizabeth Taylor—was a multitalented explorer, translator, writer, and spy. He was also a first-class crank, the sort of man who could find the one dark cloud in an azure sky but also would complain that it was not quite dark enough. In Britain, Captain Sir Richard Burton—he was knighted—is remembered today largely for his attempt to find the source of the Nile. He wrote forty-three books about his world travels and translated thirty major works. Among these was an X-rated (for the time) *Arabian Nights* and a precisely detailed sexual how-to, the *Kama Sutra*.

His own books were extremely detail-oriented, with a scientific bent. Burton was no aesthete—he served in the army and was a spy in India, and as an explorer and writer he risked death countless times. He was an expert on everything from bayonet charges to sex, and seemingly adept at all of it.

Burton is primarily known to Americans—at least those studying the Old West—for a book he penned just as the Lincoln letter was passing through Nebraska, a 574-page tome on a trip from St. Joe's to Salt Lake and beyond he took a few weeks before the election.[5] The book is one of the most literate descriptions of the era available, its descriptions almost unfailingly detailed and, within reasonable parameters, accurate.

It is also one of the snottiest comments on America ever penned. Burton was a master of the drive-by put-down. A sample:

> *Passing by Marysville, in old maps Palmetto City, a country-town which thrives by selling whiskey to ruffians of all descriptions . . .* [6]

That's a mild one. Somewhat accurate, though: Marysville was well known as a place for horse racing, gambling, drinking, and—did we mention drinking?

Another:

> *At 12 45 P.M., traveling over the uneven barren, and in a burning sirocco, we reached Lodge-Pole Station, where we made our "noonin."*

The hovel fronting the creek was built like an Irish shanty, or a Beloch hut, against a hill side, to save olie wall, and it presented a fresh phase of squalor and wretchedness.

The mud walls were partly papered with "Harper's Magazine," "Frank Leslie," and the "New York Illustrated News"; the ceiling was a fine festoon-work of soot, and the floor was much like the ground outside, only not nearly so clean.[7]

This is his almost-fair description of the Pikes Peak stage Russell et al. owned:

The conductors and road-agents are of a class superior to the drivers; they do their harm by an inordinate ambition to distinguish themselves. I met one gentleman who owned to three murders, and another individual who lately attempted to ration the mules with wild sage. The company was by no means rich; already the papers had prognosticated a failure, in consequence of the government withdrawing its supplies, and it seemed to have hit upon the happy expedient of badly entreating travelers that good may come to it of our evils. The hours and halting places were equally vilely selected; for instance, at Forts Kearney, Laramie, and Bridger, the only points where supplies, comfort, society, are procurable, a few minutes of grumbling delay were granted as a favor, and the passengers were hurried on to some distant wretched ranch, apparently for the sole purpose of putting a few dollars into the station-master's pockets.[8]

Burton happened to meet Alexander Majors when he began his journey in St. Joe. He admired him . . . almost:

. . . a veteran mountaineer, familiar with life on the prairies. His meritorious efforts to reform the morals of the laud have not yet put forth even the bud of promise. He forbade his drivers and employees to drink, gamble, curse, and travel on Sundays; he desired them to peruse Bibles distributed to them gratis; and though he refrained from a

lengthy proclamation commanding his lieges to be good boys and girls,
he did not the less expect it of them. Results: I scarcely ever saw a sober
driver; as for profanity—the Western equivalent for hard swearing—
they would make the blush of shame crimson the cheek of the old Isis
bargee; and, rare exceptions to the rule of the United States, they are not
to be deterred from evil talking even by the dread presence of a "lady."[9]

Harsh, but in the main probably accurate.

Burton liked little that he saw, criticizing even the bridles on
horses, though he paid grudging tribute to a cowboy's spurs for their
effectiveness. The Brit made a habit of studying what he considered
exotic religions and unusual sexual practices; he was heading to Salt
Lake City and the Mormons hoping to encounter one or the other. He
crossed paths with Pony Express riders at least twice on his trip; alas,
it seems to have been only from a distance. This is the most detailed
report, from near South Pass, Wyoming:

Advancing over a soil alternately sandy and rocky—an iron flat that
could not boast of a spear of grass—we sighted a number of coyotes, fit-
test inhabitants of such a waste, and a long, distant line of dust, like the
smoke of a locomotive, raised by a herd of mules which were being driven
to the corral. We were presently met by the Pony Express rider; he reined
in to exchange news, which de part et d'autre *simply nil. As he pricked*
onward over the plain, the driver informed us, with a portentous rolling
of the head, that Ichabod was an a'mighty fine "shyoot."[10]

Burton seems to have been mildly disappointed in America, even
as a target for his wit; maybe he found the language more difficult
than the Arabic and twenty-eight other tongues he is said to have
known. Even one of the continent's notorious achievements suffered
in his opinion: scalping.

Burton was a connoisseur of scalping, a devotee of the art whose
dissections—excuse the pun—raised it to a place above dance and
sculpture in his opinion. Seemingly no reference to Indians seems to

lack a mention of the possibility, and after talking about the "rite," he explains how to detect counterfeits. Burton was expert enough on the art to publish an article about the subject a few years later. It begins by succinctly summarizing the matter:

> *It is generally, but falsely, supposed that only Americans scalp; the practice is Asiatic, European, and African. The underlying idea is the natural wish to preserve a memorial of the hated foeman done to death, and at the same time to dishonour his foul remains.*[11]

Hard to argue with that, much less the pages traipsing through human follicles that follow.

Burton, taking all precautions, is said to have shaved his hair close before his American travails, not wanting to tempt fate or the natives.

THE TWAIN MEET

As sharp as Burton could be, he can't quite make the cut against another writer far more familiar to American readers. This was Sam Clemens, better known as Mark Twain.

Despite Clemens's professed loyalties to the South, his older brother Orion had connections to the Union and Republican James Nye, a New York senator who was appointed in the winter of 1860 to serve as governor of Nevada. Nye tapped Orion to be his secretary, and Orion tapped Sam to be his assistant . . . and the money for the ride out to Carson City, the territory's capital. Sam enthusiastically forked over the $150 apiece it cost to get there from St. Joe's, packed a heavy suitcase with items that had to be mostly discarded (the weight limit was twenty-five pounds per traveler), and set out. Sam Clemens didn't intend on writing about the trip—his publishing career was still several years down the road—but it made an impression even so.

Clemens spotted Pony riders several times on the journey, though only long enough to get what he called a "ghost of a look." This is what he says he saw:

The pony-rider was usually a little bit of a man, brimful of spirit and endurance. No matter what time of the day or night his watch came on, and no matter whether it was winter or summer, raining, snowing, hailing, or sleeting, or whether his "beat" was a level straight road or a crazy trail over mountain crags and precipices, or whether it led through peaceful regions or regions that swarmed with hostile Indians, he must be always ready to leap into the saddle and be off like the wind! There was no idling-time for a pony-rider on duty. He rode fifty miles without stopping, by daylight, moonlight, starlight, or through the blackness of darkness—just as it happened. He rode a splendid horse that was born for a racer and fed and lodged like a gentleman; kept him at his utmost speed for ten miles, and then, as he came crashing up to the station where stood two men holding fast a fresh, impatient steed, the transfer of rider and mail-bag was made in the twinkling of an eye, and away flew the eager pair and were out of sight before the spectator could get hardly the ghost of a look. Both rider and horse went "flying light." The rider's dress was thin, and fitted close; he wore a "round-about," and a skull-cap, and tucked his pantaloons into his boot-tops like a race-rider. He carried no arms—he carried nothing that was not absolutely necessary, for even the postage on his literary freight was worth five dollars a letter.[12]

Twain was writing from memory some ten years after the actual trip, and his details throughout the book don't always match reality; of the Pony, he says quite seriously that eighty were constantly riding across the country, when at most two would do so; the entire army of riders might have matched that number, spending their time waiting for a relay or recovering from a ride.

KEARNY

Roughly three hundred miles from St. Joe, the future Mark Twain—and the Pony rider carrying the election news—reached Fort Kearny.

They had traveled along the Platte River, crossing to one of the main outposts on the superhighway west.

Kearny—named after General Stephen Watts Kearny but often misspelled as "Kearney"—looked more like a camp than a fort. It had no palisades, those large, imposing walls that attackers like to burn down in Westerns. It commanded no high ground to speak of. But it was convenient to the water, and to the Oregon Trail, which was the idea. The traffic west in the 1840s was such that the government decided to set up the post to protect and aid travelers—and maybe to keep an eye on them as well. It immediately became the most important stop for most people traveling out of St. Joe's; an emigrant could rest there and buy supplies, either at the fort itself or the settlements nearby.

By the time the letters detailing Lincoln's election arrived, the special run from Fort Kearny with the telegraphed results was long gone, the riders back from their mission. The news arrived at Denver a reported two days and twenty hours after leaving Kearny—possibly record time.

But the fuller results and the regular mail still had to go through. The rider rode past the fort, heading to the station near what was called Dobytown—a small settlement just outside the military camp, named for the material that the structures were built from. The hamlet and surrounding area were undergoing a mini-real-estate boom, set off by the location of the stage line and the related Pony Express relay.

The beneficiaries: Russell and company, who'd bought the land. But whatever profit they hoped to make was just a drop in the current of the nearby Platte: a fact Russell was trying to come to terms with at that moment back east.

THREAT OF DISSOLUTION

MONEY, AND LOTS OF IT

Russell realized that the idea of the Pony was bigger than the Pony itself, a means to another end. That end was money, in the form of a million-dollar contract to deliver the mail to California.

Moving mail around a rapidly expanding country could be both risky and lucrative. The risk came from uncontrollable events like Indians and winter storms. The money came from the government, and the synergy you could build using it.

If any of his banker friends doubted that there was money to be made by backing him, Russell would have gladly walked them up a few blocks from his New York offices to view an elaborate marble complex, barely two years old, complete with a railroad spur and nearby stables. It was owned by American Express, the backers of the firms that were his only real competitors out west, and in many ways his best model for the future. The company provided an object lesson in nineteenth-century fortune making, a veritable blueprint to riches. And it happened almost overnight, with a bit of help from the US Post Office.

Unintentional help, since it came first in the form of incompetence.

Official postal delivery throughout the United States had a spotty history in the nineteenth century, and even though Congress had granted the US Post Office Department a monopoly, private "express services" were numerous, right up until 1843 when Congress—arguably more concerned about losing the patronage jobs attached to the postal service than actually getting the mail through—tightened the law to discourage private companies. Even with that law, private delivery services were still the best way to get messages and packages from one place to another. There were various ways to get around the law, but quite often they operated in areas so poorly served by the US Post Office that no one dared stop them, for fear of losing all means of communicating with anyone.

The private companies were especially useful in moving valuable freight—like bank notes—which absolutely had to get to where it was going quickly and dependably. This latter business boomed with the dissolution of the Bank of the United States; in the absence of a central bank, local banks conducted any number of transactions with each other, moving small but valuable pieces of paper back and forth. There was a good profit to be made in delivering the notes, and with the banks as customers, the companies had access to potential financing if they wanted to expand.

In 1850, three businessmen in upstate western New York—Henry Wells, William G. Fargo, and John Warren Butterfield—pooled their resources and formed American Express to move mail and goods quickly and dependably in the Buffalo area.[1] The trio had already succeeded on their own with similar companies; pooling their resources enabled them not only to expand, but also to gain a distinct advantage in pricing—by not competing with one another, they could charge almost what they wanted.

Buffalo sat on the shores of Lake Erie. The city was perfectly situated as a hub to the west thanks to the Erie Canal, a three-hundred-sixty-some-mile wonder of the world that ran straight—almost—across northern New York State to Albany and the Hudson River. The Hudson connected directly to New York, and from there, the world.

Business boomed. Their company did more than move messages and goods. It collected money, shipping freight on credit for customers, to be paid at delivery. It exchanged notes payable at distant banks—the paper money of the time—for a percentage of the value. It became a banker as well as a mover of stuff and information, though its origins were embedded in the name, American Express.

Expanding rapidly, Wells, Fargo, and Butterfield brought in other investors as stockholders, formed alliances with other freight and express companies, protected their interests by cross-pollinating company boards. They had different personalities, slightly different goals, varying perspectives on the degree of risk to take and when to take it, but together they built an empire in less than decade. Despite some reverses along the way, they were a potent model for anyone wanting to get rich in America.

WELLS FARGO, BUTTERFIELD, ET AL.

American Express was well established in the Northeast by the time Russell joined with Majors and Waddell to form their mammoth freighting company. It was dominant in the Northeast, and its interests were slightly different from theirs in any event—it left freighting on that scale to specialists. But as Russell set his sights on building the business and expanding into mail, two of the conglomerate's offshoots came into view—Wells Fargo and the Butterfield Overland Stage.

VERY SOON AFTER THEY FORMED AMERICAN EXPRESS, MR. WELLS AND Mr. Fargo, two of the three main partners, saw opportunity in California, which had recently become a state and was booming due to the gold rush. When Butterfield balked—there was a good deal of animosity among the partners—the others set up the company on their own.

Like American Express, Wells Fargo moved things—messages, small packages, and, most profitably, gold. The company was good at it—and even better at advertising and PR. After the 1852 election, they rushed—a relative term—news of the results around the state and got credit for it in the local newspapers.

Mail moved along stagecoach lines established by the firm or contracted by it to other lines. Wells Fargo did not have a contract to deliver the US Mail. But the company found a loophole: Congress in 1852 allowed express companies to carry mail in stamped envelopes sold by the Post Office, and the company made good use of these by buying a large supply of envelopes, franking them with their own stamp, and then reselling them at one of their one hundred or so offices around California.[2] You could drop off a letter at a Wells Fargo office and have it picked up at the post office, and vice versa—a real convenience in areas like the mining camps where there were no post offices. Any businessman who had to send an important note would gladly pay the double or triple price premium to ensure his letter was delivered.

Wells Fargo made a profit on the service, but its true value was in helping to bring in other business.[3] The company moved people, goods, and gold via stagecoaches, generally though not always the same ones that moved the mail. And then there was banking. Wells Fargo purchased and sold gold dust and handled financial transactions: issuing notes that could be cashed for gold, and cashing notes from other banks—important business at a time when banks were printing their own money. While Wells Fargo's banking business briefly imploded with the rest of the state's businesses in a panic during 1855, it quickly revived. Synergy between the different services, efficient management, and superior capitalization—the principals had deep pockets—helped the firm steadily grow.

BUTTERFIELD

Butterfield soon realized he'd made a mistake by not getting into California with his partners. But better late than never: he decided to start his own company there in 1857, and to do so with a bang; he snagged a huge contract from the US Post Office Department to deliver the mail to California.

If you put Russell, Majors, and Waddell together in a single person, you would have the perfect nineteenth-century entrepreneur: physically tough, outwardly visionary, solidly practical, and financially astute.

Or you could just look at John Warren Butterfield, who encompassed all those qualities, with a few added features like steely resolve and occasional quarrelsomeness for good measure. Born in the upstate New York town of Berne near Albany in 1810, Butterfield had begun driving stagecoaches as a teenager. By the 1840s, he headed one of the principal companies dominating upstate New York transportation of people, goods, and messages. He joined with Wells and Fargo at the end of the decade and was soon a partner in one of the richest companies in America.

THE '49ERS OUT WEST COULD HAVE SHARED A FEW THOUGHTS ON HAPpiness and the solace of wealth, had he asked. They had plenty of time to contemplate both, though experiencing either was often more a matter of luck than hard work.

Digging up rocks is a lonely business, especially when you've left your heart to someone three thousand miles away; you need to remind her that all these sacrifices will pay off soon. If you're a businessman in New York and have investments in Sacramento, you need to send orders occasionally just to remind your agent you're alive. Those and a million other reasons made reliable mail service between the old states and California a practical and political necessity.

Through the early part of the 1850s, steamers taking the mail or goods from east to west could take as many as six months for a trip; the construction of a Panama railroad helped narrow this time to about a month, if the weather was good and the jungle cooperated.

California and eastern business interests in Congress agitated for more and faster deliveries. The postmaster looked to save money—it cost hundreds of thousands of dollars more to send mail by steamer than the postal service could collect in postage—and to consolidate the service.

Finally, appropriations were earmarked for an overland service contract in 1857, with payment depending on frequency—do it once a week and earn $450,000; twice a week would pay $600,000. Every other week was a bargain at $300,000. Butterfield got the contract for $600,000, using a route known as Oxbow through the Southwest.[4]

From the start, his Overland Stage had a strong relationship with American Express and Wells Fargo. Not only was the principal stockholder one of the founders of American Express, but several of the largest stockholders were heavily invested in American Express or were directors of Wells Fargo, or both. More important, American Express fronted money to the company in the form of loans.

One important note: while American Express and its original founders had made money by running private delivery services and competing with the US Post Office, here the situation was very much reversed. A private company might make a small profit, but the only way to make a fortune delivering the mail was to get a big—very big—contract from the postmaster. The prices charged for delivering mail could simply never pay for it to be delivered a few hundred miles, let alone two or three thousand. Subsidies were necessary, though even a healthy subsidy alone would not guarantee a profit.

GOLD AND AN EMPIRE

Butterfield's service was generally considered excellent, but his line had a fatal political flaw, or feature, depending on your point of view: it traveled south, through areas that could be easily controlled by Southern states. As the country continued to divide in two, that left Northern congressmen uneasy. There was support in Congress for an alternative route that traveled to the North, and several congressmen were clamoring to revisit the contract, even though it had years to run.

The overland mail contract to California was substantial and potentially would help Russell fill the hole that the government had put him in. But he saw it as part of a larger opportunity, one made possible by the discovery of gold—not in California, but Pikes Peak, Colorado.

Shortly after getting the first acceptances from War Secretary

Floyd in 1858, Russell traveled back to Missouri and Kansas to talk with his partners. He had barely arrived when news came of the gold discovery. The breathless reports spoke, as such reports always do, of unending riches. Russell knew optimism when he saw it, and for him, this news reports meant one thing: there was going to be a new gold rush.

He expected that it would be every bit as big and lucrative as the California gold rush a decade before. That meant he could make big money moving things around. A stagecoach company to transport people from Missouri to Denver and the surrounding areas was a must. And a mail contract would be a huge bonanza—the stages would bring the mail as well as people and goods.

Majors and Waddell were skeptical, and so Russell formed another company with his old partner John S. Jones to set up a line and take advantage of the rush he expected. Russell, Majors & Waddell continued freighting through the area, and Jones kept his own business going as well. The partnerships were intertwined, but not exclusive.

On paper, Russell's stagecoach idea looked great, even without a mail contract. A stagecoach ticket covering the entire trip from Leavenworth to Denver cost $125. Shorter trips were charged at the rate of twenty-five cents per mile. Throw a mail and package business on top—a quarter for a letter, a buck for a package—and it could add up, especially if there was a gold rush.

There *was* a gold rush; a traveler reported seeing as many as fifty quartz-crushing machines entering the area in one month alone.[5] But even though Russell needed only a few hundred people a month to use his stages, the customer base turned out to be far smaller. Most people heading toward the mineral fields used their own transportation. And there were other stage lines, which made it difficult to raise prices.

No matter. Russell was after the big picture: the mail contract and a monopoly on transport through the area. He saw an opportunity to achieve this when J.M. Hockaday & Company, itself badly pinched, offered to sell its contract to deliver mail from St. Joseph,

Missouri, to Salt Lake City. Russell paid about $144,000 for the contract. No cash actually changed hands—the sale was arranged by allowing Hockaday to collect money owed by the US Post Office Department and giving that firm the rights to $121,250 that would be paid out through 1860. That freed up cash flow and probably saved Russell from having to get outside financing or more investors to complete the deal.

Russell now had an operation over half the route to California: a strong argument in favor of being awarded a new contract. He viewed the purchase as another step toward a monopoly. Majors and Waddell saw it as something else—a financial debacle.

But in truth, they were already in the middle of one.

THE SINKHOLE

The crisis that had started with the Utah War got only deeper in 1859. Facing cash shortages, Russell found that he couldn't pay off the acceptances Floyd had already given him. He went back for new ones, using them to replace those he'd already gotten. It was like paying off a mortgage with another mortgage, except that the new mortgage had a higher interest rate (or to use the financial term, "discount rate"—the difference between face value and what was handed over by the bank).

One other problem for Russell: this was all short-term debt. It was expected to be paid off quickly, generally within a few months.

The debt was starting to become unmanageable. It didn't help that when Russell went to Congress to petition for money owed, his firm was roundly criticized as war profiteers, even though they had lost money—fairness was not a requirement for newspapers or politicians even then.

Russell shuttled back and forth between Washington and New York, working feverishly to get Congress to pay, lobbying for the mail contract to be rewritten, and, most important, arranging for new financing. Back west, his decision to expand into the Denver area proved to be a mistake, or at least ill timed. He had added more obligations without adequate income against a speculative future payoff.

The fact that Majors and Waddell were right about the stage line to Denver didn't help them. The convoluted nature of their partnerships and the interwoven business plans meant the partners were deeply entangled with Russell. So when the line went quickly into the red, they reluctantly found themselves backing Jones, Russell & Company. Recognizing the interdependence, the firm was reorganized as the Overland California & Pikes Peak Express Company, with Majors and Waddell as stockholders.

Now the million-dollar mail contract wasn't just the seed of an empire; it was salvation.

You might think all the trouble collecting money from the War Department and Congress would have soured Russell on any dealings with the government. But Russell didn't see it that way. He had friends in Congress, and he believed they would help him get the contract.

His most important friend, when it came to the mail, was California senator William Gwin. He was a powerful, but mercurial, ally to have.

SENATOR GWIN

William McKendree Gwin was a nineteenth-century mover and shaker, a doctor whose Methodist father had served under Andrew Jackson. Born in Tennessee in 1805, Gwin had graduated from Transylvania University—in Kentucky, not Romania—and practiced medicine in Mississippi until deciding he liked politics better than curing people. A Democrat, he served a term as a congressman from Mississippi and was the superintendent of the construction of the federal customs house in New Orleans—a political plum straight from President James Polk.

What he really wanted, though, was wealth and power. With the American annexation of California—and the gold rush—he decided that was where he could get it. He moved to California, bought land in Paloma, and set up a mining operation that made him rich. A prominent Democrat with money and connections to Washington made him a player in the still sparsely populated territory, and in September 1850 he became one of California's first US senators.

Gwin was considered a visionary when it came to the West, and he relentlessly advocated for expansion—and a reliable connection between the East and the West. He was also a slave owner, aligned with interests in the South. He owned slaves in Mississippi even after moving to California. Not by accident, either. If you asked him, he'd tell you slavery was the "foundation of civilization."[6] But politics being politics, he voted *against* the establishment of slavery in California, possibly because he didn't think the climate there would support it (which he claimed in his memoirs later on), but more likely because he knew he wouldn't get the nod as senator otherwise.

Gwin backed initiatives to fund a transcontinental railroad and a telegraph line, both of which required heavy government subsidies. He also wanted a quicker, dependable mail line connecting east to west, and though he ended up being a Southern sympathizer when the war came, he favored a central route—the same route Russell came to control.

SOME HISTORIES OF THE PONY EXPRESS CREDIT GWIN AND BENJAMIN Ficklin (usually said to be working for Russell at the time) with the idea for the Pony Express, saying that they had discussed a cross-country express mail service on a stagecoach trip. If the trip was made in 1859, it's likely that Russell had already discussed it with the secretary of war back in Washington; if it was much before that, it's hard to see how they happened to run into each other or credit the discussion as anything more than a pipe dream.

One way or another, the idea itself wasn't unique—express services had been around since the beginning of the nation in one form or another. What set the Pony Express apart were two factors:

1. Russell wanted to use it to demonstrate that mail service over the central route could work; and

2. The Pony Express was longer, by far, than any other express service in the West, or the nation.

While politics had clearly been involved in selecting the route—the postmaster at the time was aligned with the South—there were still practical reasons to favor the Oxbow route to California. The Postal Service had tried moving mail over northern routes; most of those operations had been less than satisfactory, if not outright busts. While those failures had many reasons, there was one problem with the route that was hard to overcome: winter. Snow on the northern plains, the Great Divide, and especially in the Sierra Nevada played havoc with deliveries.

Russell, who had never been to the Sierras and probably hadn't even gone as far west as Denver, was confident the weather wouldn't be a problem. The best way to prove that, he and Gwin agreed when they discussed the mail contract in Washington, was with an express service, one that would grab headlines by delivering mail from Missouri to California in the unheard-of time of ten days.

The Pony Express.

Gwin loved the idea. *Deliver the mail in ten days*, he said, *and I'll twist enough arms to make sure that contract is yours.*

SPECULATIONS AND PROMISES

Historians have never satisfactorily explained why Gwin, who would later defect to the South, was so in favor of awarding a contract on a route that would benefit the North.[7] It's possible that he saw the issue completely divorced from sectional conflict, or that he simply encouraged any plan that would bring California closer to the East. California politics were not known for their high ethical standards, but there's no indication that Gwin was going to benefit personally from the contract. His property was closer to Sacramento than the Oxbow route, but it wasn't near enough to benefit directly from the move.

Whatever his motives, Russell firmly believed he could deliver—and so he panicked when Majors and Waddell told him the Pony Express was a no-go.

MAJORS AND WADDELL MUST HAVE REACTED WITH SOMETHING CLOSE to nausea when they heard the plan. They saw the Pony Express as a huge expense that would simply deepen the dark financial hole they were being sucked into. Russell knew the Pony would lose money, but that wasn't the point. They needed the mail contract to stay afloat. And after that contract, undoubtedly there would be more. They'd be in good with the government, they'd clear their debts, they'd have a monopoly on delivery services through the area.

Their real estate and other investments would benefit. The whole tangled mess would be straightened out.

Russell tried convincing his partners, but they weren't in a convincing mood. Finally, he told them they had to go ahead.

I promised we would do it. I gave my word. We have to.

His partners gave in.

THE IDEA THAT A MAN'S WORD, HOWEVER FOOLISHLY GIVEN, IS HIS bond is a romantic notion. To think that an important business decision that led straight to bankruptcy and ruin was made because of it is equally romantic.

There is evidence—letters between the partners—that it was the case, though, or at least there's no good evidence that it wasn't. Majors and Waddell were clearly angry with Russell at this point and plainly thought the Pony would be an expensive boondoggle. Yet they went along with it. Maybe at this point they concluded there was no reason *not* to try a Hail Mary play. The tangle of interests and companies they were running needed to do something to bring money in quickly, and the mail contract and its large prize looked as if it would be awarded in 1860. Stumble along until then, and salvation might be at hand.

Russell's abilities as a salesman of the future, a man who had a vision of riches and could share that vision with others, must have been a factor. And the Pony was a grand idea—in every way except financially. Delivering mail across country in ten days got people excited. The enterprise was bold and romantic, and you couldn't pay for the publicity it generated: positive press, unlike the negative mudslinging they were getting from Congress and the newspapers back east.

Even so, it's hard to shake the notion that by this point, with losses mounting, the partners must have felt more like hostages than fellow visionaries. For whatever reason—desperate optimism, disguised despair, blind faith—they went along. They were all in on the Pony Express.

THE COSTS

The actual numbers have been lost if they were ever written down, but the cost for the horses alone—five hundred—would have been in the area of $87,500.[8] Even with most of the home stations already part of the stage line, there would have been expenses to set up the exchange stations and hire the riders, extra supervisors, and substitutes. Estimates for the total operation have run as high as $700,000.

Against that were revenues from the Pony itself. Again, the actual projections Russell and others may have made have been lost, but at five dollars a half ounce, fifty pounds of mail per trip would have brought $8,000 into the coffers. A year's operation with once-a-week trips would yield $416,000. A more realistic estimate of fifteen pounds per trip—roughly five hundred pieces of half-ounce mail—would have earned $2,400 a week, or $125,000 annually.[9]

The Pony carried a total of 34,753 pieces over its eighteen-month life span. If each were a half ounce, and if each half ounce netted $5— far above what we know the average to be, as the price was dropped to encourage use as the service went on—the total revenue for the entire operation would have been under $175,000.

Russell was not horrible at math, and he knew as well as his partners that they were going to lose money on the Pony Express. But he was banking on the publicity to get him the mail contract. And besides, the hoopla was contagious.

When the service launched in April 1860, it looked like Russell's vision would work. Everyone was talking about the service, along the line and back east. "A spontaneous celebration took place at every town through which the Pony passed," the *New York Times* reported on May 1, 1860. Newspapers not only sang its praises, but prominently reported dispatches delivered "BY THE PONY EXPRESS."

The public response was enthusiastic—right up to the point of plunking money down to use it. Most people simply didn't feel the need to spend two or three days' worth of pay to send a letter to Aunt Joe or Nephew Bill. There wasn't enough official business to keep the mochilas filled, either. Missives going east outnumbered those coming west two-to-one, perhaps demonstrating how much more important the connection was to California than the rest of the country.

None of this daunted Russell. The publicity was fantastic. He managed to win a contract to deliver mail from Salt Lake City to California, taking over from George Chorpenning when the postmaster general declared Chorpenning hadn't properly fulfilled the contract.

This was probably a political move, and undoubtedly an unfair one—Chorpenning was a pioneer on the route, had run it successfully through the winter, and had set a record in 1858 delivering James Buchanan's second annual message to Congress from Salt Lake to California in seventeen days. But he lacked the connections Russell kept wining and dining.

Russell and company now had a complete route from Missouri to Sacramento; they had contracts along the route, infrastructure, and fame. The contract wasn't due to expire for a few more years. But congressmen, not least of all his friend Senator Gwin, were agitating to revisit the agreement, ordering the US Post Office Department to tear up the contract and give a new deal to Russell, Majors, and Waddell.

Maybe.

Russell trusted Congress and Gwin about as far as any reasonable man ought to; in other words, not at all. So rather than relying on Gwin et al., he went directly to the postmaster and started negotiating on his own. The contract that carried mail to California via steamer expired; Russell suggested that his service would replace it. Among his many plans—there were a number—was a proposal to provide overland mail service to California six days a week for $900,000. It was a plan nearly as ambitious as the Pony Express—and one that would require even greater capital—but no one ever accused Russell of thinking small.

THE UNION TEETERS

Dissolution and secession were on everyone's mind in New York, even as the Pony riders were taking word of the election results westward. The results were already well known in the city, and the papers briskly reported the South's talk of secession. Some were optimistic that it wouldn't happen; some were more realistic. The *Evening Post* declared the latest speech of South Carolina governor William Henry Gist a "menace," while praising Georgia's governor Brown for not being quite as bombastic.[10] No one really knew what to expect, which put a damper on business dealings around town.

Southern states had been talking about leaving the Union for months, espousing a theory that several states in the North had themselves voiced during the War of 1812—namely, that union was voluntary, and as such the country could be dissolved at any time by a simple vote of a state's legislature. Or at least, a state could decide to leave, just as a man could leave his company or a marriage. Messy, maybe, but doable.

Sentiment around Wall Street was decidedly mixed. New York had gone for Lincoln, but many there had business and family ties to the

South, and even those who weren't sympathetic to slavery were un-easy about the results. New York had abolished slavery in a series of fitful, halfway measures beginning in 1799, and even allowed black men who owned significant property to vote—a stricter requirement than for white males, who enjoyed universal suffrage, but something considered revolutionary at the time.[11]

But there were limits to New York's "liberal" view: a referendum had been held at the same time of the presidential vote, asking voters whether the property requirements should be removed.[12] The result was a landslide against. The city was firmly opposed; the only strong support was in the upstate rural areas.

Like the city around him, Russell was conflicted about the election and the country's future. He'd worked to make Kansas a proslave territory and state. Some of his best political contacts were from the South.

On the other hand, the votes he needed for the mail contract were mostly in the North.

There was one more complication, one he felt acutely in November. It had to do with bonds whose face value amounted to $870,000, but would be worthless if the war came.

ROUGH MEN

Russell's financial gymnastics were as distant to the men carrying the letters west as Washington and New York were. Their concerns were far more tangible and immediate than hypothecated bonds. The trail beyond Fort Kearny over the Great Plains grew ever more lonely, and potentially more dangerous. Vast herds of buffalo moved south, a hazard for riders. Indians, though generally peaceful, remained at least a theoretical danger. Horse thieves lurked in the settlements, and in the wide-open space in between. But the biggest danger was simply the weather. Winter was rolling through the mountains to the west, and cold wind blew across the plains. It had already snowed, though it was more a distraction than barrier.

Fort Kearny and Dobytown marked the western boundary of the Pony's Division One.[1] From there, the rider took the mochila and headed northwest, following the Platte River. Rider James Moore held what may have been the speed record through the Division Two section of the trail, once taking the mochila between Midway Station and Julesburg, arriving to find that an important government dispatch was waiting to go east. With no one else to take it, Moore grabbed a fresh horse and set up, returning to Midway fourteen hours and fifty-six minutes later—an average speed of sixteen and a quarter miles an hour.[2]

The riders in this section always moved quickly. For they were traveling through the domain of the most effective, and murderous, division superintendent employed by the Pony, and perhaps anyone else: Jack Slade.

JACK SLADE

Jack Slade was the sort of rough SOB who built the Old West and the legends it still thrives on. He was more famous in his time than Bill Hickok, and with more reason. He, too, was a killer and occasional drunkard—those two went together in his case—but most of all an exceptional middle manager.

Which also may have connected well with the murderer part. Because there was no question that if you got on Jack Slade's bad side, you were in definite need of a good health plan, if not a cemetery plot.

The area of Division Two stretched from Kearny clear through Colorado and the tip of Wyoming to Horseshoe Station near Fort Laramie.[3] The route from Kearny ran aside the Platte River to the South Platte before cutting back north to the North Platte. Though well traveled by wagon trains, both of emigrants and freighters, it was notoriously lawless. An especially favorite spot for horse thieves happened to be near the river crossing near Julesburg. There was a stage stop there, and a stable, both made of cedar logs. There wasn't much more, a blacksmith and a store, maybe a little house or two. But it was positioned well for travelers, a convenient stop some two hundred miles from Fort Kearny. Those headed to Pikes Peak and the gold mines would follow the South Platte to present-day Denver. Settlers sticking to the Oregon Trail—and Pony riders going west—would trek north along Lodgepole Creek and then out to Fort Laramie.

The stage stop at Julesburg was set up and run in 1859 by a fellow named Jules Reni. Jules was the informal mayor of the hamlet, whose skills included baking whiskey-bread—a combination of whiskey and flour, mixed and processed in procedures that remain a mystery today. Jules was also well known as a bit of roughneck—some would say bully. He was reputed to have killed several men. But he was the law, such as it was, around Julesburg.

Somehow, though, he was ineffective when it came to catching horse thieves. Evidence—or rumor—pointed toward Jules as the main source of thievery, an especial problem for the stage line when

Russell bought it. With their stock and equipment constantly turning up missing, Joseph "Jack" Slade was appointed area superintendent and told to straighten things out.

Slade may or may not have employed the most refined investigative techniques when he showed up to assess the situation. Jules apparently didn't like the nature of Slade's questioning, and the two argued, with the upshot being that Jules was removed as manager of the station.

Slade then discovered horses being used by Jules that were supposed to be company property. Jules disputed this. Slade took matters—and horses—into his own hands, returning them to the company stables.

Jules decided to skip the formalities involved in repossessing them and got straight to the source of his problem. He and some friends ambushed Slade a short time later, unloading a double-barreled shotgun on him and leaving him for dead.

Death came too easy on the frontier . . . but not for Jack Slade. To Jules's everlasting regret, he lived.

BORN IN 1829 IN CARLYLE, ILLINOIS, SLADE IN HIS YOUTH WAS REPUTED to be both prankster and murderer: as the story goes, the thirteen-year-old and some friends decided to have some fun on a neighbor by overturning his outhouse—with the fellow in it. In the ensuing argument, Slade had thrown a rock, killing the man.

Flight to Texas followed. During the war, he fought on the Texas side and was reputed to have slain nine Mexicans during a reconnaissance near enemy lines.

Take those stories with a grain of salt, but this one is far more reliable: working as a freighter after the war, Slade got into an argument with a friend named Andrew Farrar as they traded drinks. Slade drew his gun; Farrar dared him to shoot.

That was the last dare Farrar made. Slade gladly obliged.

Sorry that he had shot his friend before they'd finished paying for their drinks, Slade sent for a doctor, but it was too late and Slade was far too good a shot; Farrar died soon after.

—

BY THE TIME HE WENT TO WORK FOR RUSSELL ET AL., SLADE HAD BUILT a solid reputation as a world-class hard-ass. Two loads of buckshot from Jules's gun were not going to kill him. They did send Slade to St. Louis, however—a trek probably as painful as the buckshot—to recuperate. In the meantime, stage line and Pony superintendent Ficklin heard what had happened, and administered some frontier justice: he had Jules hanged.

But Jules was tough himself; even better, he had friends: as soon as Ficklin rode off, the friends appeared and cut him down.

Or so it's said. In any event, prudence declared that the best thing to do was for Jules to abandon his burg, and he and his companions headed west, setting up near South Pass, Wyoming, another crossroads for travelers and presumably a better place to practice the fine arts of thievery and skullduggery.

Slade made his recovery in due course. Always a man to pay his debts, he decided that he would personally return the borrowed buckshot. Recruiting a half dozen or so friends—and apparently alerting the authorities, such as they were, to his intentions—he rode out to find Jules.

They met at Pacific Springs, which despite its name was nowhere near the Pacific, but rather a wet patch in the dry scrubby rocks southwest of South Pass. Seeing a ghost or just not in the mood for confrontation, Jules kicked his horse and tried to get away. Slade drew a pistol and shot him out of the saddle.

A beating ensued, followed by target practice, with Jules immobilized against a fence post. At some point, Slade either got tired or ran out of bullets. He took his knife and relieved the corpse of both ears. One, he nailed to a fence post. The other he kept as a souvenir.

CLEANING UP

Slade then resumed his duties for Russell, Majors & Waddell. When a rancher tried shortchanging the company's hay—rather outrageously hiding brush under it—Slade convinced the man to abandon his stake for the sake of his health. Horse thieves in his domain, suspected and otherwise, were burned out.

Historians tell the story of a gang of four who made the mistake of robbing a stage in Slade's division. He found their hideout and walked in, uninvited.

Three of the men left feetfirst, carried out to their shallow graves. The fourth saw his future in the smoke from Slade's pistols and jumped out the window. He soon joined his friends, pushing up whatever passed for daisies on the lonesome plains.

But even a badass has a tender side, and Slade had his. He married a woman named Virginia—he called her Molly—and named a station stop after her. The couple adopted a "half-breed" as a son . . . possibly because Slade had killed his father; the adoption record is unclear.

Whatever inklings of romance and sense of duty guided him when sober, by all accounts Slade had a terrible temper when drunk—which was pretty much his default state soon after entering a saloon.

"Give me change for this," he'd say, slapping down the ear on the bar. He'd laugh. The bartender would pour. Things would go from there.

Slade's sprees were as wild as any good Western movie might depict them. He would rile up without provocation, remove his pistol, and start firing at mirrors and windows. Fellow patrons would generally make a quick exit; even friends would pay dearly if they tried to stop him.

Next day, hungover or not, Slade would show up, apologize profusely, and offer to pay the damages.

For Russell and company, Slade was too valuable to fire, and too ornery to be given a talking-to. Besides, his reputation kept things settled along his part of the trail.

And then there was publicity value, if only by word of mouth—everyone who rode the stagecoach line heard about Slade and couldn't wait to see him, though preferably in the bright light of morning and from a distance.

Among them was Sam Clemens, on that trip to Denver.

I cared nothing now about the Indians, and even lost interest in the murdered driver. There was such magic in that name, SLADE! Day or night, now, I stood always ready to drop any subject in hand, to listen to something new about Slade and his ghastly exploits. Even before we got to Overland City, we had begun to hear about Slade and his "division" (for he was a "division-agent") on the Overland; and from the hour we had left Overland City we had heard drivers and conductors talk about only three things—"Californy," the Nevada silver mines, and this desperado Slade. And a deal the most of the talk was about Slade. We had gradually come to have a realizing sense of the fact that Slade was a man whose heart and hands and soul were steeped in the blood of offenders against his dignity; a man who awfully avenged all injuries, affront, insults or slights, of whatever kind—on the spot if he could, years afterward if lack of earlier opportunity compelled it; a man whose hate tortured him day and night till vengeance appeased it—and not an ordinary vengeance either, but his enemy's absolute death—nothing less; a man whose face would light up with a terrible joy when he surprised a foe and had him at a disadvantage. A high and efficient servant of the Overland, an outlaw among outlaws and yet their relentless scourge, Slade was at once the most bloody, the most dangerous and the most valuable citizen that inhabited the savage fastnesses of the mountains.[4]

Clemens's version of Slade's history differs in some particulars from what historians have much settled on, but that doesn't necessarily mean he was wrong and they were right. And being Mark Twain, his version sounds better:

. . . two thirds of the talk of drivers and conductors had been about this man Slade, ever since the day before we reached Julesburg. In order that the eastern reader may have a clear conception of what a Rocky Mountain desperado is, in his highest state of development, I will reduce all this mass of overland gossip to one straightforward narrative, and present it in the following shape:

Slade was born in Illinois, of good parentage. At about twenty-six years of age he killed a man in a quarrel and fled the country. At St. Joseph, Missouri, he joined one of the early California-bound emigrant trains, and was given the post of train-master. One day on the plains he had an angry dispute with one of his wagon-drivers, and both drew their revolvers. But the driver was the quicker artist, and had his weapon cocked first. So Slade said it was a pity to waste life on so small a matter, and proposed that the pistols be thrown on the ground and the quarrel settled by a fist-fight. The unsuspecting driver agreed, and threw down his pistol—whereupon Slade laughed at his simplicity, and shot him dead!

He made his escape, and lived a wild life for awhile, dividing his time between fighting Indians and avoiding an Illinois sheriff, who had been sent to arrest him for his first murder. It is said that in one Indian battle he killed three savages with his own hand, and afterward cut their ears off and sent them, with his compliments, to the chief of the tribe.

Slade soon gained a name for fearless resolution, and this was sufficient merit to procure for him the important post of overland division-agent at Julesburg, in place of Mr. Jules, removed. For some time previously, the company's horses had been frequently stolen, and the coaches delayed, by gangs of outlaws, who were wont to laugh at the idea of any man's having the temerity to resent such outrages. Slade resented them promptly.

The outlaws soon found that the new agent was a man who did not fear anything that breathed the breath of life. He made short work of all offenders. The result was that delays ceased, the company's property was let alone, and no matter what happened or who suffered, Slade's coaches went through, every time! True, in order to bring about this wholesome change, Slade had to kill several men— some say three, others say four, and others six—but the world was the richer for their loss. The first prominent difficulty he had was with the ex-agent Jules, who bore the reputation of being a reckless and desperate man himself. Jules hated Slade for supplanting him, and a good fair occasion for a fight was all he was waiting for. By and by Slade dared to employ a man whom Jules had once discharged. Next, Slade seized a team of stage-horses which he accused Jules of having driven off and hidden somewhere for his own use. War was declared, and for a day or two the two men walked warily about the streets, seeking each other, Jules armed with a double-barreled shot gun, and Slade with his history-creating revolver. Finally, as Slade stepped into a store Jules poured the contents of his gun into him from behind the door. Slade was plucky, and Jules got several bad pistol wounds in return.

Then both men fell, and were carried to their respective lodgings, both swearing that better aim should do deadlier work next time. Both were bedridden a long time, but Jules got to his feet first, and gathering his possessions together, packed them on a couple of mules, and fled to the Rocky Mountains to gather strength in safety against the day of reckoning. For many months he was not seen or heard of, and was gradually dropped out of the remembrance of all save Slade himself. But Slade was not the man to forget him. On the contrary, common report said that Slade kept a reward standing for his capture, dead or alive!

After awhile, seeing that Slade's energetic administration had restored peace and order to one of the worst divisions of the road, the overland stage company transferred him to the Rocky Ridge division in the Rocky Mountains, to see if he could perform a like miracle there. It was the very paradise of outlaws and desperadoes. There was absolutely no semblance of law there. Violence was the rule. Force was the only recognized authority. The commonest misunderstandings were settled on the spot with the revolver or the knife. Murders were done in open day, and with sparkling frequency, and nobody thought of inquiring into them. It was considered that the parties who did the killing had their private reasons for it; for other people to meddle would have been looked upon as indelicate. After a murder, all that Rocky Mountain etiquette required of a spectator was, that he should help the *gentleman bury his game—otherwise his churlishness would surely be remembered against him the first time he killed a man himself and needed a neighborly turn in interring him.*

Slade took up his residence sweetly and peacefully in the midst of this hive of horse-thieves and assassins, and the very first time one of them aired his insolent swaggerings in his presence he shot him dead! He began a raid on the outlaws, and in a singularly short space of time he had completely stopped their depredations on the stage stock, recovered a large number of stolen horses, killed several of the worst desperadoes of the district, and gained such a dread ascendancy over the rest that they respected him, admired him, feared him, obeyed him! He wrought the same marvelous change in the ways of the community that had marked his administration at Overland City. He captured two men who had stolen overland stock, and with his own hands he hanged them. He was supreme judge in his district, and he was jury and executioner likewise—and not only in the case of offences against his employers, but against passing emigrants as well. On one occasion some emigrants had their stock lost or stolen, and told Slade, who chanced to visit their camp. With a single companion he rode to a ranch, the owners of which he suspected, and opening the door, commenced firing, killing three, and wounding the fourth.[5]

Clemens, by then known as Mark Twain, wrote about the trip roughly ten years after it had occurred. While there's no reason to think that he didn't meet Slade, he seems to have cribbed a few details from Thomas J. Dimsdale's work *Vigilantes of Montana.* Twain was a fair man, though, as he credited Dimsdale while quoting liberally from his book.

Dimsdale's book—another good source for writers on the Old West—began as a series of articles written and published in his own newspaper, the *Montana Post,* in 1865. He wrote about things he knew firsthand, or mostly firsthand, as he was a member of one of the Vigilance Committees that acted as police, judge, and jury in the Montana Territory. There were similar groups throughout the Pony's route, though they lacked the prestige of a scribe.

While vigilantes subsequently got a bad name, Dimsdale's book illustrates even more completely than Twain that stories about rough justice and heroism were not constructed after the Old West was tamed, but rather were already popular at the time, and not just in the East. The elements in many of the tales—rough justice, survival against all odds, individualism—say much about the readers. They knew and approved of these things, or many of them. America in the 1860s was a time of great stress and turmoil, a time of rapid change and invention as well as conflict. It's no wonder that tales that highlighted immutable values, values that Americans believed were part of the national soul, were popular. Once embedded, the tales and their morality became inseparable; one can hardly tell a story, any story, about the Old West without at least some nod toward those underlying variables.

The Old West wasn't an invention of quieter times, or even 1950s screenwriters and directors. Given the origin of the stories and their original audiences, it's easy to see why certain patterns were repeated over and over again. Bear fights, ears being cut off—these are all elements that quickly illustrate a characteristic or theme the tale teller wanted to reveal without losing the focus on the action. We're the ones who distort history, then, by taking these details out of their intended context. Of course, we blame the original writers for being inaccurate or confusing, when they had a different agenda than we do.

A FOOTNOTE: WHEN CLEMENS FINALLY MET SLADE, HE WAS SHOCKED at how gentlemanly he was. The well-known killer and scourge of the plains was a gentleman, handing over his own coffee when the pot ran out.

A bit of a letdown, apparently, but better for American literature than the possible alternatives.

SOD AND PRAIRIES AND PEOPLE

From Julesburg, the message continued across the South Platte. The river was deceptive—though shallow, its yellow-tinted water was flanked by quicksand and hidden sandbars that could grab hold of a horse's foot and not let go. But at least it wasn't raining—the water could swell suddenly, and the swift current nearly drowned a rider once, sending him and his horse far downstream before he could recover. The horse, though unhurt, was temporarily lost; the rider had to run back to the Julesburg stop and grabbed another.

Mud Springs was the next home station on the line—a small house made of sod bricks with a wooden roof; the rider could sleep in a lean-to on the side, provided there were no guests from the stagecoach that shared the stop. Sod was an ecologically correct building material before there was such a thing: thick bales of grass and dirt, cut from the prairie, that provided good insulation created from a renewable resource. The grass had to have fairly thick and deep roots, or the dirt would simply fall away; preferred varieties included buffalo grass, little blue stem, wire grass, prairie cord grass, Indian grass, and wheat grass.[6]

Sod bricks, roughly a foot wide, three feet deep, and four inches high were laid grass down and built up like Legos, alternating the courses for strength; a wall would be two or more feet thick, providing natural insulation against the cold and heat. Doors and windows were framed out with timber pegged into the sod bricks. They were rarely higher than one story. Cedar was the wood of choice for the roof poles and logs, which were then covered with a thinner layer of sod.

The interior could be smoothed over with a sandbased plaster; shelves were added on supports driven into the wall. In most cases the sod houses were seen as temporary structures, useful while you were establishing your farm or business. Once you were doing well enough to afford sawn lumber, you relegated the sod structure to some other use and built a larger house.

The prairie grassland was an ancient landscape, created after the

Rocky Mountains rose and the glaciers retreated. For a variety of reasons—including drought, lightning, and the human propensity to start fires—the plains were not well suited for massive tree growth. Instead, thick-rooted grasses became the dominant plants. That in turn created an ecosystem in which large vegetarians, such as bison, could flourish. Indians reinforced the cycle, it's thought, by periodically starting fires to control the land or the animals that used it, and in some cases to make areas more easily defended.

The soil was incredibly fertile, thick with trapped nutrients. But the thick grass roots that helped keep the nutrients in place also made it hard to farm. John Deere's steel plow, invented in 1837, was revolutionizing farming, making it much more practical to break up Nebraska's thick sod, but there were still drawbacks to farming there, especially the lack of dependable water in areas away from the rivers and streams and a growing season shorter than many from the East and South were used to. Less than thirty thousand free whites lived in the territory in 1860; Nebraska City and Omaha were the largest cities; neither had more than two thousand people living in them.[7]

White people, that is. There was a larger number of Indians, both native to the area and recent arrivals from areas overrun by European Americans.

Omaha takes its name from one of the tribes that had settled in the area from the East, having been devastated by disease—smallpox, caught from whites—and the Sioux. The Pawnee, the Otoe, and Santee Sioux, the Winnebago, the Ponca, the Iowa, the Sac, the Fox—some ten thousand Native Americans were in Nebraska when it was split off from Kansas to become a separate territory in 1856, and all were dealing with extreme pressures, both natural and manmade. The lifestyles of Plains Indians ranged from that of horse-based nomadic bands that followed bison herds to the inhabitants of relatively stationary settlements. Not all Indians were openly hostile to whites, though it's fair to say few if any welcomed the incursions or even interactions with open arms. Those interactions were varied and could be unpredictable for either side.

As a general rule, Pony riders were not harassed by Indians on this part of the trail; it may or may not have helped that the company employed a small number as helpers, tending the animals. Others who lived in or near white settlements often traded or did other business, such as tanning and preparing hides, so there was often some relationship between the local riders and station people and the Indians, one that was unappreciated or even unknown to visitors like Clemens and Burton.

The riders' principal strategy was always to ride away from any potential trouble. Out on the plains, the Indians they were likely to encounter outside of settlements were usually handfuls of warriors on a hunting party; large forces and outright war on the Great Plains was still a few years away.

Bison were a more evident danger. Massive herds roamed the plains, and a stampede could do more than take a rider off his route. There were antelope, wolves, deer, mountain lions, rabbits, prairie dogs, the occasional bobcat; bald eagles and over three hundred other species of birds flew overhead.

The land made its own mark, occasionally beckoning travelers with its upheavals and erosions. The path from Mud Springs led to Chimney Rock, a three-hundred-foot-high finger of volcanic ash, Brule clay, and Arikaree sandstone cursing at the sky.[8] The stones date to the Oligocene epoch, thirty-four million to twenty-three million years ago; this was a time after the dinosaurs had disappeared but before most of our current mammals evolved. It was a good time to be a giant tapir, which may say everything you need to know about the era.

The rock survived, and for pioneers as well as Pony riders it was an easy landmark to steer by, a lone pole rising above the Nebraska hills as they headed south. A favorite of lightning strikes, it was the tallest and arguably most stunning of the many rock formations that dotted the region. A little east, Courthouse and Jail Rocks stood side by side, the former bulky, the latter slim, together measuring some four hundred feet above the landscape. Squint as hard as you can, and neither today looks like what it was called. Early travelers' descriptions of Courthouse Rock as a ruined castle seems closer to the mark. But the notions of justice as well as civilization were apparently more prominent than the Round Table in emigrants' minds; Courthouse and Jail Rocks stuck, Old Broken Down Castle Crumbling on the Plains and Easy to Steer By didn't.

WILLIAM CAMPBELL

Novembers on the plains are always cold, but November 1860 was particularly so. As the message of Lincoln's election flew west, storm clouds gathered on the other side of the mountains ahead. The frost in the wind was so bad, the rider out of Kearny began contemplating a new line of employment.

One of the men he rode past, William Campbell, would have been happy to hear that. He'd watched the rider change horses at the area stations plenty of times, always with a twinge of jealousy. He wanted that job. In a few weeks, he'd get it: more by default than merit, though once in it there'd be no dislodging him.

Campbell had worked for Majors as a freighter on the road to Santa Fe for two years, and when the Pony was started, he had applied for a job as a rider. He was tough enough—he'd survived a brief encounter with a Comanche war party, and a far more frightening run-in with a stampede of some five hundred bison. But he was considered too tall and heavy, at six feet and one hundred and forty pounds. So he settled for other work, helping to set up the stations along the line, and bringing them supplies.

Campbell finally got the job as rider in December when the local men had all quit and the stationmaster couldn't find a ready replacement. He would end up as one of the most famous riders in the Pony's history, thanks at least partly to his good fortune of still being alive when one of the service's earliest and most reliable historians was working on his book during the Depression era. Arthur Chapman managed to locate Campbell, who by then was in his early nineties, and interviewed him extensively for his book, *The Pony Express: The Record of a Romantic Adventure in Business.*

"The boys were dropping out pretty fast," Chapman remembered. "Some of them could not stand the strain of the constant riding. It was not so bad in summer, but when winter came on, the job was too much for them."[9]

Campbell talked about the horses he rode in the Nebraska stretch from Fort Kearny to Cottonwood Springs (also called Box Elder)—nasty brutes, he said, but also strong and the fastest around. His first run in December was through a blizzard; it was an appropriate christening; the winter would bring storms so severe that the stages could not make it through. Campbell's hardest and longest ride came during one of those blizzards—starting east from Cottonwood Springs, he rode to Kearny, fighting drifts nearly to his saddle and making, at best, five miles an hour. But there was no relief there; he got back on a horse and rode toward the stage stop in Fairfield, twenty miles away. There he found another rider and promptly went to bed, having spent twenty-four hours in the saddle.

The ride back to his home station took three or four days.

The schedule often had Campbell riding through the dark, and occasionally he got lost. He told Chapman about one pitch-black night when, utterly baffled, he had to use the sound of the nearby Platte as a guide. Riding a favorite pony—Ragged Jim—he was making good time until he hit a buffalo wallow—a shallow hole that would hold water during the spring and after heavy rains, so called because bison would gather there for a drink until the water ran out.

The horse buckled and Campbell went airborne. Somehow—he didn't explain exactly how—the mail went with him. This was fortunate, because the horse vanished in the darkness. Mochila in hand, Campbell started hoofing toward the next station, a good fifteen miles away. Luckily for him, he heard a stage coming behind him a short while later and managed to flag it down for a ride.

Campbell hated wolves, but they apparently liked him. One night riding through Nebraska he happened upon a pack feasting on a dead horse. The wolves eyed him and his horse up; before they could decide which would be dessert, he spurred away. The wolves trailed a full fifteen miles. On his way back, he "doctored up the carcass of that horse with strychnine," eventually claiming a dozen victims, who were all skinned and sold.[10]

Wolves he hated, and he wasn't particularly fond of dogs, either. One in particular bothered him—a bulldog that had a nasty habit of chasing coaches and riders, yapping and growling. Great sport for the dog, annoying to his horse. Campbell finally had enough one night; as the dog came out, he drew his Colt and fired in the animal's general direction, hoping to scare it enough that it would stay away from then on.

It did stay away, but not because it was scared—Campbell had inadvertently killed it.

Its owner was not happy. Warned that the rancher was fixing to avenge his best friend's death, Campbell located an alternate route around the man's property. Some folk are just born to be cat lovers.

IRISH TOMMY AND ROWDY PETE

By legend, the Pony never faltered; riders always kept to their schedule, even riding miles and miles extra if their relief had not managed to report for work.

That's true in the main, but it wasn't easy getting the mail through on time. One stagecoach driver, "Irish Tommy"—Thomas J. Ranahan officially—remembered several occasions when one of the Pony riders fell out of the saddle at a transfer station where he and his coach had stopped. Irish Tommy would push the kid off to bed, hop on the saddle, and ride off to the home station himself. There he'd make the exchange and wait for the stagecoach and his assistant to catch up.

It was on one of those occasions, a few months after the election message had passed through, that Irish Tommy stopped in at the station at Green River Crossing in Wyoming. A crowd had gathered, which was more than a little unusual. Asking around, Irish discovered that the station keeper—who was expressing sentiments in favor of the South and disunion—had fallen out with a stage driver called Rowdy Pete.

Pete—full name has been lost to the blur of history—was a Union man, and rather proud of it: the last time he was in, he'd wrapped himself in a Union flag and all but rubbed the stationmaster's nose in it. The stationmaster had warned him not to try that again.

Rowdy Pete hadn't gotten his nickname by being a quiet man, and the crowd had come in anticipation of a good show, given that Pete and his stage were due in a matter of minutes. Irish poked through the crowd, angling for a ringside seat. Soon the telltale clomp of mule feet and the thud of wheels rose from the distance.

Eyes strained; bets were arranged.

The stage finally drove into view—bespectacled with flags.

The crowd cheered, clearly weighted toward Union men. But ultimately they were disappointed: the stationmaster slunk away, perhaps judging from the cheers that he would lose even by winning.

WHEN THE ELECTION MESSAGE REACHED COTTONWOOD SPRINGS STATION in Nebraska, W. A. "Bill" Gates took over. Gates was an Illinois boy who had caught gold fever in 1859. Heading west toward Pikes Peak, he got derailed and then enticed by the offer of a job as a rider for the Pony. Figuring gold in the pocket was worth more than whatever the ground promised, he signed on.

For Gates, most of the thrill came from the exhilaration of speed, the sensation of riding against the wind, a lone man against nature and time. He didn't have much to fear from the Indians he passed; they thought he was crazy. Why else would a man ride like lightning across the plains, frenetically galloping through the darkness?

Gates and the mail continued westward on its relentless run, heading with the North Platte River toward the border with Wyoming. With Fort Laramie ahead, Pony rider and letter were now within sight of the most famous Pony rider of all—Buffalo Bill Cody.

Maybe Bill even saw him, assuming Cody could stop mucking the barn long enough to take a look.

BUFFALO BILL

THE MOST FAMOUS RIDER NEVER

To be perfectly honest—a dangerous thing when talking about the Old West and its legends—it's not clear that Cody was mucking a barn, or even doing anything at all for the Pony that day or any day.

In fact, the Pony's most famous rider ever almost certainly never actually rode for the service. But while most historians say that with 99.9 percent *hell-no* surety, there is no one, Russell, Majors, and Waddell included, who did more for the Pony Express. If people know anything about the Pony today, whether it is right, wrong, or halfway in between, it's mostly due to Cody.

Especially halfway in between.

WILLIAM F. CODY WAS BORN FEBRUARY 26, 1846, IN A LOG CABIN IN WHAT was then Iowa territory two miles east of LeClaire. He was the second son and fourth child of Isaac Cody, a trader, farmer, and one-time freighter. The family's roots in America dated at least to the late seventeenth century; his mother, Mary Ann, numbered among her forebears a friend of William Penn, the distinguished Quaker who set up Philadelphia and was a tireless advocate for freedom of religion, peace with the Indians, and a union of colonies, foreseeing that future decades before it became a reality. In some tellings—mainly those that spring from Cody's sister Helen—the Cody clan descended directly from Mil Espáine, the Spanish hero whose sons settled Ireland, establishing it as a great kingdom before the English came and mucked things up. Probably not true, given that Mil Espáine seems to have been more myth than flesh and bones, but to see the way Bill Cody turned out, a royal lineage would have been appropriate.

Young Bill was a hoot. He and his friends made regular forays to neighboring farms, liberating apples and melons, and even adventuring to the Mississippi. A better trapper than scholar—could you blame him?—he mastered horse riding and hunting at a young age and generally lived the life of a carefree farm boy until the spring of 1854, when his father decided to take the family west to Kansas. The eight-year-old had his own horse, riding along the wagon and—in his mind, at least—keeping guard over the family.

The journey west was interrupted in Missouri, where Cody and his dad met up with his uncle Elijah; the trio took a reconnaissance into the unsettled land that the boy would never forget—buckskin-clad frontiersmen, soldiers at Leavenworth, Indians in full regalia, and an endless plain dotted with trains of wagons and herds of wild buffalo.

But it was a cousin who made the deepest impression. Among his many skills, the itinerant cousin was a horse whisperer and taught the young man how to break a pony, eventually getting it to ride steady enough to allow its owner to stand on its back while riding. It was a skill Wild Bill practiced the rest of his life.

Young Bill's father was a wanderer at heart, never staying too long in one place even though he had a young family. But he was also an entrepreneur and farmer, small-scale admittedly, but certainly one willing to take a risk if he saw eventual profit in it. He was also law-abiding, and when he heard that the Kansas-Nebraska Act had been passed, he established a legal claim on farmland in Salt Creek Valley west of the wandering Missouri—twenty-five miles as an eagle flies, if he goes in a straight line, from St. Joe's. The claim was said to be the first legal claim in the not-yet state.

This was the summer of 1854, around the same time that Russell et al. were encouraging development in Leavenworth—and hoping that development would bring settlers who would vote to make Kansas a slave state. Passions—pro and con—were high. Kansas had not yet earned the adjective "Bloody"—but it was heading that way.

SEPTEMBER 18, 1854: BILL'S FATHER, ISAAC, RODE OUT FROM HIS FARM ON some errands. On the way, he passed a trading post operated by M. Pierce Rively.

Rively was a friend; he and Isaac had cosponsored a picnic that past July Fourth, treating local whites and Indians to barbecued buffalo and firewater. He was also very pro-slavery, which didn't bother Isaac, particularly. The elder Cody's views on the issue were between the two poles: no abolitionist, he was not for spreading slavery, but also not for abolishing it where it already existed.

Ambling by the post, Isaac heard the hails of some of his neighbors, who stopped him and invited him to talk for a bit on the status of slavery and coming vote for a state constitution. Isaac soon found himself atop a soapbox, speaking his mind.

Having come from Iowa, he thought it a good model for a state—a *white* state, he emphasized. But like that white state, Kansas, too, should be free of slavery. Let the states that had slaves keep them; as for the others—

Isaac's speech was interrupted by a man with a bowie knife. Two large stabs to his chest followed.

Rescued by a neighbor, Isaac was hustled inside the trading post, severely wounded, his lung punctured. Taken away by wagon to his home, he lived to orate another day.

HISTORIANS HAVE HESITATED TO CALL ISAAC AN ABOLITIONIST, BUT newspaper editors at the time had no such compunction. The *Democratic Platform*—a short-lived pro-slavery newspaper published by Robert S. Kelley across the river in Independence, Missouri—reported:

> *A Mr. Cody, a noisy abolitionist, living near Salt Creek, in Kansas Territory, was severely stabbed while in a dispute about a claim with a Mr. Dunn, on Monday week last. Cody is severely hurt, but not enough it is feared, to cause his death. The settlers on Salt Creek regret that his*

wound is not more dangerous, and all sustain Mr. Dunn in the course he took.[1]

Once labeled an abolitionist, a man became a target in Kansas. Isaac's horses were driven off; a store of hay he planned to sell to the army burned. A judge showed up at his house while Isaac was away, sat uninvited in a chair and honed his knife, promising to kill husband and father when he returned. The man settled on thievery instead, taking away a saddlebag (or a horse, depending on which family member's version you believe).

But Isaac was not without allies. He helped establish Grasshopper Falls (Valley Falls today), some thirty miles west of Leavenworth. He was part of a group that encouraged Free-Staters to relocate into the territory. He built a sawmill and a gristmill. An attempt at setting up a school in his old home was foiled by pro-slavery thugs who scared off the teacher.

Isaac became a member of the anti-slavery legislature—there was a pro-slavery version—and after surviving at least one other attempt on his life, died of pneumonia or its complications in 1857, leaving his wife to care for five children, including eleven-year-old Billy.

Rambunctious, tall for his age, blessed with fair skin and blond hair, the precocious adventurer put his energy to work for his family.

THE PONY

Young teenagers often went to work even if their families weren't desperate for cash like Cody's. Mom started taking in boarders; Billy got a job helping tend a neighbor's hay wagons on a trip to Leavenworth. After working on one or two larger trains heading west, he heard about the Pony Express.

Bill's version of what happened, told years later, went like this:

The great Pony Express, about which so much has been said and written, was at that time just being started. The line was being stocked with horses and put into good running condition. At Julesburg I met Mr. George Chrisman, the leading wagon-master of Russell, Majors & Waddell, who had always been a good friend to me. He had bought out "Old Jules," and was then the owner of Julesburg ranch, and the agent of the pony express line. He hired me at once as a pony express rider, but as I was so young he thought I would not be able to stand the fierce riding which was required of the messengers. He knew, however, that I had been raised in the saddle—that I felt more at home there than in any other place—and as he saw that I was confident that I could stand the racket, and could ride as far and endure it as well as some of the older riders, he gave me a short route of forty-five miles, with the stations fifteen miles apart, and three changes of horses. I was required to make fifteen miles an hour, including the changes of horses. I was fortunate in getting well-broken animals, and being so light, I easily made my forty-five miles on time on my first trip out, and ever afterwards.

I wrote to mother and told her how well I liked the exciting life of a pony express rider. She replied, and begged of me to give it up, as it would surely kill me. She was right about this, as fifteen miles an hour on horseback would, in a short time, shake any man "all to pieces"; and there were but very few, if any, riders who could stand it for any great length of time. Nevertheless, I stuck to it for two months, and then, upon receiving a letter informing me that my mother was very sick, I gave it up and went back to the old home in Salt Creek Valley.[2]

But the bug had caught him, and Cody soon thought of reupping. He enlisted an acquaintance at the parent firm, Lewis Simpson, and prevailed on him for an introduction to William Russell. Russell was so impressed that he wrote a letter of introduction for none other than Jack Slade, telling him to hire the lad.

Slade was a skeptic.

Man's work, he told the boy.

Billy told him he'd already ridden for the Pony farther west, in Bill Trotter's division. Slade chewed on that a moment.

"Are you the kid they said was the youngest in the service?" asked Slade.

The same, replied Billy.

Welcome aboard, said Slade, though he tempered his offer by telling Cody he'd be tending stock if he didn't make it.

Slade assigned Cody a section of the trail from Red Buttes—near Fort Caspar, Wyoming—to Three Crossings near Sweetwater, Wyoming, with Three Crossings as his home station.

One day, riding east, Cody arrived at Three Crossings to find that there was no relief—the scheduled rider had had a fatal disagreement with someone the night before. Cody took his place, riding to Rocky Ridge, where after exchanging the mochila he grabbed the eastbound mail and rode all the way back to Red Buttes, a distance of some 322 miles.

Slade offered him a raise after that, and the fun was just beginning. Not long after, Billy found himself pursued by fifteen Indians out near Horse Creek. He spurred his big roan, flattened himself against its back, and sped off toward Sweetwater Bridge. But the station had been raided, the tender killed, relief ponies gone. Billy kept on to Plant's station, swapped out mounts, and completed his relay.

This was the start of Indian trouble in the area, with raids on stages, including one that left a driver and two passengers dead. An assistant division agent was wounded. The service was halted for several weeks until peace could be restored and the miscreants run off.

Bored by lying idle, young Billy joined a party headed by none other than Wild Bill Hickok that set out to reappropriate the horses. They headed north toward Powder River, worming through the arid, mostly barren hills. Narrow areas of green hugged the dried creeks, wandering gradually west. The men found evidence that the party of Indians they'd set out after had joined with another; the old trail hounds declared they were no more than a day ahead.

This was perfect ambush country, and even with forty men, the whites were nervous. But as luck would have it, the Indians were arrogant—so far from European civilization, they didn't bother to post pickets when they camped.

Wild Bill concocted a plan: they'd wait until twilight, then charge down on the camp, free the horses and skedaddle before the natives could organize a defense. As night beckoned, Wild Bill led the charge. Guns, screams, thundering horses—the surprise was so complete the whites carried off the horses without a single loss.

Sweetwater barely survived the celebration when they returned, as the forty or so members of the party gave it a victorious working over. Slade, in town to supervise, added to his reputation by settling an argument with a stagecoach driver at the point of a gun. The unfortunate fool was buried soon after—pretty much the usual reward for being dumb enough to argue with Slade when he was drinking.

Slade liked Billy, though, and when he was sober transferred the youngster over to Horseshoe Station, where he was given lighter duties as a substitute rider. This allowed him a lot of leisure time, and his mind naturally turned to hunting. One day he loaded his gear up on a horse and rode up in the direction of Laramie Peak, looking for a bear.

THE HUNTING PARTY

Antelopes, deer, rabbit—Buffalo Bill saw nearly every animal under the sun except for a bear. Unwilling to go back to Horseshoe empty handed, he shot some prairie chicken for dinner and breakfast and looked for a place to camp.

He'd just found a spot by the water and tied up his horse when he heard a horse whinnying up the trail. Deciding to investigate, he walked in the direction of the horse, rifle in hand, until he saw a little dugout hut. There were voices inside: trappers, he thought.

Young and foolish, he walked up and knocked on the door.

A human wolf in the form of an ex-teamster, current thief, and murderer opened the door.

Enter, young man, and be seen.

There were eight men in the hut, hardened criminals all. The horses Billy had heard whinnying were their latest haul, taken from a rancher in the vicinity. The man's objections had been silenced; he was now sharing them with the angels.

Just passing through, said Billy, adding he had seen the hut and decided to say hello. Asked about his horse, the boy volunteered to go get him, thinking he'd make his escape.

We'll come with you, said two of the thieves.

Cody left his rifle and showed them down to the horse, looking for an opening to escape. Retrieving the hens he'd killed, he trudged back up the hill, one of his guards leading the pony.

Desperate, Billy dropped one of the birds. As one of the thieves stooped to pick it up, the boy pulled a pistol from beneath his coat and clonked the criminal on the head as hard as he could. Whirling around, he saw the other thief drawing his gun.

Billy got his shot off first. By the time the thief hit the ground, Cody was aboard his horse and making tracks.

The rest of the gang charged from the hut. It was hard going in the thick pines, and even though his pursuers were on foot, Billy realized he wasn't going to get away. He slipped off his horse and hid while the pony clomped off into the darkness.

The thieves followed the horse. Billy slipped away, trekking twenty-five miles in the dark to the station. A subsequent search of the area found a fresh grave: Bill Cody had notched his first kill.

THE *BUT* . . .

Young Bill Cody's adventures were exciting and unusual, which you'd expect from the man whose name is synonymous with much of the Wild West.

But . . .

Those are all wonderful stories, and there are undoubtedly a few nuggets of truth to them—there was a Jack Slade, there was a Pony

Express. But there are so many holes in the tales contained in Cody's 1879 autobiography, which these are drawn from, that historians have had a field day pointing them out. There's testimony from a sister that Billy was in school when some of this happened, the timeline seems longer than the Pony Express was in existence, Russell was not the one who generally did the hiring (and spent most of his time back east besides), the Indians did not shut down the trail at that time . . .

In short, there is exactly zero evidence that any of what Cody says in his book about his days in the Pony Express is true, and plenty of evidence that it's not. The circumstances of his being hired, the Indian chase, the adventure with the horse thieves: none of those stories fits well with what we know of the service's history, even if it could be plausible in the context of the times. Cody probably did work for Russell, Majors, and Waddell—or at least one of their companies—though most likely as a messenger or as a hand helping one of the supply trains, or a kid working in the stables. He was exceedingly young to be a Pony rider, even as a substitute.

But if his tales can't be proved, they can't be disproved by the legal standard either. No less a writer on the West than Larry McMurtry takes it on faith that Cody rode with the Pony; he even accepts most of Cody's stories as only slight exaggerations.[3]

Faith and the Old West have always had a tight relationship; to appreciate the latter you need at least a bit of the former, be it blind or not. Young Billy Cody was exactly the sort of young man the Pony *did* hire as riders—though those we think we're sure of were nineteen and above when they rode. A love of adventure and a good dose of toughness were requirements for the job.

Dubious claims about having ridden for the Pony are plentiful. It's what Cody did afterward that set him apart.

A GUIDE'S GUIDE

Fifteen years old, Bill Cody found himself in Leavenworth some six months after the message of Lincoln's election passed through

Wyoming.[4] His family history leaned Union; so did he. Cody joined an independent force headed by a man named Chandler. While the unit was one of several supposedly defending against raids by Southern-leaning guerrillas, from Cody's description they were guerrillas and thieves themselves, stealing horses and harassing Southern sympathizers.

When the young man's mother found out, she hit the roof. Cody was ordered home and didn't ride with the unit again. About this time, the boy ran into Wild Bill Hickok, who, fiction aside, does seem to have been a family acquaintance. Hickok hired Cody as an assistant on an ox train from Leavenworth to Rolla, Missouri, and from there to Springfield, Missouri. Back in Rolla, Wild Bill had the boy race a horse he'd bought. The stakes were high: the horse and all the cash they had.

They lost. Wild Bill went to work for the army as a scout; Bill Cody went home to earn his keep. He enlisted in the army in 1864—he claims while drunk, which wouldn't be unique. Cody's Seventh Kansas regiment was a cavalry unit, and Cody's duties may have included scouting—or spying, as some of his tales indicate he was wearing Confederate gray while on horseback in open territory.

With the end of the war, Cody married and started a family. But he spent little time at home, and after more or less failing at running his mother's house as a hotel, he went back to working as a scout.

Scouts at the time were human GPS systems, tasked with taking army units from point A to point B with a minimum of bother. They would also hunt for fresh game, carry messages, and occasionally recon enemy positions. It was dangerous work, glamorous only in the aftermath, assuming you survived.

Cody was working at Fort Hays on Big Creek in Kansas when an army officer tasked him to lead him from Hays to Fort Larned, about fifty miles or so south.

The officer was George Armstrong Custer. Cody showed up to meet him and his party of ten on a mule.

I want to get there quick, Custer told him. *And a mule isn't going to do it.*

My mule will be faster than your horse, answered Cody.

Custer didn't believe him, but he let the young man give it a try. It was a good race for the first fifteen miles or so; then things turned in Cody's favor. By mile twenty-five, Cody was holding his mule back. As Cody proved, the animals were often better suited to long-distance travel over open country than horses, especially if the way was hilly or rocky.

Following his mission with Custer, Cody had a series of adventures, including a stint as an army detective in which he collared the notorious horse thief and future stagecoach robber William Bevins. In 1869 he was reassigned with the Fifth Cavalry to Fort McPherson in Nebraska. He distinguished himself in action against the Cheyenne, working in one of the most, if not the most, dangerous areas at the time. He won great respect from the Pawnee by wheeling a herd of bison and killing the animals one by one—thirty-six were dead when he finished, four more than the band of Indians had managed to kill before he took up the challenge to do better. And in the Battle of Summit Springs—an engagement on the South Platte in Kansas with a renegade band of Cheyenne led by Tatonka Haska, a.k.a. Tall Bull—he engineered a critical US victory.

Tall Bull and his force, who went by the tag "Dog Men Society," had raided local white settlements, destroying them and taking two women prisoners in a raid on a settlement along the Solomon River. A government force of about three hundred men, including a unit of Pawnee scouts, all under the command of Eugene Carr, set out to rescue the women.

Cody helped direct Carr after the Indians were spotted, and the force successfully maneuvered into a position where they could attack. At the last moment, the element of surprise was lost, but the force was still close enough to rout the Indians—fifty were killed. Unfortunately, one of the captives was killed as well, tomahawked by Tall Bull's wife; the other, a Mrs. Weichel, survived the ordeal and light wounds.

Cody did more than guide the troops to a strategic spot. He was in the middle of the battle and is generally given credit for shooting and killing Tall Bull. If Cody did kill the Indian chief—as with nearly every story about him, there are doubters—he didn't realize who it was until after the action: he was after the impressive bay horse the Indian was riding, and the status of its owner was an afterthought.[5]

It was within a few weeks of this engagement that Cody met Edward Zane Carroll Judson, a self-styled colonel and insanely prolific writer, better known to history as Ned Buntline.

NED

It's not true to say that there would have been no history of the Old West—be it of the Pony Express, Indian battles, or even Buffalo Bill—were it not for Ned Buntline. Things happen regardless of a man writing them down; a tree that falls in the forest still hits the ground.

Then again, if that history hadn't existed in the first place, it's a fair bet that Ned Buntline would have invented it.

Born in upstate New York, Edward Judson lived with his parents in Pennsylvania as a boy. In 1834, he ran away to sea at eleven or thirteen (the date of his birth is in dispute); jumping into the water to rescue the survivors of a ferry crash earned him a promotion from sailor to midshipman. He left the navy in favor of a career as a hunter and fur trader out west, but he found his true calling as a writer, both as a freelancer and as the editor of his own magazine.

He dueled, he captured criminals, he instigated riots against the English. He married—at least five times. But most of all, he wrote as Ned Buntline. His novels of heroes, generally though not always out west, were bestsellers at a dime a pop; he wrote some four hundred in his lifetime. He supplemented his income, and scouted for material, by traveling west and giving lectures in 1868 and 1869.

Cody was already a legend when he was introduced to an easterner who was to accompany a patrol Cody had been tasked to guide. A bit portly, the man walked with a limp and wore enough medals on his coat to stop a cannonball.

Ned Buntline.

Cody and the writer, brothers in yarn as well as action, got along famously well; Buntline spent much of the expedition grilling him. The result was published in a series of stories debuting on December 23, 1869, in the *New York Weekly* entitled "Buffalo Bill, the King of the Border Men."

The stories started off with a bang—Buffalo Bill, age ten, confronted border ruffians immediately after they killed his father. Trouble and adventure multiplied from there.

The story eventually made its way to book form a few years later, but by then Cody's fame had exploded beyond the West. Besides helping the army battle Indians, he was a popular guide on VIP hunting expeditions, including at least one where the party was attacked by Indians and Cody rallied the resistance. Word spread, and he did what he could to encourage it by being as memorable as possible. Guiding a party that included several important newspaper editors, Cody debuted an outfit that would forever be identified with him: a buckskin suit trimmed with fringe, an embroidered red shirt, and a sombrero. Finally, he had a visual to match the narrative.

MEDAL OF HONOR

April 26, 1872: Spring hadn't quite gotten its grip on the Nebraska sod as Cody led a company of soldiers to the south fork of the Loup River. They'd been riding for two days, tracking a party of Indians who had struck an outpost near McPherson, killing two or three men and stealing horses. While the rest of the force rested, Cody and a half-dozen men forded the river to look for the Indian camp.

They found it barely a mile away. Rather than returning to the main force, Cody and the sergeant in charge decided to see if they could surprise the half dozen or so Indians camped there.

They almost made it.

Spotting them when they were about fifty yards away, the Indians started to retreat. Cody began firing, killing one warrior instantly.

Two others fell before the main group made it across a stream where they had stashed their horses. Separated from the other soldiers as he charged, Cody killed two more Indians before the rest rode off.

Cody's courage was by now so well known that the officer writing up the citation for the engagement barely had to write "Cody" to justify his praise. The engagement earned him the army's highest praise—and the Medal of Honor.

There is a post note on the medal: because Cody was a civilian, the award was revoked, Cody's name stricken from the rolls. It was restored after his death, and he remains one of the very few civilians so recognized.

WILD WEST

Buntline's genius wasn't restricted to writing books or fighting duels. In December 1872, he convinced Cody to come to Chicago and star in a show he called *Scouts of the Prairie*, based loosely on the story he'd written about him.

The show was never going to win literary awards, but the shoot-outs, Western action, and Cody's soliloquies on bravery, the frontier, and Injun trouble immediately struck a chord with audiences. As Robert A. Carter puts it in his biography, *Buffalo Bill Cody: The Man Behind the Legend*:

> *By obscuring the fine line between make-believe and reality, between his and [Texas Jack, another Western Scout and friend of Cody's] actual experiences, on the frontier and the derring-do they improvised on the stage, he was unknowingly creating the myth of the Wild West, the archetype of the Western, a genre that persists to this day.*[6]

The show traveled to Cincinnati and then New York, continuing to Philadelphia, Richmond, and elsewhere. When it closed that summer in Port Jervis, New York, Cody was a star equal to today's film idols.

The following year, Cody began mounting his own yearly shows, which he called "combinations." These were essentially action-filled skits based on things that had happened or might have happened or could have happened to Cody or someone he knew or someone he could have known, sort of. They were maybe real, if one adjusted for the fact that they were being re-created in a theater in an environment nothing like where they might have happened, compressed for time, and enhanced for maximum entertainment.

Whatever. People loved them.

Cody's theater season ran from fall through spring; he traveled by train from city to city in the East. But every summer he went back west, back to being a military scout and private hunting party leader.

There are no parallels today: Imagine a highly decorated navy SEAL taking a break from chasing terrorists to appear in movies and on TV for eight or nine months at a shot, then returning to Undisclosed Locations to track down ISIS leaders. Then on weekends, he takes VIPs out to hunt bears.

In 1883, Cody pushed his theatrics to the next level, taking the show outdoors, where he had more room for horses, stagecoaches, rampaging Indians, and heroic cowboys. Always a little different, the show featured Western personalities and personal friends, from Annie Oakley to Sitting Bull, with each season a little different.

Except for one constant: a vignette featuring the exploits of the Pony Express riders always opened the show.

The Pony and its riders were not unknown before Cody began touring, but his shows, which lasted into the next century, enhanced and enshrined the service in the American memory. It's hard to understate the impact of the Wild West Show as popular entertainment; it was like the Super Bowl arriving in your own hometown. Cody, larger than life whether on the frontier or the stage, was both a real hero and the age's equivalent of a rock star. Anything and anyone associated with him gained a permanent glow.

Buffalo Bill inspired many liars of the purple sage, but few had the sheer genius for showmanship that he did. Buntline gets a lot of credit—the man could stampede words together and gave no quarter to reality when he had a gust of fantasy at his back. But Cody climbed scales generally inaccessible before the advent of true mass media. Ultimately, he defeated time just as the Pony did: he outran history, creating legends still with us today.

There were precedents. It was in general a time when entertainment involved lecturers visiting around the country, getting paid to talk. Samuel Colt, struggling to find himself before perfecting his revolver, gave lectures on laughing gas. More seriously, the poet and essayist Ralph Waldo Emerson spun an entire philosophical and art movement, transcendentalism, out of talks he gave. But most of these were on far smaller scales.

P. T. Barnum, perhaps the best salesman America or the world has ever known, toured Europe and America with two major acts before the Civil War, then created the "Greatest Show on Earth," the best parallel in scope and impact to Cody's Wild West Show a few years later.

Barnum's attraction was curiosity: animals you never saw, freaks you hadn't even read about. Cody, on the other hand, sold things you *thought* you knew: heroes and legends from the West, skilled at murder and other blessed acts of endearment.

Why were these stories so successful? What were people tuning into?

The nineteenth century was a time of violent, dramatic change. There was the Civil War, and the end of slavery. America ceased being a collection of individual states and divided regions, knitting itself together into a world power. At the same time, everyday life changed dramatically, in ways difficult to fully appreciate because they're now so familiar to us: the amount of light in an average room, the height of buildings, the ability to communicate with someone half a continent away in a matter of days—these were radically different before midcentury, even as we take them for granted today.

Wild Bill's stories about the West reminded people of what wasn't changing, values that they saw as important. Heroism, individualism, a love for adventure. Wrap it in an exotic cloak, throw in some gunplay, and you have not only the heart of the Wild West Show, but one of America's strongest foundation beliefs. Call it a myth, but in doing so remember that myths are of value only when they express a universal truth.

The Pony Express was an integral part. Its heroes—ordinary teenagers for the most part—fought Nature and Time. They were heroes everyone could identify with, no matter their political views, no matter their philosophies, no matter their cares. William Frederick Cody may or may not ever have ridden for the service during its scant eighteen months of operation, but he rides the trail forever in the nation's collective memory of its achievements.

UNBONDED

THE STORMS THREATEN

But that was posterity. William Hepburn Russell had more immediate things to worry about that November. His own future, for starters.

Midfall is uniformly cold on the plains; that year there was snow. Early November in New York, by contrast, is a changeable time. There are warm days, teases of the summer past. And then there are cold days, warning of the approach of winter blizzards. The changes are enough to drown the mood of even an optimistic man like Russell, whose moods had been swinging high and low for months.

Now at his office, a letter arrived from Washington that froze even his indomitable spirit. It was from a clerk he barely knew, but who held the fate of his company—and him—in his hands.

The letter was about bonds, and when they would be returned.

The short answer—the one he couldn't give, not really—was never.

RUSSELL HAD STAVED OFF DISASTER SEVERAL TIMES OVER THE PAST several months. As acceptances came due early in the year, he managed to get new ones, trading one debt for another, larger one.

Finally, that past July, he reached a point where he could get no more. Shuttling between Washington and New York, he realized the $150,000 he needed to pay off the debt coming due would not come from John Floyd, in cash or acceptances. The war secretary had problems beyond Russell's contracts. And President Buchanan, having learned of the acceptances, had put an end to them.

For a moment, it looked as if the mail contract might come through.

But it didn't. Worse, as the days passed, the banks holding the acceptances Russell had already pledged began threatening to cash them in. If that happened, Floyd would undoubtedly be liable for some sort of prosecution. Scandal would follow.

Worse, Russell wouldn't get paid.

As the country teetered on the edge of dissolution, financial panic was setting in. Russell's house of cards—or Ponzi scheme, to be unkind and use a term that wouldn't be invented for a few decades—threatened to collapse.

Desperate to raise money, Russell was on a train back to Washington when he chanced to meet Luke Lea, a friend, banker, and a partner in Russell's Leavenworth bank—and not coincidentally, a man who had helped him place acceptances before. He explained the entire situation to Lea, asking first for a loan, which Lea wouldn't provide. He then asked if he knew of anyone or any way he could help.

Lea had been the commissioner of Indian affairs during the Taylor administration; as commissioner, he knew of bonds that were kept in trust for several tribes. Though the bonds were technically under the jurisdiction of the secretary of interior—a different department—they had been kept in a safe in his office.

What role that knowledge had in the proposed solution Lea offered Russell was never explained, but it seems hardly coincidental that, after arriving in Washington, Lea approached the current clerk in charge of the bonds, a man named Goddard Bailey.

Bailey, a lawyer, was related to Floyd by marriage. Lea went to him and warned that the acceptances were about to be turned in to the government for payment—technically "protested." He made it clear that Russell couldn't pay or substitute new ones for them. This, both men knew, would present an immediate problem for Floyd.

So if Floyd couldn't come up with the money to cover the charges Russell said were still owed from the Mormon War, or pay actual money on the freighting contracts still in effect . . . what could be done?

The very next day, Bailey turned up at Russell's offices a few blocks from the White House.

They talked about the situation; Russell told him that he needed $150,000 to make good on the acceptances or they were sure to be presented, and Floyd was sure to be ruined. Bailey agreed to help, and in short order produced $150,000 worth of Missouri and Tennessee bonds to take care of the acceptances. They were a loan, though one without interest. Russell gave him a note for them and returned to New York.

PAYMENTS DUE

The face value of the bonds, which were from the states of Tennessee and Missouri, was $150,000. At this point they were not worth anywhere near that much; Russell ended up raising only $97,000 against them.[1] Still, he was able to retrieve the acceptances and stave off disaster, for him as well as Floyd.

But increasing worries about the country's financial situation—and the fact that the bonds were from two states whose loyalties and ability to pay might be questioned—lessened their value. Worse, the failure of Congress to award a new mail contract, the continued losses by Russell, Majors & Waddell—some of which were due to the Pony operation—multiplied Russell's problems. In September, he returned to Washington to talk to Bailey. He proposed selling the bonds. Bailey freaked.

The bonds, he said, belonged to the Indian Bureau, not the War Department; they had to be returned.

Russell was shocked, or so he would claim later.

The two men arranged for more bonds—$387,000 worth, at face value—to be used to redeem the Missouri and Tennessee bonds and cover other acceptances coming due. These bonds were also heavily discounted, and Russell had to swap ones guaranteed by Florida as they were considered worthless. But once more a crisis had been averted.

Partially. To continue going at least until the mail contract was awarded—an unrepentant optimist despite everything, he had good hopes it would be let when Congress reconvened—Russell began looking for more conventional funding, trying to arrange $400,000.

But even that wasn't going to be enough. More acceptances were coming due, and the worth of the bonds he'd placed continued to drop.

And Bailey was worried about the whole deal, as his letter made clear. When will the bonds be returned?

It was a question Russell couldn't answer. The best thing to do, he thought, was to let them be sold, then buy them back when their value reached rock bottom.

Which, with the way things were going in the country, might not be that long at all.

THE GREAT DIVIDE

THROUGH WYOMING

The Pony's trail through Wyoming began at a relay and stagecoach stop called Cold Springs in the eastern part of the state near present-day Torrington, Wyoming, running west along the North Platte past Fort Caspar before cutting over to follow the Sweetwater River through Pacific Springs on toward Fort Bridger. The rider was moving at top speed toward the great fissure that lay at the heart of the continent, one that connected east to west, a geological accident that was essential to America's development: the Great Divide. From the back of his horse, it was invisible, far off in the distance, and impossible to discern amid the close hills or even the snow-capped mountains towering above them. And while it made his route and his job possible, all he knew was to ride.

The things he noticed were closer in. Settlements were sparser, with conditions away from the rivers increasingly more difficult. Grass grew thick on the plains, not yet decimated by the herds of cattle that would fill the space a few years after the Civil War.[1] The primary fact of the territory was space—vast and empty, running off to hills and mountains that underlined a seemingly endless sky. Each night the sinking sun painted the mountains red, its rays glaring in one last blaze, going down in glory.

The route west out of Nebraska into Wyoming was gradually uphill, the way increasingly spartan. Pole Creek Station Three in Nebraska (east of present-day Sidney in Cheyenne County; as the name suggests, there were two others) was a dugout hovel on the hillside; the tender waited on a box for the rider to arrive.

In the middle of this wilderness, a virtual metroplex loomed in Wyoming: Fort Laramie.

FORT LARAMIE

The fort was located near the intersection of Laramie River and the North Platte. Named after a French fur trapper, Jacques La Ramee,[2] the Laramie River flows south to north, unusual in the United States as well as Wyoming. A fort was established here in 1834; it changed hands twice in the next two years, en route to becoming a major trading post.

The word *fort* conjures a certain set of images today, especially when associated with the Old West: palisades and lookouts, cannons at every corner, mounted steads at the ready. A grand building sits at the center, lording over several dozen lesser buildings, mustered in military rows and bristling with squared-away troops.

The original Fort Laramie—Fort William as it was christened—was more general store than fort, a far cry from the grand image of historical imaginations. There was a wooden palisade, but it enclosed a tiny space, reportedly only 150 square feet, with a few low cabins making up the buildings.[3] A large block house guarded the gate; there was a single cannon.[4]

The post did great business for six or seven years, serving as an important resting spot for travelers and, more important, the favorite of Sioux Indians with goods to trade. But when competition to the north cut into its business in 1841, the American Fur Company decided to do what many modern strip mall owners might—they abandoned the old complex and built a shiny new one nearby, complete with adobe or masonry buildings and all the modern conveniences, including double doors at the entrance.

The opening of the Oregon Territory and the subsequent migration changed Laramie from the equivalent of a strip mall to a megaplex.

In 1849, the government bought the fort for $4,000, only to realize it had purchased a rat-infested slum. Once more the old was abandoned; what rose in its place next door was a complex much closer to your imagined fort: an impressive set of buildings arrayed over a wide area, with a neat officers' row at one end, a secure guardhouse at the corner, and enlisted barracks in the middle. There were no palisades; the main danger from Indians was theft and annoyance—loners and the occasional small group would beg items from travelers, which annoyed them no end but did not present physical danger.

That changed in the middle and latter half of the 1850s, with more migration and more chances for misunderstandings. Incidents at the fort and nearby settlements and trails led to conflicts with the Sioux and Cheyanne tribes. These were not pretty; in 1854, a boneheaded second lieutenant in charge of thirty or so men precipitated his own death and that of his entire company by insisting that twelve hundred Sioux warriors violate a treaty by turning over an alleged cow thief without due process. The Indians underlined their point by ransacking the fort. In response, the army launched an attack the following year that resulted in the massacre of women and children in a Brule Sioux village.

Of course, if you read the newspapers at the time, you would think the whites were the ones who were wronged and find no mention of the Indian village, whose only offense was being in the wrong place at the wrong time.[5] A new treaty was signed in 1856, pretty much on terms dictated by the whites. The peace that followed still lingered, uneasily, at the time of the Pony Express.

The Pony "office" at Fort Laramie was probably at the sutler's store, a civilian structure located at the corner of the property that functioned as a commissary for nonmilitary items and gear. You might buy coffee or flour, or maybe a nice bolt of calico and some straight pins for your wife. Made of stone, the building was one story with a large attic; there was a stable nearby, and a cluster of other civilian houses, including the doctor's.

The real palace, at least in terms of Pony Express and stagecoach stops, was two exchanges down the line at Horseshoe Station, where even the notorious cranky Brit, Richard Burton, was impressed by the number and seeming expense of the buildings. It was a palace fit for a badass: Jack Slade owned it.

The house had a large whitewashed veranda, "Floridian style," said Burton with some approval, since he valued the porch for its coolness. The wood was a change from the dull adobe structures common along that part of the trail, and the house was far grander than the hovels and "whiskey houses" the stage passengers generally were treated to.

Burton being Burton, he couldn't stay content for long. His next paragraphs turn to Slade's wife, Virginia, or rather, turn against Slade's wife, something he probably felt safe in doing only after he had an ocean between them:

> The Bloomer [Mrs. Slade] was an uncouth being; her hair, cut level with her eyes, depended with the graceful curl of a drake's tail around a flat Turanian countenance, whose only expression was sullen insolence. The body-dress, glazed brown calico, fitted her somewhat like a soldier's tunic, developing haunches which would be admired only in venison; and—curious inconsequence of woman's nature!—all this sacrifice of appearance upon the shrine of comfort did not prevent her wearing that kind of crinoline depicted by Mr. Punch around "our Mary Hanne." The pantalettes of glazed brown calico, like the vest, tunic, blouse, shirt, or whatever they may call it, were in peg-top style, admirably setting off a pair of thin-soled Frenchified patent-leather bottines, with elastic sides, which contained feet large, broad, and flat as a negro's in Unyamwezi.[6]

Beauty was surely in the eyes of the beholder. Burton describes common dress for a frontier lady of reasonable means. Brown was very common; the pink, purple, and mauve chemical dyes popular in Europe had only recently been invented. Crinolines were very much the rage, achieving their peak in popularity just as they reached their

maximum bell-like dimensions. Pantalettes—an undergarment covering the legs so no flesh appeared between the shoes and dress when
sitting—were relatively recent in style.

Slade by all accounts loved his wife; the following summer he built
a new house for her in northern Colorado that he named Virginia
Dale. She was reported to be voluptuous and pretty, tall, and a good
rider.[7] While it would have been difficult to match her husband's temperament, she was strong-willed enough to handle him.

TREATY OR NO, PROBLEMS WITH SMALL BANDS OF INDIANS IN THE AREA
increased west of Horseshoe. Henry Avis, a St. Louis boy, worked as a
wagon and stagecoach driver for Hockaday before Russell took over
the line. Staying on, the twenty-one-year-old graduated the following
year to the Pony, riding between Mud Springs (Nebraska) and Horseshoe (Wyoming). He'd landed at Horseshoe one day to find that there
were reports of a Sioux war party near Deer Creek Station farther
west. The Pony rider scheduled to take the mochila from Avis refused
to go on; Avis changed horses and went in his place.

By the time Avis arrived, the station's horses had been run off and
the men inside were in no mood to try to retrieve them. Huddled inside the house was the eastbound rider, who declined to risk his neck
with the mail. Avis took it instead, retracing his route to Horseshoe
Station.

Not that he did it entirely out of a sense of duty: The stationmaster
guaranteed him $300 for the ride—or so Avis later claimed. Maybe he
exaggerated, maybe he happened to hit the station when its master
was flush; in any event, he finished the ride with both mail and body
intact and collected his booty.[8]

SEEING RED

Tonight, twenty-six-year-old Charles Becker was waiting at Deer
Creek Station in Wyoming for the election dispatches.[9] He was so agitated he couldn't read any of the magazines he habitually studied be-

tween rides, let alone the thick science text he practically memorized during the long days and nights while he waited to take the mail.

The Pennsylvania native had apprenticed as a butcher before giving up the cleaver for the sea. Working as a cabin boy on the *Augusta*, a side-wheeling steamer that sailed between New York and Savannah, he heard stories of the West that fired his imagination.[10] He left the sea and ended up in Leavenworth, working as a freighter.

His very first trip west was one in which Russell et al.'s trains were raided. Captured by Mormon guerrillas, he was stripped of his rifle and pistol, then marched with other drovers to Salt Lake City. After several weeks under guard, much of it working as a servant, he was blindfolded and packed off with other prisoners via mule from Salt Lake City to a spot on the Bear River some thirty-three miles from Fort Bridger, a trip that took several days. Freed in the icy winter wilderness, they survived by eating the meat of an ox they discovered—after building a fire to defrost the meat. It took four days to reach Bridger.

Taken on as a Pony rider about a year and a half later to work a route closer to Fort Laramie, Becker was a thoughtful young man, someone who welcomed solitude—probably a must for success on the long stretches of the trail he worked. He loved nature and would stare at it for hours—except when he rode. There was a lot to look at. Once seabed and swamp, the ground west of Laramie spread toward massive, bald rocks. Chiseled stone jutted in the distance; far-off mountain barriers, capped white by daylight and glowing from the moon at night, looked more like backdrops to a painting than actual mountains.

Becker changed horses at a station at the upper crossing of the North Platte. The future home of Fort Caspar, the station was barely a year old, established by Louis Guinard as a trading post and stop for travelers west.[11] Known as Platte Bridge Station, Guinard had built a house and stable to complement a bridge crossing he built over the river a short distance away. The bridge went over a shallow patch of the river favored by Mormon pioneers—and not coincidentally was situated to compete with another toll crossing a few miles away.

Guinard was married to a Shoshoni Indian woman, which brought him into conflict with other tribes and renegade bands that increasingly roamed the area. Just a few weeks before, Guinard's son was killed by Hunkpapa and Sans Ar Lakota while tending his father's horse and cattle.[12] With the perpetrators gone, there was nothing to be done now but grieve.

Becker continued down to Red Buttes, a small home station near yet another crossing on the North Platte used by settlers taking the Oregon Trail. A gently worn hill or "butte" sat north of the station about five miles. In the right light, from the proper angle, it looked like a castle turret, its red walls topped by a white ring, as if the battlements had been done in thicker bricks. The hill gave a good vantage of the river valley and was said to be used by Indians, outlaws, and all manner of voyeurs.

Independence Rock, Devil's Gate, Split Rock, Sweetwater—the Pony stations west took their names from emigrant waypoints, named by people eager to be anywhere but where they'd been. Independence Rock—a double hump of easily carved and thus graffiti-covered sandstone—was a landmark that had to be reached no later than July 4 if you were going to get to Oregon before the snow. Devil's Gate was a narrow pass that looked like the doorway to hell. Split Rock was a notch in the rocks that could be seen for miles, a natural compass. Sweetwater was the first dependable source of fresh water since leaving the river, and a far sweeter source at that.

Three months before, the wide plain to Sweetwater would have been crowded with wagons and pioneers. Now in early November it was empty, with nature rushing to cover the evidence of their passing, first with prairie grass in the rills where their wheels had rolled, and lately with hard frost, bits of ice, and snow. But there were reminders harder than wagon ruts to remove: crude crosses and mounded rocks that marked the graves of those who had died along the way.

Cholera and dysentery, passed by bacteria in food or drinking water, were the classic killers. In the days before antibiotics and vaccines, measles and the like were often fatal. Contagious diseases had no frontier, and the world was more connected for germs in the nineteenth century than we realize. A cholera outbreak in Bengal led to a worldwide pandemic—an epidemic on a global scale—which included a mass outbreak on the Oregon Trail around the time of the gold rush. Hard conditions on the trail weakened people's immune systems, making it more difficult to recover once infected.

How many people died? The most common estimate is that, of the 350,000 emigrants believed to have used the Oregon and California trail from 1841 to 1869, from 6 to 10 percent got a serious disease. Some thirty thousand died . . . roughly fifteen per mile.

Disease wasn't the only killer. An accident in the wilderness could often be fatal. Childbirth in the nineteenth century was inherently risky for mother as well as child.[13]

> *We have just passed by the train I have just spoken of. They had just buried the babe of the woman who died days ago and were just digging a grave for another woman that was run over by the cattle and wagons when they stampeded yesterday. She lived twenty-four hours, she gave birth to a child a short time before she died. The child was buried with her. She leaves a little two year old girl and a husband. They say he is nearly crazy with sorrow.*[14]

The stories of deaths in travelers' journals are heartbreaking and cruel, even more so for their brevity and the quick acceptance. Orphans wander near wagons left by the trail after a father died from an accident and their mother died of disease. Children fall from the wagon and have their skulls crushed by nearby wagons. Emotional calluses were an important tool for survival as emigrants pressed on to beat the winter.

SOUTH PASS

To this point in Wyoming, all the Pony riders had been riding generally along the emigrant trail, which followed a route that had been discovered less than forty years before by Robert Stuart. That route pivoted through South Pass, a fortuitous hollow through the Rocky Mountains that connected the two halves of the continent.

Stuart, a fur trader working for Jacob Astor, set out in the summer of 1812 from Fort Astoria at the mouth of the Columbia River west of present-day Portland in search of a passage easier than the treacherous one on the Snake River known as Union Pass. Stuart and his party of six wandered for days through the area of the Rockies, chasing ghosts and rumors—and eventually a guide and stolen horse—until the mountains seemed to open up before them.

Stuart's journey ended in the spring of 1813; it wouldn't be followed in great numbers for nearly thirty years, but it opened the way for all. His path through what became known as South Pass was a middle passage, neither scorching and parched like those south, nor frozen and equally treacherous like those to the north. Choices multiplied beyond the pass—Oregon, Utah, and California beckoned—but the roughly twenty-mile wide bowl and its crannies were the essential gateway.

The pass was a connection but was also the mark of division. Beyond the pass was a new world bereft of old possessions, sold or jettisoned to make the journey. As hard as the trip had been to that point, it would get even harder very soon.

And so it was for the country the pass connected.

LINCOLN

The man freshly elected to hold together the country's soul if not its geography was home in Springfield, Illinois, pondering his next steps. He was very much aware that he had won less than a majority of votes: 40 percent, compared with Douglas's 30, Breckinridge's 18, and Bell's 12. Lincoln had an electoral landslide, but it was a landslide of the Northern states only.

How to cross the country's divide was his great question. To Lincoln, the moment required action—something the present occupant

of the White House did not understand. To see a crisis and not act—
that was un-American.

But what action was the right one? On the one hand, Lincoln was
against slavery. On the other hand, he was in favor of the Union. He
knew intuitively that the contradiction could not continue indefi-
nitely, yet as he pondered how to set up his cabinet, he considered
men on both sides of that divide. He thought of including his old
friend Joshua Speed, not only because of their friendship, but Speed's
political registration—Speed was a Democrat. It would turn out that
Speed couldn't afford to take the job. Lincoln would end up with no
friends in the cabinet, and no Southerners, though there would be
plenty of conflict from what the historian Doris Kearns Goodwin
would later term a "team of rivals"—prominent Republicans who had
competed with him for the party designation: William H. Seward,
Salon P. Chase, and Edward Bates.

Each morning this November, Lincoln rose and went to the state
building, working with his aide John Nicolay. By ten, he would open
the doors and the public would pour in—fans, job seekers, the press.
Anyone could come, and just about anything could be said or asked.
The doors closed for lunch at one; there was another open house
free-for-all from 3:30 to 5:30. Over a hundred and fifty people milled
through the room each day.

Lincoln greeted most with energy and pizazz. As the door to the
room flew open, he lunged forward, grabbing the first person's hand
and leading him off for a private moment.

"Get in, the rest of you," he would shout over his shoulder.

They'd follow, amused, taken off guard, but eager to make whatever point they'd come to make. Lincoln would listen, but also play
the crowd the way he had played the juries in the courts he'd worked
the past twenty-four years. Sharp asides sent the room into fits of
laughter; no one laughed louder or harder than Lincoln himself.

He was more politician than comedian; push him on a subject that
he didn't care to speak on, and Lincoln would easily deflect it. Some-

one who pressed him would be asked, with a guffaw, if he had read "my speeches."

He didn't want to be pinned down in large part because he was still trying to figure it all out.

Somehow the Union must be preserved. Action was imperative, but what action?

The newspapers were filled with stories about angry Southerners clamoring for division from the Union. Violently if necessary. The *New York Tribune*, a staunch Republican paper run by Horace Greeley, declared that the South should be left to go off in peace.

Lincoln disagreed, but for the moment he made no public statement, not even in his jokes, not even in reaction to the dreary news from Washington.

BUCHANAN

If there was a man who could keep America together, it was not the present occupant of the White House, James Buchanan, who by this point in 1860 was well hated by just about everyone who was anyone in the country.

Four years before, the native Pennsylvanian surely would have looked like a great choice. Six feet tall, good-looking, with a calm and friendly temperament, he had a deep résumé in service to his country, starting with his enlistment at age twenty-three to fight against the British in the War of 1812. He'd served in the statehouse and in Washington, been minister to Russia and Britain, and served as senator from 1834 to 1845. He'd been in Polk's administration as secretary of state, a job for healing divisions if ever there was one. He knew personal tragedy—his fiancé had committed suicide following a quarrel; the death broke his heart and may have influenced his decision to remain a lifelong bachelor. But he knew the importance of families: he adopted his orphaned niece, raising her as his own daughter.

Buchanan had even crossed political divides, beginning his political career as a Federalist before becoming a Jacksonian Democrat. Though he hailed from Pennsylvania, he was aligned with the Southern half of his party. This was a double contradiction, considering his attitude toward slavery—he was not only philosophically against it, but he freed slaves he acquired in Washington by bringing them to Pennsylvania, a free state.

For all his personal and political experience, Buchanan could have been a Punch and Judy doll and gotten the same results. By this point, he might have taken fewer bruises. He'd seen disaster for his party in Douglas's nomination and worked against it; the worst had now occurred—and even worse was threatened.

In the wake of Lincoln's election, Buchanan called an unprecedented series of cabinet meetings, asking for advice on how he might proceed in the face of threats from the South to secede.

South Carolina was the most immediate problem. On October 20, more than two weeks before the election, the state had mobilized the Washington Light Infantry of Charleston—in effect calling out an army to prepare for combat. Five days later, a group of state leaders met to discuss what to do if Lincoln won. The results of that meeting were now clear: all federal judges and the members of the grand jury in the state resigned the day after the election, making it impossible to charge anyone there with a federal crime.

On November 7, the governor asked a friend to pose a question to Buchanan: *What are you going to do about the four state forts on state soil?*

Only a blind man would have missed the signs that dissolution was coming, and the president's eye problems—one eye was farsighted, the other near—let him see perfectly well, even if he did have to cock his head to one side to keep people in focus. What he couldn't see was a way to avoid it.

IN BUCHANAN'S MIND, THE NORTHERN STATES WERE AS MUCH TO blame for the break as the South; more so, since they'd gone first, openly defying the federal Fugitive Slave Act by passing their own laws to supersede it, or simply failing to enforce it.

The act directed citizens throughout the country to help capture and return runaway slaves. If you didn't, you could be jailed and fined. Signed by Millard Fillmore in 1850, the law was part of failed compromise that had nonetheless headed off a nationwide fissure. A harsher revision of a 1793 bill—which itself was not particularly popular—the Fugitive Slave Act provoked widespread resistance in the North. It also doomed Fillmore to one term and hastened the breakup of the Whig Party.

But it *was* the law, and it was based on section 2, clause 3, of the Constitution: "No Person held to Service or Labor in one State, under the Laws thereof, escaping into another, shall, in Consequence of any Law or Regulation therein, be discharged from such Service or Labor, but shall be delivered up on Claim of the Party to whom such Service or Labor may be due."

Vermont passed a contradictory law requiring state officials to protect escaped slaves; Wisconsin declared the Fugitive Slave Act unconstitutional. Most other states in the North simply refused to enforce the law. Juries "nullified" it by failing to convict people brought up on charges.

To Buchanan, this was horrendous. Nullifying the law was, in effect, nullifying the Constitution; pick and choose which parts you want, and eventually the whole falls apart. He was against slavery, but for law, and of the two held the latter a higher good.

Even if it had been possible to overlook local jury nullifications, the implications of the *Dred Scott* case, decided by the Supreme Court in 1857, made prolonged political conflict inescapable. The seven-judge majority declared that Scott was not a citizen and had no rights under the Constitution. As bad as that was, the majority opinion also declared that Congress had no right under the Constitution to limit slavery; at best, the matter had to be left up to the states and territories. The immediate impact was Bleeding Kansas.

Some believed—or feared—that the ruling meant there was no right of *anyone* to ban slavery, though nowhere was that stated. The logic, though, was simple: If a man wasn't a man, if he couldn't be a citizen, then what would keep him from being treated like a piece of broken furniture no matter what part of the Union he was kept in?

Sectional interests and party politics added to the mixture of anger and fear that both sides felt as the implications settled in, but slavery was the main issue for both Northern and Southern politicians. Compromise was a nonstarter for politicians: being weak on the issue, on either side, meant you lost votes, which meant you went home. Northerners preached open defiance of the Fugitive Slave Act; Southerners, realizing they were politically outnumbered, talked of leaving the Union by force.

Buchanan was a man of law, and law meant courts, not guns. But it was growing apparent that force would be the only way to keep the country together.

THE DAY AFTER THE ELECTION, A SMALL GROUP OF SOLDIERS WERE stopped by a Charleston wharf owner when they attempted to take arms from the federal armory and transport them to Fort Moultrie, a fortification on Sullivan's Island that helped protect Charleston Harbor. A crowd had gathered, and the soldiers retreated. The next day the commander managed to have the weapons moved without incident. But word of the conflict alarmed Buchanan. There were four forts in South Carolina, and all would be vulnerable to attack.

He asked the cabinet what he should do. They couldn't decide. Buchanan suggested that he would deliver a message to Congress declaring that he would protect federal property—which meant the forts.

Mmmmmm . . . not so fast.

John Floyd, the secretary of war, thought that was too strong. Instead, he suggested the president replace the present commander at Fort Moultrie and the arsenal with officers from Charleston, a bit of a compromise that would show the federal government was sympathetic, though not 100 percent gutless.

Buchanan agreed to send Major Robert Anderson to the fort and Colonel Benjamin Huger to the arsenal; both men were seen as more sympathetic to the South than the present command. But he doubted the change would be the end of it.

How much further does the law allow me to go?

Can I shoot people?

Should I shoot people?[15]

Legalities aside, Buchanan wanted to know: What could he do to prevent an attack without provoking one?

There was no good answer to any of his questions. Buchanan asked his attorney general, Jeremiah Black, to answer five questions about presidential power. The last was the most difficult: Could military force be used in a state that had no federal judges or other officers?

Force over law? It was a possibility that filled him with dread.

Attorney General Black, charged with answering questions about whether it was legal to keep the Union together by force, came by the White House to discuss informally the policies he thought the president should follow.

I don't want advice, Buchanan snapped. *I want information. Answer the questions: I'll decide what to do.*

JIM BRIDGER

The conflict between North and South, between slave and not-slave, had been baked into the Constitution. But the national DNA also contained the sort of determination and force of will that it took to overcome tremendous adversity. If the struggles were rough and even violent, so were the people; necessarily so. The explorers and frontier entrepreneurs who had blazed the trail the Pony rider took through the Great Divide were a perfect example.

One in particular had given his name to the next major stop on the route: Fort Bridger.

JIM BRIDGER = MOUNTAIN MAN.

End of story. Because whatever a person can imagine a mountain man to be, that will pretty much define Bridger. And then some.

Born in Richmond, Virginia, March 17, 1804, Bridger was orphaned at thirteen after his father had moved the family to St. Louis. He began earning a living to support himself and a younger sister, first as a ferryman, then as an apprentice blacksmith. At age eighteen, he joined a fur-trapping expedition headed by Andrew Henry to the far West. The trip transformed his life, and those of countless other Americans.

Battered and bruised from mishaps and encounters with hostile Indians, the small party spent the winter near the Yellowstone River in present-day Montana. They later moved down the Big Horn River and in 1824 rediscovered South Pass, whose location had slipped from popular white memory.

That summer, the party was moving up Grand River in what is now North Dakota when one of its members, Hugh Glass, happened upon a bear. Attacked before he could fire his gun, Glass was horribly mauled. He was near death when the rest of the group found him moments later.

The party had been constantly harassed by Indians, and Andrew Henry worried that if they didn't move on quickly, they'd be ambushed. But Glass wasn't quite dead. He couldn't be buried. He could be carried. He couldn't be left to die.

Eighty dollars to stay and take care of him, said Henry, looking around the party. *Stay, and I'll give you eighty bucks.*

Most likely he'll die. But if he lives, bring him back to the trading post. Easier for one or two men to hide, than a whole party.

Eighty bucks. I need two volunteers.

Bridger was one of those who stayed. Neither he nor his partner thought it would be for very long. But five days on, Glass was still alive.

Doesn't make any sense to hang around here, said Bridger's companion. *He's not getting better. Sooner or later, the Indians'll get us, too.*

They decided to leave. Catching up to the main group, they claimed Glass had passed away and showed his rifle as proof.

But Glass hadn't. In fact, he'd crawled from his deathbed in the heavy woods and begun struggling toward Fort Kiowa, a hundred miles and infinite hardship away.

IF THAT STORY SOUNDS FAMILIAR, IT MAY BE BECAUSE THE 2015 MOVIE *The Revenant* was based on a book of the same name, which was based on the Glass story.

Kinda. The way movies and books are based on *any* story, the same way legends are based on real life.

As the original story goes, Glass found Bridger and forgave him because he'd been only a kid. Then he went after the other man, but rather than killing him—supposedly because the man was in the army, and the penalty would have been death—merely asked for his rifle back.

Historians, of course, will insist on saying that the tale can't be proved. But by the same token, it can't be disproved. And one thing's for certain: by the time of the Pony, it was in wide circulation and accepted as true.

BY THAT POINT, BRIDGER WAS HIMSELF A LEGEND. PART OWNER OF THE Rocky Mountain Fur Company, he had explored Yellowstone and the Great Salt Lake; just as important, he had shared what he saw with the world, both in personal conversations and in newspaper interviews. At least some of those interviews weren't printed because the descriptions, especially of Yellowstone, seemed too wild to be believed.

Bridger earned his glimpses of America's exotic beauty the hard way and had the scars to prove it.

In 1832, a rival group tried to use him and a friend as bird dogs to find rich trapping grounds in the Rocky Mountain foothills. Bridger caught on and with his companion led the rivals into Blackfoot country. The Blackfoot, or Niitsitapi, were feared even by their most ferocious Indian rivals, and it didn't take long for a small band to find Bridger; the fight ended with Bridger and a chief going mano a mano. Bridger was shot with his own gun and got away with two arrowheads in his back—but he got away. He didn't stick around to record what wounds his enemy sustained.

The wounds were payment for the effect Bridger intended: the trappers following them walked right into Blackfoot territory, not realizing it was a trap. The one we know of was treated with the loving kindness that the tribe often showed enemies who violated their territory: his bones were stripped of flesh and then thrown into the river.

Bridger went on to have other encounters with Blackfoot; he and Kit Carson narrowly escaped from an ambush in 1837, thanks not only to their superior firepower but probably also some luck besides. In 1843, he set up a small post on the Black Fork of the Green River, near the trails used by Mormon and Oregon pioneers. Bridger's fort included a blacksmith as well as a store; he had good relations with the local Indians, trading for beaver pelts.

Those good relations may have come because he sold alcohol to them—or so it was charged by Mormons. It was a serious charge, as the law forbade such sales, even if it was common practice. The fort was either sold to or stolen by the church (Bridger maintained the latter; the church has a deed, but it's signed by a supposed power of attorney) during the 1850s. During the Utah War, the fort was burned down by Mormons who didn't want the army to occupy it. The army took over the ruins and rebuilt.

Presented with the question of who owned the land—Bridger or the Mormons, the government took a stance worthy of King Solomon, declaring neither did: it was government property, and if you don't like it, sue.

Bridger did. The case wound around to a decision some thirty years later. The government forked over around $6,000 to pay for improvements he'd made, but the court decided it owned the land.

TO THE PONY RIDERS, AND EVERYONE ELSE WHO STOPPED AT THE FORT or passed nearby, Bridger was more than a legend—he was living, breathing, older fella who could tell real-life, valuable stories about tromping through the woods and fighting hand to hand with some of the fiercest warriors in the world. It was like having Neil Armstrong as your older uncle, except that Neil could tell you the quickest way to the moon, and even offer to get you there. He'd joke with you, tell stories you barely believed, and some you shouldn't believe. Mixed in with them were tested words of advice on how to successfully negotiate with Indians, when to scare a bear, and when to run.

The Pony riders—and the unexplored American wilderness— were barely a generation removed from a time when it was impossible to get across the continent. Now they were doing it in ten days.

TO UTAH

Fort Bridger stood in Rush Valley in the southwestern corner of Wyoming. While numerous sources say it was a stop—and there's even a static display of a pony stable at the modern museum that stands on the grounds—the two most rigorous historians of the Pony Express, Raymond and Mary Settle, claim the service didn't use the fort as more than a quick stop, hello and good-bye, pop your horse's head into the sutler's shop and off you go.[16] According to the Settles, the home station was at Muddy Creek, between ten and twenty miles west of the fort, depending on how straight you rode.

You couldn't go too straight, given the hills in the way. Willows and cottonwoods clung to the hillside; above them, sheer rock.

The country was wild, the road crooked—but the stages were steady, running regularly up to Salt Lake City. They made their way over precariously perched log bridges, detouring around unmovable rocks and other obstacles so often that the regular riders and stage drivers must have had a million fantasies of dynamiting their way clean through. The Bear River Station—named for where it was— was a high sliver of narrow plain between formidable rows of peaks east and west. This was the eastern end of Division Three, ruled by James Erwen Bromley with the same efficiency if less boozy aggressiveness than Slade's to the east.

Bromley had worked the area earlier, setting up the stage line for

Hockaday. The names of the small exchanges in the region are suggestive of animals, plants, and most of all the land: Bed Tick, Box Elder, Elkhorn, Echo Station.

Thomas Owen King was one of Bromley's riders, starting from the very beginning. He earned his pay that first ride: not more than twenty miles out of Echo Station—he was heading east to Bear River—the weather suddenly changed on him. What had been a beautiful spring day turned nasty mean in the mountains. His horse slipped on a curve near a cliff, and off went King . . .

And the mochila. King nearly broke his neck retrieving the mail from below. He managed to make up the time, somehow, arriving on schedule for the exchange.

Many riders could tell some variation of that tale, and undoubtedly brag about the length of their greatest journey (King's was 110 miles, farther west in the division, from Salt Lake City to Ham's Fork, in thirteen hours). The service itself had a well-deserved reputation for getting the mail through and meeting its aggressive timetable for doing so. The riders deserved the credit—but not all of them, and not all the time. More often than the service's storied reputation would have it, riders were absent, sick, waylaid, just gone. The stationmasters— middle and low-level managers—kept things together, finding substitutes, cajoling faithful employees into pushing on past what they'd signed up for.

Not an unfamiliar scenario in any industry, then or now.

FORT BRIDGER, NOW IN THE STATE OF WYOMING, WAS PART OF THE Utah Territory in 1860. As the riders and their mochila headed west in the direction of Salt Lake City, threading through high ranges and mountain passes, they rode into a promised land established in the best and oldest traditions of American history, though only after a large share of toil and blood. Not quite a land of milk and honey, it was nonetheless a place where its inhabitants could practice their religion with a minimum of interference and prejudice.

Mormon country.

SAINTS

THE NEW RELIGION

It seemed like everyone was getting religion in the spring of 1820. The Second Great Awakening had taken hold of America, with preachers vying everywhere for converts. Membership in the country's Protestant sects boomed, as thousands and then millions found faith an emotional antidote to the cold rationalism threatening to push God out of everyday life. The furor of faith spread even to the small village of Palmyra in upstate New York, east of Rochester on the still-being-constructed Erie Canal.

Joseph Smith, then barely fifteen, felt the call of God—but wasn't sure which preacher to follow, what church to join. His mother was pulled toward the Presbyterian Church, but he didn't share her enthusiasm. Confused, he went into the woods to pray.

He came out with a revelation so great he feared to share it.

As Smith later wrote, a "pillar of light above the brightness of the sun at noon day" shocked him, forgave him his sins, and then told him that mankind had turned away from God:

> The world lieth in sin at this time and none doeth good no not one they have turned aside from the gospel and keep not my commandments they draw near to me with their lips while their hearts are far from me and mine anger is kindling against the inhabitants of the earth.[1]

Later, Smith was told by an angel that golden plates were buried not far from his house; the plates—thin gold sheets written in a forgotten language and bound together like a book—contained the text of prophets who'd gone to America six centuries before Christ. Smith found the plates, but the angel prevented him from taking them, commanding him to wait four years before returning.

He hunted buried treasure in Pennsylvania; not finding jewels, he settled for a wife. He farmed, he did odd jobs. Eventually, he recovered the plates and began translating their message from "reformed Egyptian" with the help of "seer stones"—rocks that for the spiritually gifted functioned as Google Translate before Google or computers.

The result was the Book of Mormon, named after the last contributor, the father of the angel who appeared to Smith. Published in March 1830, the book would become the foundation of a new—or in the eyes of believers, a reinstated—religion. It told how a group of Israelites were guided from Jerusalem just ahead of the Babylonian conquest and led to a new land—implied but not stated as America. A new kingdom is established. Kings and wars, the occasional sermon—the civilization rises but then begins to falter, teetering as it rots from within, the heads of commoners and VIPs alike swelling with arrogance. Their sinful ways doom them to destruction at the hands of their longtime enemies, a civilization they had always considered more evil than their own.

GOLDEN PLATES, TRANSLATING ROCKS, HIEROGLYPHICS NO ONE ELSE could read, angels they never heard of—this wasn't a formula to win over skeptics, then or now. Most Christians who heard Smith laughed or worse.

The spiritual message of the book, though, was more difficult to dismiss, especially for American Christians. It declared that Jesus was the eternal God, accessible to all. It declared that America was a promised land, exceptional among the world's nations. The righteous would be rewarded; the poor must be cared for; the wicked would be destroyed.

As he spread the word, first to a group of perhaps forty or fifty, Smith found his audience growing. His church—the Church of

Christ, better known as the Mormons—expanded through families, then beyond. According to the church's teachings, Native Americans had descended from the people who had escaped Israel. Convinced that Christ would soon return to the righteous, Smith decided that a shining city on a hill, a Zion, had to be built to welcome him. This was both literal—a *real* city, majestic buildings and all that—and a *metaphorical* city, a community of humble faithful who believed in Christ and practiced what he taught. Smith and his followers abandoned their homes in New York to settle in Kirtland, Ohio, a few miles from Lake Erie.

Kirtland was one Zion; Smith and his missionaries found another on the edge of the frontier: Independence, Missouri, the same area where the Pony Express's owners lived.

As the church grew and Smith's revelations continued, the founder and his closest associates organized a hierarchy that mixed priesthood and governing together. Growth of the church in Independence bestowed considerable political power on the Mormons in the sparsely settled county around it, worrying the citizens who weren't part of the church. Among other things, they interpreted Smith's welcoming of black converts to mean they were anti-slavery—not a popular stance in 1833.

Following a town meeting that July, the leading non-Mormon townsfolk went to church leaders and told them to get. When the Mormons asked for more time, the citizens burned down the house and office of the Mormons' printer, then tarred and feathered the bishop.

An aborted attempt at resistance and some scattered violence later, the Mormons relocated to land in Caldwell and Davies Counties, Missouri, northwest of Independence. The community grew quickly; in 1838, it numbered five thousand in Caldwell alone.[2]

But prosperity was short lived. Once more the church was seen as a political force at odds with the rest of the community. Fighting both external pressure and internal dissension over financial decisions, the church faithful hunkered down. Open warfare broke out with the locals; a five-hundred-member Mormon militia attacked the leaders of a Missouri "vigilante" group that had raided Mormon homes. Fifty buildings were burned before the governor called out the militia, declaring the Mormons enemies of the state and directing the state forces to exterminate them.

The violence peaked on October 30, 1838, with a massacre at Haun's Mill that killed seventeen Mormons, including two children and a man aged seventy-eight. A number of women were assaulted in the aftermath; houses were robbed; dead bodies were desecrated and cut to pieces.

Joseph Smith surrendered to state authorities. The church agreed to leave the state, this time traveling to low land along the Missouri River north of Quincy, Illinois. The exodus was led by Brigham Young; Smith remained in jail.

Once drained, the mosquito-infested river swamp became a city called Nauvoo. Within years, it was one of the largest in the state. It was here that Smith first announced—and fulfilled—the practice of "plural wives"—a.k.a., polygamy. The practice was controversial even inside the church, which by now was called the Church of Jesus Christ of Latter-Day Saints. Nauvoo became a "theodemocracy," in which government and religion existed as one. Dissenters were persecuted; non-Mormon neighbors saw the Mormons as a political threat.

Criticized by a dissenters' newspaper, Smith and the Nauvoo city council voted to suppress the paper, seizing and destroying its presses. Not only the dissenters but non-Mormon critics of Smith and Nauvoo went wild, threatening to riot and burn Nauvoo down.

The governor personally intervened, suggesting that Smith give himself up for a hearing on charges that he had incited a riot when the city council ordered the newspaper be destroyed. Smith reluctantly agreed to be tried—it was either that or his followers would be killed, he decided—and went with his brother to nearby Carthage.

Smith agreed to answer the charge of inciting a riot; for reasons somewhat murky—but probably to make it hard for Smith to get bail[3]—the local justice of the peace added the charge of treason against the state. On June 27, 1844, two days after he and his brother were locked up in Carthage, Illinois, a mob stormed the jail and murdered them.

Did the governor order the murder, or simply hope and look away? Did the local "militia" assigned to protect Smith instead plot his murder? Were there one hundred citizens in the mob? Two hundred?

Five men were accused of organizing and participating in Smith's murder—prominent state and local military officials and an anti-Mormon newspaper editor; they were acquitted by a jury that included no Mormon members. The man whom a witness claimed actually shot Smith escaped prosecution the old-fashioned way—he ran away.

EXODUS AND WAR

If the local citizens and the state authorities hoped killing Smith would make the Mormons go away, they got what they wanted, eventually. But their bigger wish—that the church would disintegrate into oblivion—went unfulfilled.

Small splinter groups broke off from the main body after Smith's murder, but the main group followed the Quorum of Twelve, elders Smith had appointed as apostles to proselytize and help guide church affairs. Brigham Young, as the president of the Quorum (later first president), became the church's de facto leader.

For roughly a year, an uneasy peace settled over the areas of Illinois where the Mormons and non-Mormons lived. But in September 1845, attacks began again. Young asked for state protection; he and the Twelve had already decided that the church would leave, seeking a new promised land in Utah, beginning the following year.

Camps and way stations were set up along the way to help the emigrants, but the trip was more difficult than the leaders had imagined. Progress was a few miles a day. Leaving from a temporary camp in Iowa on March 1, Brigham Young crossed into Salt Lake Valley July 24, 1846. The emigrants who followed made barely better progress.[4]

—

AT THE TIME OF THE MORMON MIGRATION, THE VALLEY BETWEEN THE mountains and the great Salt Lake belonged not to the United States but to Mexico. But the two countries were already on the brink of war; by the time Young set up camp, Zachary Taylor was selling captured Mexican artillery for scrap and American forces were well on the way to victories that would force Mexico to turn over much of the northern continent.

That was fine with Young, who suggested that a state named Deseret be created from the Mexican territory. This was a huge hunk of land, taking in everything between the Rockies and the Sierra Nevada, from San Diego to southern Oregon, Arizona, New Mexico, Nevada, and, of course, Utah. (California west of the Sierras was left to itself; ditto the land east of the Rockies.) The proposal was sent to a congressional committee, where it got the usual committee treatment: kicked around, discussed endlessly, the territory was downsized and renamed; the end result was the Utah Territory, created in the fall of 1850, and including Nevada and parts of Colorado and Wyoming as well as Utah. Brigham Young became the first governor.

The population, concentrated around Salt Lake, was predominantly Mormon. Religious and political conflict continued, both in the territory and the nation at large: the 1856 National Republican Party platform put polygamy—a.k.a. "plural marriage"—in the same category as slavery.

In 1857, President Buchanan decided to show that the feds, not the church, were the ones in charge of Utah. He fired Young and appointed Alfred Cumming as governor. Then, realizing this was going to be about as popular as telling people to eat dirt, he sent twenty-five hundred troops to make sure Young vacated.

That was the start of the Mormon, or Utah, War. Aside from the financial disaster inflicted on Russell, Majors & Waddell, the war was a fizzle, ultimately settled by a compromise that took the church officially out of power but still in practical charge. One key event occurred that non-Mormons would point to for decades as a sign of Mormon treachery: the massacre of about 120 migrants in a wagon train moving through the country at Mountain Meadows.

A Mormon "militia," the Nauvoo Legion, wiped out the train, leaving only children under the age of seven, who were adopted by Mormon families. The Mormons tried to make the attack look as if it had been carried out by Indians, but the truth was quickly found out. "Mountain Meadows" would be a byword and bogeyman for years to come, surfacing whenever sentiments were roused against Mormons. (The atrocity was as bad as it sounds, and many historians blame Young for provoking it, if only indirectly.)

An unintended effect of the war was to concentrate the Mormon population around Great Salt Lake City, as it was then called. The census of 1860 found a little more than eleven thousand people living there; had the state been incorporated, it would have ranked in the top one hundred cities in population, ahead of western New York's Auburn in the area where Smith had started from. (New York City was by far the most populous, with 813,669.)

SALT LAKE CITY

The election results the Pony Express rider brought in November 1860 were neither denounced nor particularly cheered. The church's stance toward slavery had moderated, at least slightly. While Brigham Young said flatly that he thought slavery could not be sustained in Utah, he made his arguments on "practical" grounds, saying it would be unprofitable. He criticized abolitionists and what he called "black-hearted Republicans." There was a small number of black slaves in Utah in 1860; the church forbade enslaving Indians, whom it saw as descendants of one of the lost tribes of Israel.[5]

In Salt Lake City, Brigham Young insisted that the territory would remain loyal to the Constitution—in its own way, as the church leaders wrestled with federal authority practically every day in a low-simmering power struggle. Ultimately, he saw war as God's judgment; if it came, it was only because the true word had not been followed.

Despite its particular history and connection with the church, Great Salt Lake City looked for the most part like most other frontier cities, bigger than many, far more organized and neater than most, but made up of the same types of houses and buildings the Pony riders would have seen from the start of the trail. A range of industries, from carpentry to paint manufacturing and a nail factory, had been established early on to aid development and make Salt Lake as self-sufficient as possible. As they had done in the East, the church fathers had established a strong relationship between church and government from the very beginning. The church set prices; political parties were outlawed or discouraged as divisive.

The center of the city was Temple Square, which the rest of the city marked itself off from. The ten-acre parcel was surrounded by a timber wall. The Mormon Tabernacle dominated the southwest corner. This was a long adobe structure with a deeply sloped roof used for various church assemblies and functions, including concerts by the not-yet-famous Mormon Tabernacle Choir. One hundred and twenty-six by sixty-four feet, the rectangular hall held between two and three thousand people, but it was already considered too small. (The more famous structure with its domed roof would be built a few years later.)

There was an Endowment House—used for temple rituals—and the Council House, a square two-story building that housed the territorial government.

The city streets were laid out in a grid that followed a plan set out by Joseph Smith years before; the streets accommodate ten-acre wards, forty by forty rods square. (A rod is five and a half yards.) Smith's plan for Zion—the perfect Mormon city, followed virtually everywhere possible by Mormon settlers—called for houses to be built twenty-five feet from the street, with a nice little lawn or "grove." They were to be single-family houses, only. They were offset, so that when you looked out your front door, you saw greenery, not your neighbor's front door. Barns and stables were segregated away from the houses, with enough farmland in each ward to supply the residents of that ward.[6]

The Utah capital had moved temporarily to Fillmore from 1851 to 1856, but by 1860 Great Salt Lake City's primacy was uncontested. It would lose the word *Great* in 1868; by then its importance was so obvious it didn't need the adjective.

LET 'EM RUN

The Pony trail out of Wyoming led to Echo Canyon. From the station at its mouth—called, not very creatively, Echo Canyon—the trail was smooth and the grade gentle, which meant stages as well as Pony riders could race down at top speed. The red rocks above made it seem as if you were racing through the ruins of a castle; if you were foolish enough to close your eyes, you might even imagine yourself back in medieval Europe. The trail then turned up Weber Canyon, following its curve—there was a station at Weber and Echo Canyon.

James Bromley, the Pony district superintendent, lived in Echo; he ran Weber Station, which was the first one over from what is now Wyoming. The home station was a large stone building about seven years old that nudged between a rock and the path, a spit and a half from Echo River. Bromley's stables were extensive; he'd purchased many of the ponies used on the line himself. The trail followed the river northwest to Big Mountain Pass, where Salt Lake City came into view.

The descent was so steep that the Pony rider had to rein his horse back, slowing him down to keep from falling into a terrible tumble. But he was lucky: at different times of the year, special wagons with four or five yokes of oxen would clog the path down from the quarries, carrying loads of foundation stone for the church buildings rising at the center of the city.[7]

The city suddenly spread itself out from behind the mountains. Two miles wide, it reminded the English sourpuss Richard Burton of Athens . . . without the Acropolis.

If Athens was made of adobe, and colored brown and gray:

> in some points it reminded me of modern Athens without the Acropolis. None of the buildings, except the Prophet's house [the Tabernacle], were whitewashed. The material—the thick, sun-dried adobe, common to all parts of the Eastern world—was of a dull leaden blue, deepened by the atmosphere to a gray, like the shingles of the roofs. The number of gardens and compounds—each tenement within the walls originally received 1–50 square acre, and those outside from five to ten acres, according to their distance—the dark clumps and lines of bitter cottonwood, locust, or acacia, poplars and fruit-trees, apples, peaches, and vines—how lovely they appeared, after the baldness of the prairies!—and, finally, the fields of long-eared maize and sweet sorghum strengthened the similarity to an Asiatic rather than to an American settlement. The differences presently became as salient. The farm-houses, with their stacks and stock, strongly suggested the Old Country. Moreover, domes and minarets even churches and steeples—were wholly wanting, an omission that somewhat surprised me. The only building conspicuous from afar was the block occupied by the present Head of the Church. The court-house, with its tinned Muscovian dome, at the west end of the city; the arsenal, a barn-like structure, on a bench below the Jebel Nur of the valley—Ensign Peak; and a saw-mill, built beyond the southern boundary, were the next in importance.[8]

Burton, maybe somewhat misinformed about "plural marriage," reported that he looked in vain for the harems he believed he'd find. He was happy to discover that, while Mormons generally frowned on the use of alcohol, there were places where gentiles such as himself could discreetly partake.

Great Salt Lake City's finest hotel, Salt Lake House, stood on East Temple Street (now Main Street) across from the Express's office. A long, two-story building with a wide balcony across its front façade, the hotel offered accommodations so fine that even Burton spared it his worst complaints. Not far away, the foundation for the new temple was being redug. After work was suspended during the Utah War, the engineers discovered that much of the sandstone they used was only a little better than sand as foundation material. The temple, walled with white quartz monzonite, would be decades in the making.

If Salt Lake City was the promised Zion, its occupants were not so heavenly as to go around unarmed. Burton claimed everyone had a pistol; bowie knives were just as popular. Non-Mormons owned some of the stores in the city, and a good number of travelers at the inns, rough or refined, were not members of the faith, but Mormons were by far the majority, and they could be just as hot tempered as anyone else. A few months before the election, a pair of reputed horse thieves were gunned down in broad daylight; the murderer had not been discovered.

The Pony Express tied Salt Lake City and the Mormons to east and west more effectively and efficiently than earlier private mail services had. When the service began, the *Deseret News* boasted of the shortened time for news to arrive from Washington—six days—which compared more than a little favorably with the previous time of three months.[9]

The crowded business center—buildings jostled next to each other, a shoe store next to dry goods, next to furniture showroom and so on—was popular with stagecoach travelers, but the Pony riders merely made a quick stop there, continuing on to the Rush Valley station run by Doc Faust. Faust's farm was an important facility, supplying hay for the stations farther west, where the desert made it impossible to farm.

MAJORS AND THE MORMONS

Alexander Majors, the Pony's whip-cracking principal, had known Mormons from his early days in Missouri; his father had led one of the groups that had helped run them out of Independence. The Utah War and the Mormons' capture of his wagon trains had set him and his partners on the way to financial ruin. But he seems not to have blamed them for those troubles, or at least had forgiven and somewhat forgotten by the time he wrote his memoirs. Even during the Pony's days he was doing business with the church and hiring Mormons to work for him.

Majors felt that the root of the trouble in Missouri was religious arrogance: the Mormons claimed that they'd received special instructions from God, and these instructions overrode anything anyone else might want. They'd been told to settle in the area. They'd been told to build their own city. They'd been told an apocalypse was coming; they'd been told anyone who wasn't with them was going to perdition. And they weren't shy about saying any of this.

People who didn't believe in Smith's prophecies didn't like the insinuation that they would burn for all eternity. Nor were they particularly pleased when the Mormons promised to, in effect, populate the land and run the place their way. In Missouri and elsewhere, the Mormons were accused of voting in blocs, electing their own, and running ramshod over everyone and everything.

Some of the political accusations were exaggerated, but there was no doubt that Mormons mixed theology and government, voted for their own, and tended to shun non-Mormons as outsiders. The conflict that had led to Joseph Smith's death was tailor-made to demonstrate the dangers of autocratic church rule, even if the reaction of the non-Mormons was just as arbitrary.

But Majors was perceptive enough to realize that a lot of the resentment was merely because the Mormons were different, and their religion brand-new; if people were used to them, he thought, they might just have been laughed at rather than persecuted. He had a high regard for their ethics, saying that as a rule church members were gracious and honest. If only they weren't so righteous about what they believed.

Majors met practically every important Mormon leader alive

during his lifetime, with the apparent exception of Smith. "A fairer, more upright set of gentlemen I never met," he declared. He even heard several preach and was quite impressed by Young:

> *I was present . . . when he was preaching to a very large congregation, and he said to them:*
>
> *"Brethren, we have thieves, scoundrels, perjurers, and villains in our church, but the day will come when the tares will be separated from the wheat and burned up with unquenchable fire; if this were not so, however, we could not claim to be the church of Jesus Christ, for he said that the kingdom of God was like a great net, which, being cast into the sea, brought all manner of fishes to the shore." He was the only preacher I ever heard make such remarks to his own people, and recognize the church as being the true one because of the tares that grew among the wheat.*[10]

Majors's generous attitude toward the Mormons and Young in particular—he called him one of the smartest men he'd ever known—may have been because he lived in Salt Lake City for ten years (1869–1879) later in life. His attitude was certainly ahead of its time, though perhaps emblematic of a slow, fitful trend.

After the Civil War, the railroad made it far easier for people to get into Utah and Salt Lake City; the population of both Mormons and non-Mormons increased. Attempts at becoming a state stalled, however, despite the territory's obvious desires and the fact that it was sitting between two (and then more) other states. The wedge issue was "plural marriage"—or bigamy, as the rest of the country considered it. Congress in 1882 passed the Edmunds Act, which banned polygamists from voting, holding office, or serving on juries. This created a crisis in Utah; new elections were held, and ultimately thirteen hundred men (no women) were jailed under the act, including the church president in 1906.

The law's constitutionality eventually went to the Supreme Court; when it was upheld, the church was threatened with disenfranchisement and seizure of its assets. The leadership banned plural marriage, clearing the way for statehood, which was finally proclaimed January 4, 1896.[11] Nevada (1864) and Wyoming (1890) had long since been carved out and admitted to the Union.

QUICKSAND, FLAMING EYEBALLS, AND INJUNS

Majors and his partners trusted Mormons sufficiently to hire them not only as stationmasters and riders, but to put a prominent Mormon, Howard Egan, in charge of the district line from Salt Lake west past Ruby Valley, Nevada.[12]

Born in Ireland, Egan went to Canada with his father when he was seven. The family had its share of tragedy—his mother died before they left; two sisters and a brother died soon after arriving. His father passed away when he was thirteen; Howard became a sailor working on Canadian rivers at fifteen.

He gave up the inland waterways for dry land and rope making in Salem, Massachusetts, in 1839; when he was twenty-four, he married fifteen-year-old Tamson Parshley and that same year converted to Mormonism.

Egan helped build Nauvoo and was a member of the city's militia and police; he served briefly as a bodyguard to Joseph Smith. Away from the city on a preaching mission when Smith was murdered, he returned and joined one of the early trains west. After Salt Lake City was established, he was assigned by the church to start a trading company in the Sierra goldfields.[13] He returned to find one of his three wives pregnant by another man.

He killed him.

The jury bought Egan's lawyer's justification, which basically amounted to this: things were different in Utah, and a man couldn't get away with adultery out here like he could in the rest of the country.

It probably didn't hurt that Egan was important enough to rate a defense attorney who was one of the Twelve's apostles—the highest-ranking members of the church below the president. Not to say that the jurors didn't think about it: they took an entire fifteen minutes to deliver their verdict.[14]

Exonerated under the concept of "mountain law," Egan began leading ox trains to California and found enough shortcuts to make the mule ride from Salt Lake to Sacramento in ten days; his route eventually became part of the central route used by Russell, Majors & Waddell. So hiring him to supervise the route for the Pony was extremely logical, even if he had served in the militia that destroyed their supply trains.

Egan hired two of his sons, Howard Ransom Egan (twenty) and Erastus (eighteen) as riders, but he carried the mail himself from Rush Valley to Salt Lake City on the first run, a dark and stormy night filled with rain and sleet. He was just about to the city when his horse rode straight off a plank bridge into a swollen creek. The water was above Egan's knees, but before he could utter the name of the Prophet, the pony leapt back onto the shore. Egan held on and made it to Salt Lake, soaked but proud of his time; it stood as the best on the line for quite a while.

If there was "mountain law" west of the Rockies, there was also mountain medicine. Out inspecting the mail route late the following winter, Egan stared so hard at the melting snow that he burned his eyes. He wrapped tea leaves over them for a couple of days, but they gave him no relief. Then an Indian he knew showed up at his ranch, which served as the Pony station as well as a stage stop, store, and general headquarters for the family businesses.

"Big sick?" asked the brave.

"Eyes big sick," said Egan.

The Indian grabbed Egan, pulled the bandage holding the tea leaves away, and began sucking his eye.

Egan worried he was going to suck his eyeball out of his head. Instead, the Indian came away with a mouthful of blood. He went to work sucking on the other eye; when he was done, he declared "Big Chief" would be fine in two days.

He was.[15]

—

EGAN HAD INCREDIBLE ENDURANCE. ACCORDING TO HIS SON, HIS BUSI-ness trips to California from Utah, which included a long stretch through the desert, would be made practically nonstop: one four-hour break in every twenty-four. The men with him, and more important, the mules, had trouble keeping up. On one trip he decided to sleep only after seeing buildings where he knew there were canyons.

And this was *before* the Pony, when he would have been under no obligation to keep things quick.

East Rush Valley, Pass Spring Station, Simpson's Springs—the stops west of Salt Lake City and Camp Floyd were located near water sources that had been used by Native Americans for as long as the country had been occupied. Water was always a lifeblood, especially in an area edging on the desert, but it could also be a killer. A rider was nearly swept away by a sudden river surge while riding out of Simpson's Springs in 1862. As he was crossing a dry riverbed, a twelve- or fifteen-foot-high surge of water and debris that would have rivaled Moses's Egyptian flood came down the river valley—which by that point was well overgrown with sagebrush and the like—and nearly took him under.[16]

The ground became increasingly alkaline as you rode west. Egan's son Howard described it as a "creamly alkali, sandless but sticky mud" that stuck to hooves, shoes, pants, and wagon wheels like a slop of pancake batter.[17] The ground could be like quicksand; leave the proven trail and you might make it a mile, or you might go a yard and find your horse up to his knees in mud. Go on farther, and you might find yourself in a shallow lake.

Howard found this out the hard way the first time he was assigned to take the mail from Simpson's Springs to Willow Springs. The safe route was a bizarre semicircle that took him up to River Bed, then over to Dugway before finally coming back to Willow Springs. He figured he could cut a few hours off the run by going straight across the desert. He made it, but he nearly ended up swimming in quicksand before managing it. His father bawled him out; young Howard never took the route again.

Many riders—and *almost* riders—claimed that they had gone the longest distance on the Pony trail. Young Howard's claim has most if not all of them beat. And he did it for love.

According to Howard, his brother-in-law was carrying the mail for the service in the other direction at the time. (He didn't say when this occurred, or even name the brother-in-law, possibly to protect the innocent. There were three Andrus boys.) It seems that brother Andrus had a crush in Salt Lake City—which was Howard's station. At the time, the schedule called for Howard to come west with the mail, and brother Andrus east; they'd meet at one of the stations somewhere around Rush Valley. Each would reverse course after exchanging sacks.

Unless, of course, they somehow missed each other in the night. Then they would be honor bound to continue on to the other's home station.

Which would bring brother Andrus to Salt Lake and his girl.

Howard played the game, riding one hundred and sixty-five miles . . . where he met another pack of mail that had to be taken back east. And so he made the trip all the way back to Salt Lake, some three hundred and thirty miles.[18]

Howard's brother Richard Erastus Egan—generally called "Ras"—claimed the speed record for the stretch from Salt Lake to Rush Valley at four hours and five minutes. The favored horse for the first relay was Miss Lightning, and she lived up to her name, once flashing over twenty-two miles in an hour and five minutes, which is mighty quick for the distance. (Forty-four miles an hour in a two furlong or quarter mile is considered the record, and the horse that did that was well tired when he crossed the finish line.)

The most notorious horse in the division may have been Bucking Bally. Bally was more than a handful; new riders generally were bucked off, and if that didn't work, the horse had a habit of falling backward. One poor fellow, a substitute rider, found himself hitched on a fence after being thrown by the horse; he ended up having to cut his coat off to get down. He managed to get hold of the horse and ride to the next station, but his days with Bally were done.

Young Howard lost a $300 horse to a broken neck when the animal tripped and killed itself one day while they were riding at a good clip. He ended up walking about five miles with his saddle and the mochila to get to the next station. But he wasn't in trouble for losing the horse; as he'd been told by one of Majors's men: "Boys, if you kill a horse by riding fast, we will buy you a better one."[19]

WHILE EGAN HAD A PRETTY GOOD RELATIONSHIP WITH SOME OF THE Indians, occasionally hiring them, things were never so calm between settlers and natives that either side took the other for granted. Egan's sons were constantly on guard when traveling through the country.

One night, young Howard took the place of another rider who was feeling sick. Riding from Schell Creek to Butte, about thirty-two miles, he was winding his way through Egan Canyon when he spotted Indians camped out ahead. It had all the earmarks of an ambush.

Retracing his route didn't seem like a good option—there might easily be more Indians behind him. So Howard took out his pistol and trotted forward, until he was almost on top of the Indians. Then he spurred the horse, gave a yell, and pulled his trigger.

Howard blazed through as the Indians scattered. The Indians had strung a rope across the path, aiming to trip him, but he missed it somehow. He cut down the canyon path, taking the roughest but fastest route. Later he found out that the Indians had set up an ambush to find out why Pony riders were coming through fast—what could they possibly be carrying, or doing, that required such speed?[20]

YOUNG HOWARD'S CLOSEST CALL CAME ONE DAY AFTER INDIANS ATtacked a stagecoach along his route, killing the driver and a passenger. Howard happened by as the Indians were making off with the four horses that had been driving the stage.

One of the Indians took off after him. Howard retreated temporarily, dancing out of gun range for a few moments until his enemy grew frustrated and his horse tired. At that point, young Howard took out his pistol and urged his own horse into a charge, riding straight for the Indian, who plunged off the road in the opposite direction. Howard made it to the station safely.

But the Utah man with the most intriguing encounters with Indians was a man known as Yagaiki—the adopted brother of a Shoshone chief, Pony rider, Mormon bishop, doctor, and fiddle player, Elijah Nicholas Wilson.

If you knew him well in his later years, you called him Uncle Nick, the White Indian.

THE WHITE INDIAN

Elijah Nicholas Wilson was born in Nauvoo, Illinois, in 1842. His parents were Mormons; his uncle was one of Joseph Smith's bodyguards. The family eventually joined the Mormon migration, settling in Grantsville, a small village south of Salt Lake in 1850. While the land was good, insects were a scourge, and one of Wilson's most vivid memories of his childhood was of a harvest nearly ruined by a cricket and grasshopper plague—the Cricket War—which ended only when a swarm of gulls feasted on the invaders.

The village was surrounded by a log fence; the settlers had an up-and-down relationship with the local Native Americans, the Gosiutes (or Goshutes), who would steal cattle and, on occasion, kill white men who got in their way—at least that was the whites' side of the story. Others were friendly, often working for the settlers.

Soon after the Cricket War, Wilson's father hired a young Indian named Pantsuk to help herd the sheep. Pantsuk was about Wilson's age, and for two years they chummed together, hunting chipmunks, birds, and rabbits and getting into whatever light mischief preteens could find on the frontier. Their big excursion: trying to ride a ram. It didn't go well.

Wilson learned to use a bow and arrow, and to speak Gosiute. But his friend got sick and died, leaving the eleven-year-old Wilson heart-broken.

Some months later, in August 1854, entranced by the offer of a horse, Wilson did what many boys only fantasized about: he ran away and became an Indian, joining a small band of Shoshone, whose language was similar enough to Gosiute that he could easily talk to them.

Adopted by the chief's mother, Wilson learned to break horses and gradually fit into the band. Early on he was named "Yagaiki" by the Indians. The word means "sobbing"; Wilson said he was given it because he was mocking the way some girls cried, though it doesn't really sound like much of a compliment and you have to wonder if he earned it during an early bout of homesickness. Still a young teenager, he became an excellent rider and rescued a girl from a bear, earning respect from the rest of the tribe.

When rumors that Wilson's father was gathering an army to go after him reached the Indians, Wilson, by then fourteen, reluctantly agreed to return to his original family. He arrived just in time for the Utah War. The family survived that, but soon afterward, his father died of an illness.

Young Wilson's skill with horses led Dr. Faust, who was gathering horses for the Pony Express, to offer him a shot at a job. All he had to do was break the "outlaw"—a horse that until now had allowed no man on his back for more than a buck or two.

This is his debrief after the job interview with another of Faust's hands and "outlaw":

> I mounted the bronco. He went off very peaceably for a little way, and I thought that they were making a fool of me; but pretty soon the old boy turned loose, and he fairly made my neck pop. He gave me the hardest bucking I ever had; but he did it straight ahead. He did not whirl as some horses do, so I stayed with him all right.
>
> When he stopped bucking, I sent him through for ten miles about as fast as he ever went, and when I got back to the ranch I rode up the cor-

ral where the man [who worked for Faust and had taunted him earlier]
was saddling another horse. Standing up in my saddle, I said, "Do you
call this a bad horse? If you do you don't know what a bad horse is."

The fellow did not like me very much after that. I got along very well
with the old outlaw; but I had to give him some very hard rides before
he acknowledged me his master.[21]

The Pony Express changed Wilson's life, ending his thoughts of returning to his Indian family. Howard Egan—by now known as "Major Egan" because of his duties with the Mormon militia—assigned
him to the Ruby Valley Station in Nevada run by William Smith. It
was a green trough between the hills, but a major settlement in the
wilderness. The army had located a camp at the same location, and
the 1860 US Census taken in July found more than a dozen "mail carriers" living in the vicinity. (Presumably those were Pony Express riders, though there was no standard census entry for the occupation.)
The carriers ranged in age from seventeen to twenty-nine; between
station keepers, cooks, and the like, there were thirty-four people associated with the station, all male. (Neither Wilson nor Smith are
listed on the handwritten census report.[22])

Wilson loved the station and the life. It took about two weeks for
riders to get used to the pace and the toll it took on your body, but
after that you were good—or you quit.

A lot of the horses Wilson rode that November were new to the
Pony, having just replaced the first batch—all "played out," in his
words. The horses were mostly wild Californians, and a lot of them
were broken by Peter Neece, who was keeping one of the home stations.

Kind of broken. Neece would ride them a time or so, then hand
them off to the Pony riders to smooth them out another notch or two.
"Generally, when a hostler could lead them into and out of the stable
without getting his head kicked off," said Wilson, "the broncos were
considered broken. Very likely they had been handled just enough to
make them mean."[23]

Even though he'd lived among Indians, Wilson had more than his share of run-ins with the tribes and renegade bands southwest of Salt Lake.[24] Carrying mail east one day, Wilson rode into the home station at Deep Creek, Utah, to find that the rider coming west had not yet arrived. Knowing he needed to make the swap and not wanting to wait, he began riding in the direction of the next station, Willow Springs.[25] There he discovered that the other rider had been shot and killed, apparently by Indians.

The rider had managed to get the mail to the station before dying—Wilson never said how—and Wilson had to take it on back west. But needing to rest his horse—Wilson also didn't mention why there wasn't another pony waiting—he hung out for a bit. Shortly before he was ready to take off again, seven Indians came into the station, looking for something to eat.

The station keeper—the same Neece who broke the horses—offered them a sack of flour.

A sack for each, responded the Indians.

Out, yelled Neece. *No flour for you, you greedy so-and-so's.*

The Indians walked off, grumbling about stingy white folk. There happened to be an ancient, lame cow out beneath the roof of an old shed near the station house; the natives decided to test their archery skills on it.

Neece, clearly an animal lover, pulled out his pistol and shot two of the Indians dead. The others ran off.

Wilson decided he'd stay at the station a bit after that. Willow Springs was not large; according to Burton, it was a "little doggery boasting of a shed and a bunk, but no corral."[26] (No whiskey either, which to his way of thinking would have been more of a handicap.) But its walls provided better protection than the open trail.

One of the men in the station with Wilson was a fellow named Lynch. Wilson had known him for a while; he'd always come off like a hard-ass, talking tough and bragging about what he would do if the Indians attacked. Now that things were tight, Wilson felt glad that he was around.

Until Lynch started to weep with fear.

Unnerved, Wilson suggested a strategic retreat before the Indians showed up for revenge.

Hell no, said Neece. *Load up your guns. There are thirty of those bastards out there and only four of us, but we'll stand them off.*

Neece led them out of the station to a spot where they could surprise the Indians when they came up to attack the building. Ducking them down into the grass, he told them to shoot, then move, shoot and move—if you kept moving, the Indians wouldn't have a good target in the dark.

Sure enough, the Indians thundered up a while later. Guns blazing, the Pony men began firing, jumping from one position to another, firing again.

All except Wilson. He remembered the jumping part; it was the shooting he had trouble with. For some reason, he just couldn't get his finger to work.

No matter. He jumped and jumped, continuing until he fell down a shallow ravine, landing in a large puddle at the base. He lay in the water, listening as the shooting continued.

And continued.

Finally, there was silence. He waited a while, then a while longer. At last, Wilson crawled up out of his ditch and went slowly toward the house. He knew the Indians had fired enough to kill all his friends. His best plan was to take his horse—or any horse—and ride east, hopefully to safety.

Except, there was someone in the station.

Wilson got his gun ready. Light shone through the cracks in the wall.

Would the Indians see him if he grabbed his horse? Were there guards nearby?

He screwed up his courage and got closer. Then he heard somewhere nearby talking.

In English.

The others had survived, without a scratch. Wilson showed himself.

"How far did you chase them, Nick?" asked Neece. "I knew you would stay with them."[27]

Wilson didn't bother to enlighten them on his actual travails.

LIKE A LOT OF ACCOUNTS FROM PONY EXPRESS RIDERS WRITTEN LONG after the fact, Wilson's stories are vivid, but hard to place into an exact time frame; most locate them around the time of the Pyramid Lake War, which would have been in the early summer of 1860. He says that shortly after this incident, he was ambushed by four Indians led by a "one-eyed, mean-looking old rascal"[28] on another part of the trail. Fortunately, he recognized one of the men as an acquaintance and was able to escape with a promise that he wouldn't ride that section of the line again. He got to the next station safely, and his bosses arranged to transfer him farther out west in the desert.

Which was a bit like going from the frying pan to the actual fire.

SAND AND SILVER

SALT AND WATER

From the distance, it's a gleaming mirage, a bright light stricken from the sky. Up close, it's an alkaline moonscape, part waste, part miraculous oasis of exotic-looking plants and the occasional iridescent stone.

The Great Salt Lake Desert is like no other desert in America. It crusts regularly, its soil so salty that a good rain or snow leaves a sheen of crystals on its skin. Located at the tip of the Great Basin, the desert edges against Salt Lake, perhaps signaling what its fate will be in a few million years. Both are the leftovers of the once massive Lake Bonneville, a paleolake that extended through the Great Basin into Idaho and Nevada. Formed during an ice age, the lake had no natural outlet; it collected runoff and rain and sat placidly, or at least as placidly as a lake can sit. For over ten thousand years, the lake dominated the local ecosystem, its levels fluctuating, its shorelines constantly changing. Then, some 16,800 years ago, the lake's water level rose high enough to overflow on Red Rock Pass.

The overflow led directly to its demise. The waters cut through the pass and created a channel toward the Snake River. The channel and surrounding area flooded; when they drained, the lake had dropped 375 feet.

Where did all that salt come from? In the Pony's day, many people believed that the water had once been part of the Pacific Ocean, and that the ground had cut it off. In fact, not a few very early explorers thought the salt water they tasted meant they had reached the Pacific. But the salt is actually due to evaporation of water from the lake over thousands of years, leaving behind salt that had been washed in from tributaries. The same thing happens to the oceans, though on a much larger scale.

The Pony route skirted the southern edge of the Salt Lake Desert, wiggling through the hills westward toward Nevada. While the stations there were usually located as close as possible to water sources, the ground became ever more arid as you rode west; in a few places, water had to be carried in by wagon for the horses and men.

The Great Basin is its own landlocked drainage system; rain falling between the Sierra Nevada and the Wasatch Mountains will flow into the middle (or more precisely, into one of the sub-basins, like the Salt Lake). But weather patterns mean there isn't all that much rain to fall. Most of the basin is high desert, just under four thousand feet above sea level at its lowest points. Besides the sagebrush, there are juniper trees, pine, and curl-leaf mahogany on the skirts of the mountains. If you see cottonwood, you know there's water nearby.

Animals? Pronghorn, mule deer, mountain lions, sometimes elk and bighorn sheep. Rattlesnakes. Gopher snakes.

Most of the animals a rider was apt to see were dead, their bones picked clean. When Mark Twain wrote of his trip across the desert, he claimed that for forty miles the road was white with the bones of oxen that had died.[1] Not far off the trail, petrified wood and oxidized iron showed where wagons had ended their days. Amid the ruins, crude markers—sometimes wooden crosses, often just piles of stones—marked the graves of pioneers and other travelers who'd died and had the good fortune to be buried rather than scavenged by birds of prey.

Only a small number of European and American explorers came through the area before the 1840s. In 1843, Colonel John C. Frémont set out on the first of a series of expeditions that would map much of the western parts of the country, from Kansas into California. Frémont had the good luck to meet Kit Carson while journeying up the Missouri; Carson had spent years living and exploring the Rockies and environs, fighting everything from grizzlies to Blackfeet Indians, and he ended up enlisting with the expedition. Carson led the army officer through South Pass westward, helping him map the Oregon Trail; they would take two more journeys together and become trusted allies. When Frémont needed a man to help overthrow the Mexican government, Carson was there; when Frémont needed secrets carried back to Washington, DC, Carson took the mission.

Carson lives on today in the popular imagination, thanks largely to the dime novels and other exaggerations that were written about his exploits. But it was Frémont who left a deeper stamp on American history, not only mapping much of the West but also helping bring California into the Union.

Some of the men who followed Frémont, like James H. Simpson, found the deserts of the Great Basin beautiful in their starkness. Despite the fact that it is a desert, Frémont and the naturalists who followed him cataloged a wide variety of plant and animal life. But for most other white Americans through the mid-1800s, the western stretches of the Utah Territory were a place to get through as quickly as possible en route to California.

That changed—for some at least—in 1859, but only after an odd, twisting route of fate and missed fortune typical of the West.

THE COMSTOCK LODE

One fine day in May 1849, a small group of fortune seekers packed up some supplies and set off from Salt Lake City. They were heading toward the California gold fields when they stopped near a bend in the Carson River, not all that far from where present-day Dayton, Nevada, now stands. At the time, the spot was called Ponder's Rest, because from that spot you could follow the river south and then head west, or keep going west and make your way through the hills. Even if your mind was already made up, it was a decent place to water the oxen and gird your loins after crossing the worst of the desert, gearing up for the push through the Sierras toward your final destination.

A twenty-two-year-old Mormon named Abner Blackburn looked at the hills and said to his friends, *Why isn't there gold here?*

The answer was along the lines of: there's none because no one's bothered to look.

The next day, Abner decided to do something about it. He took a pan and a knife and went out into the hills while his friends played cards. Amid the pebbles and grit, something gleamed.

Gold.

Not a lot, and apparently not enough to keep the train from moving on to California, where word was you could find piles of gold dust on every inch of ground.[2] The following year, another train headed for California was blocked by snow in the Sierras. The company retreated to wait out the melt. Three men in the train—the aptly named John Orr, William Prows, and Nick Kelly—went back over to the creek.[3]

Orr spotted a nugget in the rocks and dug it out. It weighed 19.4 grams, a bit more than two-thirds of an ounce. While that's not a particularly big nugget—worth maybe $8 to $12 at the time—it was enough to start rumors, and with a few years a small community of perhaps a hundred men panned what Orr had dubbed Gold Canyon, netting about five dollars a day for their work.

The easy gold soon petered out, but men kept poking and panning the earth, certain of finding something. Several came tantalizingly close to a real fortune. Others moved on after only a few days. "Gold Canyon" gave birth to a small mining town as well as Mormon Station, a tiny hamlet serving emigrants on the California Trail.

Gold came out of Carson Valley for nearly a decade, but never in amounts large enough to generate a hysteria. The miners were only scratching the surface of the mineral treasure, and looking for the wrong stuff at that.

Around about 1857, two brothers from New York who had come east from the California gold fields built a stone house at a spot called

American Flats. It was a bit removed from the rest of the prospectors, but then the brothers were a bit removed as well. Ethan Allen Grosch and Hosea Ballou Grosch spent their evenings in the cottage reading; days were devoted to working through rocks up beyond the locally renowned Devil's Gate. The two young men were poking into blue rocks that didn't promise gold, but rather silver. And unlike nearly every other prospector in the area, they were doing it on purpose.

After working the hills for three years, they found silver in 1856; the next year they wrote to their father that they were sure of two deposits, one modest, the other rich. The richer vein was difficult to mine, but they were sure they were on to their fortune.

They were right. By dint of hard work and rare luck, they had made a discovery for the ages. Then their luck turned. Viciously. Hosea struck his foot with a pick; he died of complications only a few days later. Grief-stricken, his brother left the mountain to go to California. But it was already late November, and the snow in the Sierras first confused him and his companion, then gave him frostbite. Ethan died of exposure, apparently before telling anyone where the silver was.

Two years later, one James Finney walked up the highest point of the mountain overshadowing the valley. A refugee from Virginia who loved to drink, hunt, and pan for gold, in that order, Finney was known as "Old Virginny" because of his birth state. The forty-two-year-old had spotted a yellowish hill during one of his hunting trips in the area while taking a break from panning. Believing the color of the rocks might mean there was gold there, he and three friends hiked to the low-rising hill January 28, 1859. They cleared the snow off the ground and broke out their pans.

The bits of dust they found when they washed the grit away promised there might be more. With miners' optimism, they staked some claims, dubbing the place Gold Hill.

You have to dream.

By spring, a number of other miners from the small mining town nearby had staked out claims as well. Stripping the soil with picks and shovels, the men had worked about ten feet off the surface when they found quartz studded with gold.

It was a good strike; a man could earn twenty dollars a day with his shovel and pick, but the bigger find came in June, when two men working nearby on land that had already been mined dug out a creek and discovered a vein of gold. They were examining the gold when a local character wandered across them and, after congratulating them, asked what the hell they were doing digging on his land and using his and his partner's water to fill their pans.

A partnership was formed, and the two miners went back to work. Very shortly, they found some very strange rocks, blue-gray quartz that they'd never seen before, at least not around there. The blue stuff made its way from miner to friend to rancher to assay.

Silver ore. And rich ore at that. The first tests valued it at $840 a ton; soon after it was assayed at $3,876 to the ton, with about three-fourths silver, the rest gold.[4]

The coot who'd claimed the men were on his land was Henry T. P. Comstock, a former trapper and guide, occasional miner, and oft-times bragger and bully. If Comstock had any real claim to the land, he hadn't bothered with the legal niceties to secure it, but the others left him on as a partner, and it was his name that ended up attached to one of the great precious metal deposits in the West, the Comstock Lode.

As precious metals go, this was the Mother Lode, a vein of riches beyond pretty much anyone's dreams. The statistics alone are crazy. From 1859 to 1882, a conservative estimate posits that seven million tons of ore were removed from various mines that worked the lode. This yielded almost $300 million dollars; that's maybe $6.5 to and $8.5 billion today, depending on how you play with inflation.[5] And it covers only the major mines, and part of the lode's history.

It's hard to have this much money swashing around without conflict, and even harder to keep the lawyers away. By the time of Lincoln's election, the attorneys had moved in, and legal action over conflicting claims would suck up a good portion of the profits through the Civil War and beyond. Following the war, the Bank of California muscled in, dominating the fields for a decade until a group led by John Mackay and James Fair struck a new lode richer than any of the others. Stock manipulation, busted companies, dividends up and down, petty corruption—all the usual hallmarks of boom-and-bust America would be in evidence over the next few decades.

Russell and his partners were among the thousands of enterprising capitalists trying to make a buck off the boom. The problem for many—including Russell et al.—was that the boom was never quite as big as they hoped. Whereas the California gold rush unleashed a massive exodus to California, Comstock attracted a much smaller crowd. There were many reasons: timing, the difficulty of extracting the ore, and the desert. Living in the western Utah Territory wasn't anywhere near as easy or pleasant as living in California. Farming was . . . a fantasy for the most part, and industries other than mining had easier times locating just about anywhere else. The mass of population that had driven California's economy after the gold rush's peak never arrived there.

Which isn't to say that the Nevada area at the desert's fringe remained empty. The discovery of gold and silver brought many into the territory. Whether because of politics, religion, or the prospect of controlling all that gold and silver production, both the new residents and Congress began contemplating splitting Nevada away from the rest of the Utah Territory. The appointment of a new territory governor in early 1861 was one of the last things Buchanan would do in office.

Sam Clemens's brother was that governor's secretary. If things had worked out and the job Sam had been promised materialized, Mark Twain might never have been. Huck Finn, Tom Sawyer, and all the rest would have remained locked in their creator's brain, perhaps emerging over cocktails in some Washington bar as tall tales to ease the monotony of lobbying for a government contract.

EMPTY NEVADA

Riding from South Pass to California, the Pony rider and just about everyone else went in anything but a straight line. After leaving Salt Lake City, emigrants heading west would go south to Camp Floyd, then west through Faust before weaving through the hills and canyons to the Humboldt River Valley. The Pony route, most of which had been surveyed by James H. Simpson, cut considerable time and distance off the route George Chorpenning had been using—140 miles, according to Simpson, who took umbrage when newspaper editors criticized the route and its alleged lack of water. As he put it, "I have the gratification to know that mail company, as well as the Express, have been running successfully on my . . . route."[6]

Simpson could be forgiven if he sounded both proprietary or even overproud. Besides the road the Pony took, he surveyed the road from Fort Smith, Arkansas, to Santa Fe; aside from people like Majors who had walked the paths most of their lives, Simpson knew the southern and middle routes across the country better than practically anyone.

The Humboldt River led the way to Elko, seesawing through Carlin Canyon. High water there would make it impassable for wagons, and not necessarily fun for Pony riders, either, as the jagged stream had to be forded several times. Greenhorn Cutoff, Emigrant Pass, Gravelly Ford—the names document the people who used them and what they were about.

Past Battle Mountain, around to Winnemucca and down again to Lovelock and the Humboldt Sink: this was the California Trail, discovered by whites less than forty years before, but by now a major thoroughfare thanks to waves of would-be miners.

The Humboldt Sink—like the Carson Sink a little farther south—is a large lake bed, usually though not always dry. The Humboldt and Carson are the remains of Lake Lahontan, which disappeared with the last ice age. The soil is alkaline; vegetation is sparse and even nonexistent in much of the sink. The surface whips into miniature tornadoes of dust at the slightest provocation. Look across it when the sun is overhead with unguarded eyes and you're likely to see only the silver shimmer of heat rising from the sand, earth blending to sky as if they disdained boundaries. But this was only the gateway to the real desert, some miles of thirst-inducing sand and dryness called the Forty Mile Desert.

It's more like seventy by a hundred and fifty. Maybe the people who named it were trying to be optimistic.

Arguably the worst part of the California Trail, the desert turned to a soft, dry muck that taxed animals and the people urging them on before finally reaching Carson River Valley. Wagon wheels choked in the sand; horses bogged down. Walking through the sand was like trudging through dry slush to your knees; heat and simple exhaustion killed many. Hasty graves and skeletons marked the path across.

The Pony rider cut farther south, through Ruby Valley across the Great Basin and along the southern edge of the Forty Mile Desert; the path looks deceptively like a straight line—on a typical map or from thirty thousand feet. On the ground, it goes up and over hills, avoiding the worst climbs only barely, hopscotching from one poorly fed spring to another before riding flat out across the barren wilderness of Sand Springs to Fort Churchill and easing into the Carson Valley area at the foot of the Sierras. Nature showed just how bizarre and austerely beautiful she could be here: there was Sand Mountain and its lesser brethren, dunes of sand that look as if they were transported from another planet, or at least a different part of this one. Other sights could bring a wandering mind back to earth: bleached bones of dead oxen and other pack animals littered the trails.

But the day-in, night-out reality for a rider was a long, dry slog, sometimes a very cold one, often a very hot one.

This fall it was cold. Very. Snowflakes first flit down on the desert in mid-September; some six inches had fallen in the beginning of October, and the cold at night would freeze little patches of water in some of the more shaded areas of the hills. Morning cold, noon warm, night freezing—the sun and the altitude made for wide temperature swings, and it was not unusual for the temperature to go from below freezing to 70 degrees before noon.

The stations, even those used as stops by the stagecoach, were primitive. Burton described the best as thirty-foot shanties with sandstone walls, porthole windows, and roofs of split cedar. The inside might be divided in two, with a room for beds—two men or more would share a mattress, which more often than not was a pile of cloth and perhaps a blanket on the floor—as well as stores of whatever food and other supplies were available. Trash was spewed around the back lot. At one station, Burton washed his hands with gravel, and dried them by evaporation.

No Bible, no Shakespeare, no Milton—only a Brit would look for the last two, or even a bookshelf—but "weapons of the flesh, rifles, guns, and pistols, lay and hung all about the house, carelessly stowed as usual, and tools were not wanting—hammers, large borers, axe, saw, and chisel."[7]

Burton was surprised to find that Indians worked or hung around many of the stations. He was skeptical of their skills with bow and arrow, though they were without exception regarded as the equal of William Tell. He claims to have tested at least one's skills and found them wanting:

> An almost invariable figure in these huts is an Indian standing cross-legged at the door, or squatting uncomfortably close to the fire. He derides the whites for their wastefulness, preferring to crouch in parties of three or four over a little bit of fuel than to sit before a blazing log. These savages act, among other things, as hunters, bringing home rabbits and birds. We tried our revolvers against one of them, and beat him easily; yet they are said to put, three times out of four, an arrow through a keyhole forty paces off. In shooting they place the thumb and forefinger of the right hand upon the notch, and strengthen the pull by means of the second finger stretched along the bowstring. The left hand holds the whipped handle, and the shaft rests upon the knuckle of the index.[8]

Not even Carson City could be said to be very large in 1860; visitors noted one main street, with a lot of blank spaces between the houses.

The buildings that were there were small, and mostly wooden; most were one story. The 1860 census found 980 in the county that became the city. Nevada had only 6,857 people, most of them in the western part of the state near the mines or along the trails to California. Carson was a wild place; Twain in *Roughing It* claimed that among the first people he and his brother met was a certain Mr. Harris, who after greeting them begged his pardon to go talk to an acquaintance.

> *"I'll have to get you to excuse me a minute; yonder is the witness that swore I helped to rob the California coach—a piece of impertinent intermeddling, sir, for I am not even acquainted with the man."*
>
> *Then he rode over and began to rebuke the stranger with a six-shooter, and the stranger began to explain with another. When the pistols were emptied, the stranger resumed his work (mending a whip-lash), and Mr. Harris rode by with a polite nod, homeward bound, with a bullet through one of his lungs, and several in his hips; and from them issued little rivulets of blood that coursed down the horse's sides and made the animal look quite picturesque. I never saw Harris shoot a man after that but it recalled to mind that first day in Carson.*[9]

America's first famous humorist was exaggerating, but not by much. Burton claimed he'd witnessed a murder for each day he spent in the city.

Otis Clemens reported for duty at the governor's house, a one-story, two-room building near the center of town, which was marked by a small open area that, had there been grass, might have been called the village green. It was more a dusty brown, its surface whipped by the wind descending the nearby hills. The Pony office, far less grand than the governor's shack, was located nearby on Carson Street, between Fourth and Fifth Streets.

WHEN NO FUNDS COULD BE FOUND FOR SAMUEL, HE HIKED OUT TO THE silver fields to seek his fortune. He soon turned his attention to a surer profession—newspapering. Sam began writing for the *Territorial Enterprise* of Virginia City using the pen name Mark Twain; before long he found his way to better-paying jobs in California. Assigned as a travel writer to cover Hawaii, he returned with stories so entertaining that he started a sideline as a traveling lecturer. His ability to weave humor into his pithy observations of life, usual and unusual, made him a popular short story writer, entertainer, and major American novelist as the century went on.

Samuel Clemens/Mark Twain was a genius-level talent and extraordinarily successful, but he labored in a relatively common profession for educated, or semieducated, men at the time. Moving from job to job was not unusual. Newspapers of the era were generally local affairs published weekly, often connected with or funded by prominent business interests or political parties; sometimes, both. Typically, they were broadsheets—29.5 by 23.5 inches or some variation, depending on the press—printed on both sides of the paper and folded so there were four pages of material. Columns, sometimes eight or even nine across, were crowded together. Stories ran together, with headlines barely bigger than regular type.

Aside from a column or two of local news, papers carried reports from different areas of the state or territory, and the bigger cities to the east.[10] News and opinion mixed freely; the writer's opinion was as essential as the facts—more so in some cases. Fiction—short stories and the occasional serialized novel—were popular in some, which is how the fictional "Jim Smiley and His Jumping Frog" helped bring Twain to national prominence.[11]

Since the country's founding, newspapers had benefited from special mail rates, intended to make it easier to spread information through the country; editors could obtain editions postage-free thanks to legislation intended to help speed information along. A lot of the inside stories, and often much of those on the front as well, came from other newspapers, which would be delivered haphazardly with the mail. Because of the low rates, bundles of papers would be

carried by stages, including those run by Russell, Majors, and Waddell. They added so much deadweight to the carriage that they would
often be chucked when the going got hard.

The Pony Express made it possible for the small newspapers to
carry dispatches that were far more up-to-date than a few years
before. Throughout the West, dispatches credited to the Pony sig-
nified news that was of the very latest vintage. A Pony dateline
advertised that the paper was on the cutting edge of events and
technology, just as the words *Latest Telegraphic News* would when
the wires reached town. It was indirect advertising for the service,
even as it helped change tastes and expectations about what "news"
meant.

FRAGMENTS OF THE REPUBLIC

The editors waiting eagerly for the arrival of the Pony with the election results added them to pages already typeset with stories about
seething Southern sentiments. There was little in the pages yet about
what was going on back in Washington, let alone Illinois. Lincoln
steadfastly refused to make any statement about what he was planning; Buchanan fumed privately.

Just before the election, Lieutenant General Winfield Scott,
the seventy-four-year-old hero of the Mexican-American War and
the commanding general of American forces, had sent a letter to the
secretary of war with his "view" of the crisis. Scott, despite a reputation as anti-slavery, said states had a right to secede. While he
wasn't in favor of breaking up the country, he declared it would
be a "smaller evil" if the "fragments of the great Republic" formed
smaller units.[12]

Scott's views had been leaked and quickly entered general circulation. Buchanan fretted, knowing they would encourage the South,
especially since they rested not only on a belief that the government
had no right to use force to keep itself together, but that it lacked that

force to do it. This Scott had made clear in a second message, listing only five companies of soldiers that could be used to quickly reinforce forts on the Southern coast—South Carolina specifically.

The small size of the army had been one of the few things Buchanan and Scott agreed on; both men had urged Congress to increase the War Department's budget, to little avail. Otherwise, the two men did not get along personally or politically—Scott was a Whig, and Buchanan had supported President Polk's attempts to undermine Scott's status during the war, hoping to prevent him from becoming a war hero and running for president. (He failed on all accounts; Scott ran in 1852, losing to Democrat Franklin Pierce.)

But Buchanan's problems with Old Fuss and Feathers were mere blips compared with the distrust between him and his secretary of war, John B. Floyd. Floyd had grown increasingly moody and resented Buchanan's criticisms that he was careless with department funds. His advice also shaded toward the South, or at least against taking strong action.

Attorney General Black was still researching the legalities of what could be done. In the meantime, Buchanan began working on an address to Congress on the crisis. He planned to blast abolitionists and the North in general, telling them to leave the South and slavery alone. But he would also say that the Union must be preserved.

Don't act in the absence of action, he would tell the South. *Don't do anything unless your rights are violated. Which they have not been, election or no.*

And then he might propose the only possible solution he saw to the problem: a constitutional convention to settle things on a quiet and fair basis, once and for all.

PONY BOB

The dispatch that had been telegraphed to Fort Kearny with details of the election arrived at Fort Churchill, Nevada, on November 14 at 1:10 a.m. The local correspondent for the *Sacramento Daily Union* grabbed his report and ran to the telegraph operator, hastily dictating what he had:

> *Lincoln is elected President.*
> Stop.
> *New York city has given the fusion ticket twenty-eight thousand majority.*
> Stop.
> *The State had given about fifty thousand majority for Lincoln.*[13]
> Stop.

The dispatch[14] had traveled well over a thousand miles in a week; some letters and notes had several hundred more to go. As the details spread around the home stations and the assorted towns and settlements along the way, the riders kept on toward California.

Nick Wilson—the White Indian—was working the stretch of the trail between Carson Sink and Fort Churchill. A flat run of land where the Carson River once emptied, the station at Carson Sink was made of thick mud bricks dug from the nearby marsh, with a framed interior, according to Burton. Fort Churchill, some seventy-five miles away over a trail of thick sand, was still being finished, but already there were quarters for two companies of soldiers. The Pony used a wood-framed building at the corner of the fort property; it had replaced a station just across the river owned by Samuel S. Buckland.[15] Within a few months the fort would be able to hold over a thousand men—at a cost of several tens of thousands of dollars, considered the outrageous military boondoggle of its time.[16]

Wilson finished his run and took out a pipe; he'd started smoking recently to relax, a habit he'd continue until the end of his days—and one that would get him in trouble with Mormon elders later in life, when he had been elevated to the rank of bishop in the church.

Even for someone like Wilson, an experienced rider and an adopted Indian, trouble was often a matter of timing, location, and luck.

Just ask Pony Bob.

ROBERT HASLAM—BETTER KNOWN TO HISTORY AS PONY BOB—WAS born in London, England, in 1840. A Mormon, he'd come to the Utah Territory in the great migration. Bolivar Roberts, one of Ficklin's deputies, hired the young man to help build some of the stations as the service was starting up. When the mail began running, Haslam was assigned to Friday's Station near Lake Tahoe; his route was typically between Friday's and Fort Churchill.

Back in May, Pony Bob started out from Friday's on what seemed like a regular run. He made good time to Carson City, where he was surprised to find his next horse gone, requisitioned by a state militia officer mustering volunteers to go after the local Indians. Pony Bob rode on, continuing until he got to Buckland's Station. There, relief rider Johnson Richardson declared that with the Indians on the warpath he wasn't going nowhere for the mail.

Station manager W. C. Marley offered Pony Bob fifty bucks to take the next leg himself.

He took it.

Riding on to Cold Springs and then Smith's Creek, Pony Bob traveled nearly one hundred and forty miles from his starting point as the eagle flies; at least another twenty or thirty with the winds in the trail.[17]

When he got to the station, Pony Bob hit the hay for a few hours, then woke to take the mochila from the westbound rider. Retracing his route, he reached Cold Springs Station, where he found that the Indians had been there the day before. The station keeper was dead, the station was burned, and whatever horses had been kept there had been run off.

Nothing to do but keep on going.

When he got to Sand Springs Station, Haslam told keeper Montgomery Maze what he'd found.

Maybe you oughta come west with me.

Good idea, said the other man.

The pair got to Carson Sink on May 13. The station house was barricaded by some fifteen men, riders, station keepers, all worried about the Indian attacks. Continuing on alone, Pony Bob returned to Buckland's, where he began the regular portion of his run, riding back through Carson City en route to Friday's Station.

He had taken the mail across the most dangerous part of the trail, just at the start of the Paiute Indian War.

INDIAN WARS

CREATION

There are many stories. One:

First, there was only water. Slowly, a mountain grew, then others, then flatter land, and finally the earth was the earth.

At first, there were four children, two boys, two girls. One boy and one girl had dark skin; the other pair had white.

The family was happy. But as in all families, the happiness was interrupted by a squabble.

Father took the children and separated them, sending the white boy and girl away.

And for a long while then, peace reigned.

Another:

Wise Wolf decided to create a new people with sticks. He would place them all around the earth, each to his own. But his brother Coyote played a trick, cutting the bottom of his sack so that people fell out together. Angrily, they quarreled.

When Wise Wolf saw what had happened, he took the few people who had not fallen from the sack and blessed them with the best place, where they could live in peace with plenty.

And another:

> The Father of All People lived in the world near the river. Mother of All heard of him, and wished to see him, but this made her husband, Bear, very angry. Bear and Mother fought until Mother got the better of him and beat him down with a club, killing him.
>
> Mother journeyed far in search of Father of All, but when she found him, she was shy and afraid. Hiding, she watched him from the woods.
>
> Father of All saw her footprints and called out. He coaxed her from hiding, offering her food at his home. He urged her to stay, but she was not so easily won over. The first night, she slept out by the fire; little by little, he won her heart, and on the fifth night they wed.
>
> Their first child was a boy, mean to others. Father sent him and a girl away; the others stayed and lived in peace. Mother cried for her lost children, and her tears became a great lake.

Still another:

> Wolf and Coyote were brothers. Wolf was stronger, and he was the People's father. Coyote liked to play. Wolf asked his brother to help make the earth, but Coyote would not or could not. Coyote had bad manners and was greedy, but he also brought fire to the People and showed them pine nuts, and when his brother caught all the animals in a cave, it was Coyote who released them, and in this way People had food to hunt. Coyote taught people to pray.

THE PAIUTE

Thousands of years ago, the ancestors of the Northern Paiute tribes came to the area whites called the Utah Territory, settling near Pyramid Lake. The Indians called themselves the People and were also called Kuyuidokado, or fish eaters, by others. They specialized in fish-ing, but in this arid, ungiving land would eat whatever was plentiful nearby: mammals, birds, and plants. They hunted with bows and arrows, picked pine nuts, poked for grasshoppers among the weeds.

The climate changed gradually, becoming drier and drier. The People learned to move with the seasons, exploring and hunting, going over the mountains and exploring lakes to the north. In time, the People and other tribes worked out the fair boundaries of their land; unlike others, they managed to live mostly in peace with their neighbors.

The world of Pyramid Lake and beyond was not Disney's, nor were the People perfect beings. The ecology of the Great Basin was neither a paradise or a hell, but something in between, and humans were part of the balance with all their customary flaws. Their location, separated from so much of the world by the desert and the mountains, isolated them from many contacts, delaying the inevitable unbalancing of civilizations as whites swept across the continent.

Contact waited until the 1820s, when European trappers and traders passed through the area. Jedediah Smith was the first European American to pass through their area, or at least the first to leave a record of it. A six-foot-tall, blue-eyed wilderness explorer permanently scarred by a wrestling match with a grizzly in the Rocky Mountain Foothills, Smith did not see the People on his excursion, and if they noticed him they did not record it.

The next white to lead expeditions in the area was different: trapper Peter Skene Ogden was reviled by the People because of the many beavers he trapped, and the large amounts of grass his horses ate. The son of a Tory lawyer who'd escaped the American Revolution by running off to Quebec, he explored the western Great Basin from 1828 to 1829. He was considered a hard man even by his employers, the Hudson Bay Company, though he was the perfect employee for their aim: to get rich and stay rich by wiping out American competition in the region. The Hudson Bay Company wanted to create a "fur desert" in the American West, a boundary of barren land that would keep competition from straying too far north, and Ogden went far in that direction, practically hunting the local beaver out of existence.

Other expeditions, with less malignant intent, followed. There was Joseph R. Walker, who found much of the California Trail along the Humboldt River and through the Humboldt Sink; in 1841, John Bidwell and Colonel John Bartleson led emigrants across Nevada to California for the first time.

By the end of the decade, the trickle became a flood. In less than a single lifetime, the land around Pyramid Lake went from being completely isolated to being traversed by thousands of whites several months of the year. Beaver, used by the Indians for clothing and shoes as well as food, were gone. The grass along the Humboldt River and its tributaries had been severely depleted. The winters, never easy, became even harder to survive.

THE NORTHERN PAIUTE BANDS IN THE GENERAL AREA OF PYRAMID Lake and the western portions of Utah Territory were neighbors with and occasionally intermingled with Shoshone tribes; the two groups shared many customs and a language, and even today some specialists note that there were very few differences between the two tribes. The English curmudgeon Richard Burton turned fashion critic upon meeting a band of Indians he called the White Knives at Willow Creek:

> The dress was the usual medley of rags and rabbit furs: they were streaked with vermilion; and their hair—contrary to, and more sensibly than the practice of our grandfathers—was fastened into a frontal pigtail, to prevent it falling into the eyes.[1]

The men he was describing were said to be Shoshones; judging from pictures and paintings of the period, Burton's "frontal pigtail" is referring to the habit of draping the pigtail forward of the shoulder rather than behind. His description could easily apply to Paiutes, at least to a white man's eyes. But so could his prejudice:

They may be a respectable race, but they are an ugly: they resemble the Diggers, and the children are not a little like juvenile baboons.[2]

Not all whites looked at the local Indians that way, but this was far from a minority opinion.

HOSTILITIES INCREASED DURING THE LATE 1840S AND 1850S AS THE LO-cals were increasingly pressured by the environmental changes. Incidents and perspectives vary. Indians stole oxen and justified it by pointing to the whites' failure to share; whites shot Indians in retaliation, not bothering to discriminate between those who attacked them and innocent bystanders. There were attempts by both sides to form treaties and enforce peace, but neither the settlers nor the tribal leaders who would meet with them ever had enough control over their own kind to fully enforce the agreements.

For the Northern Paiutes, hunger became a prime motivator, especially in the years following the winter of 1858. Harsh winters multiplied the disruptions in the local ecology. There was so much distrust on either side that gestures that would have been welcomed a few years before were now regarded as likely treachery: food provided by the territorial governor to the Paiute went untouched; the Indians felt it must be poisoned.

In January 1860, a settler named Dexter Demming was found murdered in his cabin. Strong evidence pointed to a group of Paiutes. Though they were estranged from the main group of Indians the settlers had earlier made peace with, few whites cared about the difference.

With feelings rising, the territorial governor sent two men to talk with a Paiute chief named Numaga, who had fought as an ally with the settlers against raiding rival Indians and had led the Paiute in seeking peace. At great risk, the two men rode to Pyramid Lake, and after being captured and held briefly by the breakaway group of Indians, met with Numaga and asked that the murderers be turned over to the whites, as was required under a treaty the Paiutes had agreed to. But there were too many bad feelings on both sides, and while

Numaga was in general a man of peace, he denied that any Indian could be the murderer.

In a classic case of bad timing, he also insisted that the settlers make a large payment for the use of area lands for grazing. The whites returned with less than positive feelings about the chances for peace.

They were not wrong. As winter lingered, leaders of the small bands of Northern Paiute and Western Shoshones gathered at Pyramid Lake to air grievances. Speaker after speaker complained that the whites were the root of their suffering, from the lack of food to the extreme weather, from the trampling of sacred ground to the disappearance of the grass. Something had to be done.

Numaga—the chief who had asked for payment and denied access to the murderers—alone counseled against war. He knew the whites were too powerful, and too numerous, to be opposed successfully for very long.

Each band had its own leader, and no one chief could dictate what all would do. In an important matter like war, agreement among all was generally considered necessary before action was taken. Numaga was extremely influential, a great warrior and a man who also knew the whites very well. His position was therefore a roadblock; the council continued to meet, arguing among themselves without a conclusion.

Unable to convince the others and unsure how to stop them. Numaga laid himself flat on the ground in his own camp near the shore of the lake and began to fast. He lost the strength to stand, but despite the pleas of his people and threats from other chiefs, he remained on the ground, listening for an answer to the question of what was to be done.

Before the answer came, actions miles away forced a decision on him.

RAPE AT THE PONY STATION

There are different versions of the incident that began the Pyramid Lake War, and all of them make enough sense to be true. Some involve drinking, others gambling. All end in murder.

The one most often cited is the darkest, for it includes not only murder but rape and kidnapping. It goes like this:

In 1860 when they were setting up the Pony service through the western Utah Territory, agents for Russell, Majors & Waddell selected a station on the Carson River known as Honey Lake—or as Williams Station, depending on whether you wanted to talk up the nearby watering hole or credit the two brothers who owned the building. Located between Hooten Wells and Desert Station, the stop was a one-room saloon, inn, and store; there was a barn but not much more. The Williams brothers were James, the oldest; Oscar; and David. James O. Sullivan was the station keeper.

A Paiute village was nearby, off the trail used by the Pony. One day, two Paiute girls about twelve years old went out from the village to dig roots for food. They failed to return; a search party was mustered and began tracking them.

Footprints similar to theirs were found near Williams Station. The brothers said they knew nothing of the girls; the searchers moved on.

A few days later, another Indian stopped at the station. The brothers and he struck up a deal—his horse for a gun, five cans of powder, five boxes of caps, and five bars of lead to make bullets with.[3] The brothers agreed, took the horse, and gave him the gun, powder, and caps . . . but left out the lead.

The Indian objected and went to the barn to reclaim his horse. There he was intercepted by the brothers' dog; it bit him, he kicked it, he yelled.

Someone or something answered back. It sounded like a girl's voice.

The Indian fled—to the village where the mystery of the girls still hadn't been solved. His story sent the girl's family back to the station late that afternoon. Two of the Williamses were inside, along with three or four other men.

Where is my sister?
Don't know anything about no sister.

The girls?

Don't know anything about girls.

What's in the barn?

Nothing.

One of the white men bolted. Indians grabbed him and dragged him back. Another ran to a low cliff nearby and jumped into the river. But he misjudged his jump or his ability to swim, or both; he went under and was swept away, drowned.

One of the remaining whites drew a knife; he was quickly overwhelmed, and one of the Paiute strangled him from behind.

Two men dead; no use keeping the rest alive.

After all the whites were killed, the brother of the girls and the others went to the barn. There they found the missing girls bound and gagged below a trapdoor in the floor. They had been beaten and raped. Outraged, the Indians set the building on fire. By the time the third Williams brother, who had been somewhere along the river, got to the cabin, they were gone. He rode off for help, claiming he had five hundred warriors pursuing him. In the meantime, the warriors sent a message to Pyramid Lake and the chiefs of the bands.

THE STORY AS TOLD HERE, WHILE GENERALLY ACCEPTED BY HISTORI-ans, raises many questions, starting with the nature of the horse trade and ending with a wilderness barn at the edge of the desert that's expansive enough to feature a hidden cellar. Clearly we don't have all the details, and what we do have may or may not be correct.

But whatever holes may have been obvious to the Indians at Pyramid Lake when they heard what happened, the central fact was this: whites had been killed, and their kin and neighbors were going to want revenge.

Numaga, rising from his fast, told the council that battle was the only option.

Meanwhile to the south in Carson City, whites knew only of the massacre and demanded revenge. They formed a militia of just over a hundred volunteers. They buried the dead, then set out for Pyramid Lake under the direction of William Ormsby.

Ormsby was a failed prospector who'd been sucked into William Walker's ill-fated attempt to take over Nicaragua a few years before. In 1857 he made his way to Genoa in the Carson Valley mining area and saw the future—in Carson City, where he moved and bought land near where he hoped the capitol would rise. He built a hotel, bought a store, and got himself elected judge.

He also befriended a Paiute elder, the grandfather of girls (not the ones reported kidnapped) who were living with his family when news arrived that Williams Station had been burned. The family connection didn't alter his thirst for revenge now, and his stint with Walker and his troop didn't do much for his knowledge of military tactics. Ormsby led the whites into a classic trap near the Truckee River on May 12, baited into an ambush by a few Indians fleeing on horseback. Shot at from both sides by a troop led by Numaga, the whites were mowed down; some seventy died, including Ormsby.

THE WAR

Warriors celebrated by mutilating the bodies of the dead; bowstrings were cut from sinews of fallen whites.

Pony riders were passing the mail as hostilities broke out; two rode from Buckland's Station to Virginia City with news of the first attack.[4] Service was quickly suspended. Isolated cabins used for exchanges were especially vulnerable, and most were abandoned, station keepers and the others retreating to larger settlements.

Panic hit the whites living in Virginia City, Comstock, and the rest of the western slopes of the Sierra Nevada. News of the disaster was sent from Virginia City to Sacramento via telegraph; accounts of the battle were sparse, and details of the preamble nonexistent. Whites rallied to help, not least of all because of rumors that the Mormons had incited the Paiute attack: it was the story of the Meadows Massacre come back to life, this time as false legend, firing up prejudice not just against the Native Americans but also the Mormons. Troops and volunteers, as well as guns, ammunition, and other supplies, were sent over the mountains.

In the meantime, the locals recruited former Texas Ranger John C. Hays to lead a volunteer militia against the Indians. Joining with a force of regulars under Captain Joseph Stewart, the whites pushed back the Paiute in an encounter near the Indian camps at Pinnacle Mount on June 2, 1860. Generally labeled a tactical draw, it was a strategic victory for the whites, as the Indians retreated from Pyramid Lake, avoiding conflict by entering the desert.

Serious parlaying between combatants followed. This was not a polite diplomatic exchange with tea and crumpets: in one account of the discussion for a truce, Numaga scolds the white officer who has come to talk, saying that he won't talk until darkness because the men who have come killed his warriors.

The officer—Colonel Frederick Lander—responds that he was glad some of his men had killed the chief's warriors, because the chief's warriors had killed *his* men.

And besides: *I came as a man to talk to a man. If you want to talk to a woman, I'll leave and send some back.*

It probably didn't calm things that the white translator was Jack Demming, the brother of the settler killed the previous winter, and a person known to harbor very unpleasant feelings toward the Paiute. Yet after the chest pounding was done, the two sides agreed to a truce. Numaga declared that he would make sure his people did not attack for one year, perhaps two, as long as the whites behaved.

THE PAIUTES, AND NUMAGA'S BAND IN PARTICULAR, HAD MANY LEGITimate grievances, few of which would ever be addressed. If anything, the continued influx of miners and others through the area would only make the pressures against them worse. But by that fall when the message of Lincoln's election came through, the peace was still holding at Pyramid Lake. Outrage had turned to more routine occurrences in Virginia City and beyond: the *Daily Alta California* reported that a man named Elijah Porman had been killed by A. J. Bayney, the local furniture dealer, apparently because of "improper intimacy" between Bayney and Porman's wife.

But for Russell, Majors, and Waddell, the war was one more disaster in a string of them. The two large-scale battles were only the most visible part of a low-intensity war that had their company and their people on the front lines. Service was stopped completely for a few weeks, and the effects went on long afterward.[5] Peace with the fiercest chief did not translate into peace with renegade groups.

William Finney, the superintendent of the line section just to the west, went to Sacramento in June and asked the public if they could help the line by donating money for twenty-five Sharps rifles and as many pistols.[6] Finney collected $1,500. Meanwhile, Bolivar Roberts, who oversaw the area including Pyramid Lake, gathered a force of employees to rebuild the stations; they worked their way east, rebuilding and restocking stations that had been attacked and reinforcing those that remained.

They'd been at it for less than a week when they met a Pony rider, Howard Egan, at Roberts Creek. With him was an employee of their parent firm named William Henry Streeper, whose battle-shocked expression made it clear that he had a story to tell.

DEATH AT SIMPSON'S PARK

A few days before, Streeper had saddled up his mule and set out from Diamond Springs. While there were rumors of Indian trouble, "Muggins" figured he had nothing to worry about. Emigrants had gone through the day before, and he was used to rumors as well as the frontier. Now twenty-three, he'd migrated to Utah with his family at thirteen and had been part of a Mormon rescue team that helped families stranded in Wyoming during the winter of 1856.

Streeper reached Dry Creek without trouble. Wary after being warned by a trader that some local Indians might cause trouble, he went on to Simpson Park, northwest of present-day Austin, Nevada.

Coming through the canyon and heading toward the small lake where the station stood, he saw that the building had been burned. When he reached it, he found the keeper dead in the ruins. The stock had been run off.

He continued on, heading westward. Along the way he met another mail carrier coming east; when the man heard what Streeper had seen, he turned around and joined Streeper.

Streeper and the other rider made it to Smith's Creek. After dropping off his mail, he spent the night in one of the stop's bunks. Two miners joined him the next morning as he headed back east.

The station at Dry Creek was quiet as he approached. Too quiet. He went inside and found the station keeper, Ralph Rosier, lying on the floor, dead, scalped and mutilated. The trader and another man had run off after the attack, barely escaping with their lives.

THE TIMING OF THAT ATTACK IS DIFFICULT TO PLACE, AND IT'S POSSI-ble that the story has been mistold. But it's clear that small raids and harassment continued to the east of the Pyramid Lake area after the actual war.

At Sand Springs, the assistant station keeper J. G. Kelley recalled that employees had to stand guard night and day, for fear that their horses would be run off—or worse. One night Kelley was standing guard when he noticed one of the horses acting as if there was something in the shadows beyond the wall that marked the boundaries of the corral.

An Indian's head popped up. Kelley fired, but missed. Not long afterward, one of the company's riders—"a Mexican"—rode into the station. Shot by Indians near Edwards Creek, the rider was taken in but soon died of his wounds.

Kelley was tagged to go in his place. He made it to the next station without a problem, carrying a Sharps rifle with him just in case.

The return trip was hairier. Kelley had to pass through the road at Quaking Aspen Bottom where the other rider had been ambushed.

The trail was so twisted and thick with brush and trees that for two miles, he couldn't see more than ten or fifteen yards in front of him.

He ran through quickly, spurring his horse so that he went "like a streak of greased lightning." But when Kelley rested at the top of a low hill, he saw the bushes moving. He fired his rifle several times before moving on. Days later, some soldiers were ambushed in the same place.[7]

Kelley thought it a miracle that no other riders were killed. And as murderous as the Indians might be, Kelley's narrowest escape came at the hands of "a lot of fool emigrants," who heard him riding one night and decided he must be an Indian himself.[8] Fortunately, none of the shots they fired as he rode past their camp found its target.

Nick Wilson, the White Indian who'd had trouble farther east, delivered horses to Antelope Station later that summer.[9] Starting back the next day at an easy pace, he was passing through Spring Valley when he was invited to stay for dinner. He and the two men who'd invited him in were just sitting down when they saw some of the station's horses moving across the street. A pair of Indians were running them off.

Wilson ran out, revolver in hand. Pursuing to a large tree in the meadow, he was suddenly struck above his left eye with an arrow. He fell to the ground and stayed there as the other two men from the station ran up.

There must have been a moment of hesitation—here was a man with an arrow in his head—before one of the men took hold of the shaft of the arrow and pulled. The shaft came up, but the arrowhead itself remained wedged in Wilson's forehead.

Thinking—knowing—that Wilson would soon be dead, the two men pushed his body in the brush. Then, deciding that the Indians would surely come back for them once the horses were secured, the pair took off on a run for the next station.

Possibly they ran the entire way.

Courage restored, they returned the next day with reinforcements and shovels. To their great surprise, they discovered that Wilson was in need of a doctor rather than an undertaker—though just barely.

Carried back to a station Wilson called Cedar Wells, he lay unconscious for two and a half weeks; a doctor managed to remove the arrowhead, but the rest of his treatment seems to have consisted of telling the men looking after him to throw a wet rag on the wound every so often and hope for the best.[10] Major Egan, the company superintendent, came by about a week after the incident; believing more could be done, he had the doctor hauled back in. Given the general state of medicine at the time, it's not all that likely that the doctor made much of a difference. But Wilson recovered, anyway, even to the point of riding shortly after rising from bed.

He had headaches the rest of his life.

NOT LONG AFTER HE'D DONE HIS LAZARUS TURN, WILSON WAS RIDING with the mail on the route that brought him to Eight Mile Station, where he was supposed to make an exchange.[11] He was resting at the station when he saw his opposite number approaching from several miles away. Suddenly a dozen or so Indians leaped out of their hiding spots and ambushed the other rider, shooting him dead.

Wilson and the two boys who were manning the outpost ran to the barn and brought the animals to the house so they could protect them. Twelve by twenty feet square, the house was a veritable palace compared with some of the desert hovels. It was built for fighting, with strategically placed portholes for shooting.

One of their attackers made the mistake of testing the defenses; Wilson shot him dead, though he didn't realize it at the time. Warned off, the others pulled back and waited the whites out.

Wilson and the others stayed put for three days, when some soldiers showed up and told them the way was clear.

According to Wilson, the young men he was with were still boys— one was fourteen, the other twelve. They'd been orphaned when their parents were migrating: mother dead of cholera, father killed by Indians—then left for some reason at the station. (Wilson's account of how that came to happen is confused and contradictory; teasing out the details, we can surmise that the older man in charge of the station was given five hundred dollars by their dying father to care for the boys and send them home, but he ran off instead.)

Wilson also witnessed the results of a massacre of emigrants by Gosiute Indians in Egan Canyon, a six-mile-long narrow box just made for an ambush. Seeing signs of an impending raid and knowing that migrants were ahead on the trail, he rode to warn them, but stopped when he got close enough to hear the shooting. Two men who'd escaped warned him back, racing on without bothering to say what had happened.

He rode in after the shooting stopped. The horses and mules had been taken. Men, women, and children had been slaughtered. The lone survivor, a woman, died in his arms.

Wilson went on with the mail. A short time afterward he was called to act as an interpreter and guide for the army as it dealt with unrest along the trail, and he quit his job as a rider.

TALES OF INDIAN ENCOUNTERS IN THE GREAT BASIN TEND TO BE VIO-lent, but there is also the occasional comic relief, assuming you like your laughs very dark. In October, about a month before the message with Lincoln's election passed through, a large group of Paiutes paid a call to Egan's Station. Held off by Mike Holt and a rider named Wilson—not Nick, but his first name has been lost—the Indians remained about, milling around as the two whites fired away, apparently without much success.

The whites ran out of ammunition. The Indians broke through the door. As the two European Americans backed against the wall, the chief pushed his way to the front of the crowd and uttered one word.

Bread.

"Bread," not "dead."

At least that's what Holt and Wilson heard. They grabbed whatever bread they could find and piled it on the table.

Not enough. The chief pointed at sacks of flour and told them to put it to use.

The whites went to work baking. And baking. And baking until all their supplies were exhausted.

Finally satisfied, the chief nodded . . . then ordered the men tied up outside and burned to death. They were saved from the roast by the timely arrival of a rider from the west named William Dennis—and the sixty or so soldiers he brought with him. Dennis had seen the Indians surrounding the station earlier, put two and two together, and retreated until he came upon an army patrol.

THE "BUTS" OF THE STORIES

Pony Bob's long ride was said to have occurred on May 9 or May 10, putting it at the start of the Pyramid Lake War. Nick Wilson's adventures are generally thought to have taken place in roughly the same time frame, though his original narrative is frankly so convoluted that sorting out a timeline is haphazard.

But . . .

There are plenty of questions about the details both men gave about the encounters. The story of Pony Bob Haslam's long ride overstates the length of his ride and is a little skimpy on details. There are more serious inconsistencies in Wilson's accounts. He misnames stations, for example, and talks about men who sometimes aren't linked to the stations he mentions. His timeline is messed up, though that may be the fault of the people who compiled the tales later on, as he didn't seem to care about how he was ordering things himself.

Whatever the specific "facts" of these stories—whether they happened when the people said they did, to the people involved, to others they knew—there *was* a Pyramid Lake War, conflict continued for some time afterward, and the Pony was severely affected.

The service had always been seen as a loss leader, but now to the regular operating losses were added about $75,000 worth of repair expenses—at least $2 million in today's money. Worse, the blow came at the point when the Pony had only just begun to prove that the advance publicity was deserved. The delivery schedule suffered—ten days turned into thirty-six at the height of the conflict and was more often twelve or fourteen or more through to the winter, when the snow caused more delays.

For some reason, riders tended to go west a little faster than east. In any event, a ten-day transit would be the exception rather than the rule from this point forward.

The "Mexican" Kelley referred to was probably Jose Zowgaltz. Zowgaltz is the only confirmed Pony Express rider killed during the war. But only a single mochila's worth of mail went missing during the conflict: on a trip that left Sacramento July 21, either stolen from a rider or grabbed at a station during an attack.

BOLIVAR ROBERTS

Rebuilding the line was labor intensive—stone walls were erected not just for the buildings but for corrals, and up to five men would be left at each station to fortify it against attack. The only stroke of fortune was that the man in charge was perfectly suited to the task. Bolivar Roberts was an Alexander Majors type, able to rally the riders by leading from experience as well as intellect; the man could swing a hammer as well as he could issue an order.

Bolivar had come west to Utah when he was nineteen, traveling ahead of his mom, dad, and rest of the family. According to the family genealogy, his father, Daniel, had been a doctor, practicing in a number of towns in Illinois, Iowa, and Missouri before answering the call for Mormons to locate to a place where they would no longer be persecuted. This turned out to be Provo, Utah. Bolivar went with his father and a younger brother to California in 1852 to try their luck at mining. Apparently that didn't work out as well as they hoped—his dad soon left, and rather than Provo went all the way back to Missouri. Bolivar eventually turned up in Salt Lake City, where he found a position with a mail and express company that connected with Carson City.[12]

Bolivar had a frontier entrepreneur's bent: in 1859 he built a toll bridge in the area of Dayton. His knowledge of the area and experience made him a natural as superintendent of the district when the Pony route was established.

By the time of the election, the service's reputation had been fully restored, and the Indian attacks had eased off. There were plenty of other things to worry about. Rider Henry Tuckett, for one, worried more about highwaymen. While riders generally didn't carry large sums of money in their locked pouches, on one ride Tuckett knew he would be carrying a rather large sum. Realizing that he wasn't the only one who knew, he managed to hide the money (and presumably the mochila) a short distance from the station, then traded places with another rider after telling him where the money was. The other rider was stopped by highwaymen, but they apparently let him go, not realizing he was a Pony rider.[13]

Tuckett worked to the east of the area hit hardest by the Indians, but the talk in Virginia City that fall, when it wasn't about silver or the question of war, wasn't about native troubles, it was murder by whites. The city and its environs were rather famous for conflict, and if the Indians wouldn't oblige, the whites had no trouble fighting among themselves.

Out at Smith's Creek, the station keeper, one H. Trumbo, got into an argument with Montgomery Maze, the keeper who had fled with Pony Bob months earlier. Montgomery was now riding for the service—or at least was supposed to when he and Trumbo had words. What those particular words were has not been recorded, but they resulted in an argument serious enough for Trumbo to take out a pistol and snap it several times at Montgomery.

Montgomery took the dry fire as a warning, and when the argument resumed the next day, he grabbed a rifle and shot Trumbo in the hip.

Trumbo recovered and stayed on; Montgomery was fired, though he reportedly left the station with a paper signed by witnesses saying he was not to blame for the argument.

SMITH'S CREEK HAS BEEN CURSED AS A MOURNFUL, HAUNTED PLACE, its adobe walls and willow thatch roof alleged to have witnessed the first murder punished by hanging in the Nevada territory—legal hanging, that is.

The story that has always been told in histories of the Pony Express is that the killer was a station keeper, and the victim an innocent if not entirely sweet civilian.

It's time to exonerate the service, and the keeper—he was the victim, not the killer.

Actually, he'd left the Pony Express sometime before the murder, but every Western needs a good hanging.

The real tale, told by R. Michael Wilson in *Legal Executions in the Western Territories, 1847–1911*, but apparently never connected to the Pony legend, runs like this.

JOHN WILLIAM CARR—GENERALLY KNOWN AS BILL—WAS A GAMBLER who'd come out of California to the hills near Virginia City and Carson. Gambling wasn't enough of a sure thing for Carr, and so he decided to try his hand at something with better odds: holding up emigrants on the nearby trail. After the robberies, he would repair to a stagecoach station operated by Bernard Cherry.[14]

Cherry didn't realize what was going on; business was thin to begin with, and asking questions was not considered polite or life lengthening in this neck of the Old West. But at some point, Cherry figured out what was going on and felt conscience-bound to do something about it. He stepped in and stopped a robbery. Carr moved on, but held a grudge.

Cherry sold his interest in the station and moved into a hotel in Carson City sometime around the end of the summer or early fall of 1860. Carr soon showed up and, acting like nothing had ever come between them, plied him with as much goodwill as it took to get Cherry out for a walk in the western part of the city. There Carr shot him in the back, rifled his pockets—where he found only a twenty-dollar gold piece—then fled the scene with an accomplice.

The dead man was discovered the next morning. An investigation quickly turned up two facts: Carr and his friend had been the last ones to see Cherry alive, and Carr and friend were no longer around.

A California sheriff located the duo and had them returned to Carson City for trial before Judge John Cradlebaugh. Carr's accomplice sang in exchange for immunity and a quick escape. Carr reportedly confessed when he realized the evidence was against him.

Murder was generally punishable by death, which meant hanging. Hangings weren't as common in the country as you might think, at least according to the official records we have today. Sixty-six people were hanged in the United States and its territories in 1860, nearly all for murder—not counting the three slaves hanged for "slave revolt." Of the sixty-six, exactly a third were slaves.[15]

Carr's trial lasted several whole hours. Found guilty, he was hanged by the neck until dead ten days later, the thirtieth of November, 1860, making him the first man legally executed in Nevada, quite a distinction given that the territory hadn't even been created yet.[16]

STORMS

TO TAHOE

Winter comes early in much of the West—the Great Plains, the Great Basin, and most especially, the Sierra Nevada. This year was no exception: by the time the mochila with the election letters left Virginia City, nighttime temperatures were running well below freezing, and there had been snow on the ground in the mountain foothills for weeks.

From Fort Churchill, the rider took the mochila and followed the Carson River south of Virginia City, Gold Hill, and Silver City, heading for Carson City. The route cut through ridges so steep that a newspaper reporter described a recently built toll road beyond Gold Hill by saying "the rocks on each side of the canon approach each other so closely as to barely leave room for a pass way."[1] Heavily loaded wagons often had to detour to less angled paths, adding hours and maybe days to their trip.

Carson City, the future state capital, was more a dusty dream of potential than a bustling civic center. In fact, it was largely empty, a trading post centered on a fair but fairly barren ranch. Nestled strategically in a valley on the west side of the river, Carson had been born of optimism and ambition, the vision of Abraham Van Santvoord Curry, a forty-five-year-old entrepreneur who had bought the ranch surrounding it only two years before. Curry had come east from California in 1858, looking to buy and build in Genoa, but apparently experienced sticker shock when he saw the prices; he moved down the trail a bit looking for something cheaper. He found Eagle Ranch, which included a trading post and some 865 acres. It cost him and two partners $1,000, three hundred of which were paid in gold coins. Curry lopped off ten of the best-situated acres and said, *We're going to build the capital of Nevada here*—bold, given that there wasn't a territory yet, let alone a state.

Curry and partners sold off plots for as little as $50—and sometimes nothing, as long as the buyer agreed to build. The upstate New Yorker had a developer's optimism, but his partners didn't always share his vision: they soon gave up rights in another tract two miles away for a pony and twenty-two pounds of butter.[2] Maybe they were right: Curry opened a quarry there, then used the stones to build a large hotel; it was never particularly popular with visitors. But Curry wasn't the sort to give up: when the stream of visitors he'd envisioned didn't materialize, he ended up leasing the building for use as a prison.

The discovery of the Comstock Lode in 1859 helped make Curry's vision for Carson City a reality, and far sooner than even he could have hoped. By the time the Pony rider came through, there were sidewalks, a scattering of stores, and enough houses to fill four or five blocks. So much silver and gold were taken from the ground that Curry and others would soon start campaigning for a government mint; it would be planned in 1864, though government being government even in those days, it didn't open until 1870.

From Carson City, the rider went south to Genoa and Mormon Station. Originally established in 1851 as a stop for Mormons on their way from Salt Lake to the California gold mines, a planked façade had been added to the building by 1860, giving it a *slightly* grander appearance. By then, most of the Mormons who had originally settled the area were gone, called back to Salt Lake City by Brigham Young during the Utah War. The station already had a claim to history, or at least a legal footnote—it was involved in what is said to have been the first lawsuit in the western Utah Territory.

George Chorpenning—the same Chorpenning whose mail route Russell bought—and his partnership, Woodward & Company, was sued by John Reese for $675, plus court costs of $25. (Lawyers were cheaper then.) The money was for supplies Reese had delivered while Woodward was running the mail route. Chorpenning lost the case, and the local constable held an auction to clear the debt, selling Reese four mules worth from $61 to $91, a compass and chain, blacksmith tools, and Mormon Station itself for $130—not much more than two mules. The sale raised $499.[3]

Friday's Station was maybe seven miles from Mormon Station—if you were a bird. The Pony Route, twisting through the hills, was said to be roughly twenty-one and a half. But it was almost all uphill from this direction, with a rise of some twenty-five hundred feet through Daggett Pass—and the pass itself was over seven thousand feet above sea level.

The views—if a rider dared look—were spectacular. But the road was narrow, and snow and ice made it treacherous. Easier if only by a degree or two was the longer route followed by the Carson Trail to the south. Even there, the passage was so narrow in spots that the boulders on the sides were regularly scraped by wagon wheels.

Once the rider reached the summit, it was downhill to the valley near the lake. His destination was Friday's Station, a warm inn—something not to be undervalued in midfall, let alone dead winter. The station was relatively large, a two-and-a-half-story building on a hill above Lake Tahoe that had been built by Friday Burke a few years before. Originally called Edgewater, from the very first it was an important rest stop for stages and their passengers. And a pretty one: go around the side to the back and walk through the pines—the blue crystal of Lake Tahoe shone in the sunlight, magnified by the reflection of snow around it.

Shaped by glaciers and dammed by an extinct volcano, the lake had formed some two million years ago but had been seen by whites only less than twenty years before the arrival of the Pony Express. This was Washoe Indian land; their name for the lake was *Da ow ga*—or Tahoe, if a European American slurred it.

The "official" name of the lake in 1860 was Lake Bigler, named after John Bigler, the Democratic governor of California who by then had gone on to bigger and better things—or at least things overseas, as he had been named ambassador to Chile in 1857. His name replaced, or was supposed to replace, "Lake Bonpland"—something John Frémont called it after first sighting it in 1844. Bonpland honored Aimé Jacques Alexander Goujard—better known by his nickname "Bonpland"—apparently an English botching of the French words *bonne plante* or "good plant." This would make sense, given that Bonpland was a French botanist and explorer, though why exactly it made sense to Frémont isn't clear, given that Bonpland wasn't with him, nor would be at any time in the future. Neither the Anglo nor French name had any staying power, and the whites who were elbowing out the Indians from the area had already appropriated the name by the time of the Pony.

Winter in the Sierras meant snow, powdery stuff whose first flakes might be deceptively light. The Pony added a few days to its published schedule during the winter; the miracle was that the men and horses got through at all. Warren Upson rode this stretch of the trail. The son of the *Sacramento Union* newspaper's editor, Upson had dealt with a blinding snowstorm on his very first run, even though it was in April. Taking the mochila east in California at Twelve Mile House (also known as Sportsman's Hall), he started the run in the rain; it turned to ice, sleet, and finally snow as he climbed up and down through the Sierras to Friday's in Nevada and then Mormon Station. Along the way, the snow was so deep that his boss, Bolivar Roberts, had to cut a path with a team of mules as he rode to the last stop.[4]

As bad as that was, things were worse when Upson carried the westbound mail a few days later. He found a team of mules standing in a line on the path near California's Echo Summit, snowed in place. The only way around them was to dismount, hand dig, push, and prod through the snow; it took him some three and a half hours to get beyond the mules.

THE WORST WINTER

Crossing the Sierra Nevada during the winter was brutal and at times impossible, but even midfall and midspring could be a gamble. It was cold more often than not, and the clouds that gathered over the mountains routinely unleashed massive amounts of moisture. Which more often than not fell as snow. What looked like the start of light flurries could easily end up measuring near a foot as you climbed. This was hard to fathom in late October if you came from a place where winter was brutal but snow had the decency to wait until December. The snowpack could seem obscene if you were used to measuring a storm in inches rather than yards. By March, when spring might be peeking through the frost back east, people in the Sierras could walk over the roofs of houses in snowshoes, not even realizing they were there.

It was tough for the Pony riders, but unreal for emigrants who'd just traveled across a desert where a few raindrops would have been cause for celebration. It took experience to appreciate the danger.

That, or terror.

The worst, most cautionary winter for European Americans in the mountains had come some fourteen years before, when Bolivar Roberts was barely a teenager and most of the Pony riders were toddling around. The party that endured it became famous, not as stout immigrants, not even as foolhardy travelers, but as cannibals.

Having left Independence, Missouri, on May 11, 1846, the party was headed to San Francisco. The method as well as the trail was still fresh—while trappers and ox drivers had been using South Pass to get across the Rockies for about a decade and a half, wagon trains of settlers moving across the plains together were only "invented" in 1841. Things hadn't gone particularly well on that first trip: the party of less than a hundred split up, with half going north to Oregon and the other half pushing on to California. The southern contingent left their wagons in the Great Basin as they struggled through the desert below Salt Lake, but eventually made it to California by following the Walker River.

In the two or three years that followed, Oregon was hailed as the promised land, and turning south to follow the Humboldt River into the Great Basin and then west through the Sierras was regarded as almost crazy. But word of cutoffs and the discovery of a precarious but passable path through the mountains near Truckee Lake in 1844 sent rumors eastward; a cheap way to California had been found.

The rumors were widespread by the time the Donner and Reed families headed west in 1846. They left several weeks later than accepted wisdom dictated; it was one of several fatal mistakes. The families passed Independence Rock a week and a half after Independence Day, which is to say a week and a half late, and they weren't able to make up time when they discovered one of the cutoffs they wanted was far more rumor than real. Hacking their way through the Wasatch Mountains, they fell further behind, then impossibly late in the desert.

The Donner party took a path north of the Pony to Truckee Lake, reaching it October 30; there was already snow on the ground.

They found it impossible to go on. Within days, a long-lasting storm froze them in place.

Snow in the Sierra is like snow anywhere else—white, fluffy, and cold. It's the *amount* that's different: five and a half feet in one day at Echo Summit is the record, but there are many runners-up. The cold temperatures of the mountains mean the snow that hits the ground stays there. That winter, it piled over twenty feet high.

Several attempts to break out failed. As members of the party died, starvation threatened. The survivors began doing the unthinkable: eating friends and family members.

Rumors of what happened quickly circulated. The *California Star* published a lurid, highly fictionalized account of the party in April 1847. Other followed. The stories were heard not just by whites: by the time of the Pony, Indians as far away at Pyramid Lake had heard stories that whites ate humans, and it seems at least plausible that the Donner Party was the source of those rumors.

A fascination developed, not only with the story but with the scene: visitors came to gawk at what remained of the camp. They must have told themselves they were better than the survivors—no matter how extreme things got, they would never eat their own. Yet at the same time they must have wondered at their own will to survive, unsure how far they would go to live.

"Donner" became a cautionary byword in the West, and the Sierra Nevada especially. The fact that it had happened so recently—well within a Pony rider's lifetime—must have made it all the more chilling.

And yet, it didn't deter migration to the West. The extreme hardships of the country—roiling desert and impossible winters—were accepted phenomenon. Just as radical change in the country was a fact of life, so was death and starvation. The need to survive at its most extreme might push a person to do the unthinkable. But he or she would survive.

WINTER ALONG THE TRAIL

The trail through the Sierra Nevada was consistently the snowiest and worst winter section for riders. But that didn't mean the others had it easy; things just got bad a little later in the year.

Major Egan's son Robert recalled the tale of a rider who trekked from Salt Lake City to Rush Valley one winter. He couldn't remember or at least didn't record the man's name, but the story was vivid enough years later:

> He passed the point of the mountain eighteen or twenty miles south of Salt Lake City, but as there was a heavy snowstorm raging he could not tell which way he was traveling. He knew that he had gone far enough to bring him to the river, if he had kept the right road. He went on till himself and pony were both about give out, then seeing no signs of a break in the storm, got off the pony to give both of them a little rest. The snow was quite deep and drifting. Curling up beside a sagebrush he soon was sound asleep.[5]

How the man managed to fall asleep in the middle of a snowstorm is something else the younger Egan neglects to mention. But his nap nearly turned into the big sleep. Fortunately, a rabbit apparently hopped across his face, and that brought him to his senses.

> *He found that he was very numb and cold and had a time in getting blood circulation through arms and legs. His pony was standing with his head down and back to the storm, shivering like a man with the ague. He finally started again and after some time found a light. Going up to it he found that it shown [shone] out of the window of a farmhouse, the owner of which had just got up and started the morning fire. Calling the man to the door, he inquired the way he should go to get on the right trail again.*
> *The man said, "Straight ahead."*
> *"Well, if I should go straight ahead I would ride through your door and as I have been riding all night I am very cold and would like to get warm by your fire and have a cup of coffee."* [6]

Then there was the rider who made his pony exchange in or near Camp Floyd below Salt Lake City and set off for Rush Valley to the west. He got so turned around in a storm that rather than ending up at Rush Valley, he found himself back at the fort hours later.[7] Robert himself recalled a trip where he left Ruby Valley in Nevada and headed west. He got to Diamond Springs, took a break, then set out for the next station, about twenty-five miles away. A few miles out, he got stuck in a storm so bad he couldn't see.

Every direction seemed like uphill. He and his horse—this seems to have been after the Pony Express, though it's not stated—rode around and around, rested briefly, then rode around and around some more. They spent the night doing that, until finally the sun peeked up and there was enough light for him to figure out which way he had to go.

THE SNOW THAT FELL IN THE SIERRAS JUST AFTER THE ELECTION OF 1860 did not appreciably slow the Pony as the riders brought the message of the election west. But it would continue to fall, there and all along the trail. By the time Lincoln was ready to take the oath of office in March, the mail was taking fifteen days to cross. The riders carrying Lincoln's address made the trip from Fort Kearny in Nebraska to Fort Churchill in Nevada in twelve days, a feat that is usually regarded as one of the most heroic of the service's history.[8]

It also killed a number of horses.

W. A. Cates—another "Bill," one of the more popular names for riders—rode with the president's message through Wyoming. "It was tough going," he told a historian, Arthur Chapman, in an interview years after the fact. "The message got a good start out of Kearney, but the closer it got to the mountains, the worse the conditions got. We had the best horses available—several of them were killed—and, considering what we had to fight, the record was the most wonderful ever made by the Pony Express."[9]

The next run, presumably made at a more humane speed, delivered a fuller dispatch from correspondents in better weather; it took thirteen days to get from St. Joe's to California.

CONSTITUTIONAL CRISIS

As the news of Lincoln's election traveled up through the mountains, President Buchanan continued his debate on what to do. While South Carolina was rushing toward a confrontation, it was hardly the only state in which trouble could be expected. Legislators in Mississippi, Florida, Alabama, Georgia, Louisiana, and even Texas were all talking about how they would secede from the Union—not "if" or "might," but how.

Give the new president a list of demands, including enforcement of the Fugitive Slave Act, repeals of the unconstitutional laws protecting escaped slaves, and see what happens?

Or make a quick break, new Southern Union, present the Black Republican Ape-ra-ham Lincoln with a fait accompli?

Buchanan saw secession as unconstitutional—but most of the people who were talking about leaving the Union didn't. By their theories, the original states had been sovereign to begin with; in joining the Union, they had given over some but not all their rights. The legal underpinnings were a bit trickier for states that had joined the Union after being territories, but in the worst case one could go back to the Declaration of Independence and just say, *When in the course of human events, someone tries to stick it to you, take your marbles and go home . . .*

There were other things to worry about—the route for the transcontinental railroad being among the most prominent. But the issue of secession hung over everything. Buchanan had four more months in office, every day a trial, every day another tick of the fuse on the powder keg.

And even if he had all the time in the world, did he have the right?

His attorney general, Jeremiah Black, asked for a clarification on the questions Buchanan had asked about the legal basis for preventing secession. The president wrote down his questions:[10]

1. In case of a conflict between the authorities of any State and those of the United States, can there be any doubt that the laws of the Federal Government . . . are supreme?

2. What is the extent of my official power to collect duties on imports at a port where the revenue laws are resisted by a force which drives the collector from the custom house?

3. What right have I to defend the public property (for instance, a fort, arsenal, and navy yard), in case it should be assaulted?

4. What are the legal means at my disposal for executing those laws of the United States which are usually administered through the courts and their officers?

5. Can a military force be used for any purpose whatever under the Acts of 1795 and 1807, within the limits of a State where there are no judges, marshal or other civil officers?

The first three were easy questions for Black—the feds took precedence, the president was required to collect tariffs regardless, and, yeah, you gotta protect public property.

THE DAILY TIMES.

MONDAY MORNING, JANUARY 30, 1860.

LOCAL AND TERRITORIAL.

GREAT EXPRESS ENTERPRISE !

From Leavenworth to Sacramento in Ten Days!

Clear the Track and let the Pony Come Through !

In our telegraphic columns a few days ago, there was an item stating that it had been decided by the Government to start an Express from the Missouri river to California, and the time to be ten days ; but we were not aware that our fellow-citizen, Wm. H. Russell, Esq., was at the head of the enterprise. until we were shown the following di-patch. Its importance can be readily perceived :

"Let the Pony come through": The idea of taking mail to California in ten days excited the country, most especially in Missouri and Kansas. Leavenworth, though an important hub for Majors, Russell & Waddell's businesses, lost out to St. Joseph as a starting point for the Pony Express Service. *(Kansas Historical Society)*

William Russell

William Waddell   Alexander Majors

Four riders for the service, said to be (clockwise from top left) Billy Richardson, Johnny Fry, Charles Cliff, Gus Cliff. Fry is often credited as the first rider out of St. Joseph.

One of the letters carried on the first run west. *(Courtesy of Richard Frajola)*

The Pony Express has inspired authors and artists since its inception. Many, including Frederic Remington, who painted this scene of a horse exchange, tended to romanticize the service; there was plenty to romanticize. The rustic nature of the stable in the background looks fairly authentic—though even it is more elaborate than many of the actual buildings used.

LEFT: The mochila fit over the Pony saddles and could be removed in a nonce.

Both the Patee House hotel and the Pony Express's former stables in St. Joe's are now museums. *(Courtesy of the author)*

A letter to Abraham Lincoln carried west by the Pony. *(Courtesy of Richard Frajola)*

One of the election news covers. *(Courtesy of Richard Frajola)*

Across the Great Plains: Contrary to popular belief, Indians generally were not a problem during the Pony's run—with the notable exception of the Paiute War.

Two of the best examples of structures used by the Pony Express and its parent companies are open to visitors in Kansas—a stable complex now a museum in Marysville, and a station now part of a state park. *(Courtesy of the author)*

Stage coach stations and inns, like this one in Rock Creek, Nebraska, often did double duty as Pony stops.

BELOW: While a range of revolvers were available to Pony riders, their best defense against attackers was generally the speed of their horse. *(Courtesy of the author)*

The notorious Jack Slade supervised the Julesburg, Colorado, stretch—something commemorated by modern buffs with a replica ear nailed to a post near the former station. Slade is said to have relieved a thief of his. *(Courtesy of the author)*

Pony riders shared the trail with homesteaders and pioneers in many parts of the Plains, including Nebraska and Colorado, where the Platte River and its tributaries showed the way west. The deep ruts cut by wagon wheels remain in many places. *(Courtesy of the author)*

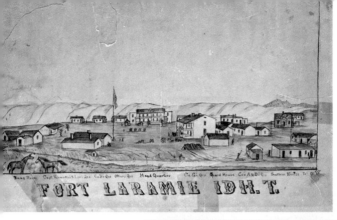

FORT LARAMIE IDH. T.

Fort Laramie, on the High Plains of southeast Wyoming. Forts were an important resource for travelers as they headed across the open territories; you could buy anything you needed for the journey. Pony stations were often located near or within the forts.

Fort Caspar in Wyoming features faithful reconstructions of the old Pony stables, as well as cabins depicting soldiers' frontier life. *(Courtesy of the author)*

Split Rock in central Wyoming was an important marker for pioneers heading west. *(Library of Congress)*

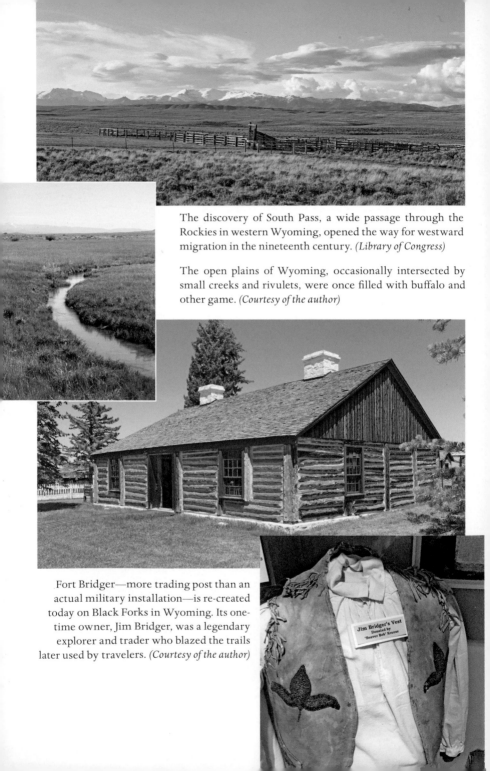

The discovery of South Pass, a wide passage through the Rockies in western Wyoming, opened the way for westward migration in the nineteenth century. *(Library of Congress)*

The open plains of Wyoming, occasionally intersected by small creeks and rivulets, were once filled with buffalo and other game. *(Courtesy of the author)*

Fort Bridger—more trading post than an actual military installation—is re-created today on Black Forks in Wyoming. Its one-time owner, Jim Bridger, was a legendary explorer and trader who blazed the trails later used by travelers. *(Courtesy of the author)*

Across the desert: Simpson Spring, Utah—a replica station near a present-day campground. *(Diane Garcia/ Shutterstock)*

"Recovered from a mail stolen by the Indians in 1860." Only one set of letters is known to have been stolen. It happened during the Paiute War in Utah Territory, and the contents were subsequently recovered in 1862. *(Courtesy of Richard Frajola)*

The ruins of an old building near the Pony trail in Nevada—not a known station, but similar to stone buildings used there. *(Courtesy of the author)*

The flat stretches of Nevada provided no relief from the sun during the summer – nor the cold winds in winter. *(Courtesy of the author)*

Whether going up or down the mountains, the jeweled Lake Tahoe teased riders and other travelers with its azure beauty. Not yet famous as a resort, the small settlement on the shores was a quiet little haven at the edge of the woods. *(Library of Congress)*

Yank's Station in El Dorado County, California, was one of the stops for both the Pony Express and stagecoach lines. *(Library of Congress)*

ABOVE: "The Pony Rider," from the July 1860 issue of *Hutching's California Magazine*. When it launched, the Pony was a subject for newspapers and magazines from California to New York.

The Hastings building in Sacramento today. The Pony Express office on the corner is now part of a small Wells Fargo museum. *(Courtesy of the author)*

THE OVERLAND PONY EXPRESS.—[PHOTOGRAPHED BY SAVAGE, SALT LAKE CITY, FROM A PAINTING BY GEORGE M. OTTINGER.]

The Last Ride by George M. Ottinger has become an iconographic print, seeming to sum up the end of the Pony at the hands of the telegraph. But the history is far more complicated. *(Library of Congress)*

NOTICE.
—
BY ORDERS FROM THE EAST,

THE PONY EXPRESS

WILL be DISCONTINUED.

The Last Pony coming this way left At-chinson, Kansas, yesterday.

oc25-1t WELLS, FARGO & CO., Agents.

The Pony died an ignoble death in the hands of its competition: Wells Fargo took over the line after the bond scandal torpedoed Russell; its parent company was already well into the red.

"Buffalo Bill" Cody may not have ridden for the Pony, but he did more for its legend than anyone, even its founders. The Pony Express was a mainstay of his popular Wild West shows, and was often featured in posters and ads.

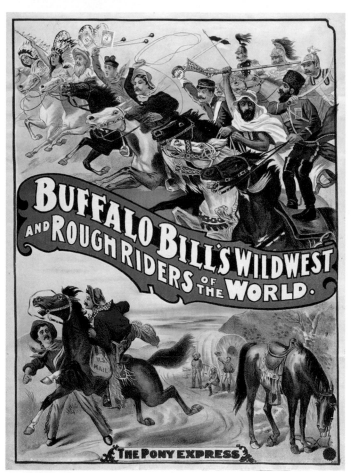

James Butler Hickok had a tangential relationship with the Pony, but "Wild Bill" played it up anyway.

Buffalo Bill Cody was legitimately a legend and a hero on the battlefield before the writer and impresario Ned Buntline made him famous.

Rider Charles Cliff (left) and Buffalo Bill at the dedication of a memorial to the Pony Express some fifty years later. *(New York Public Library)*

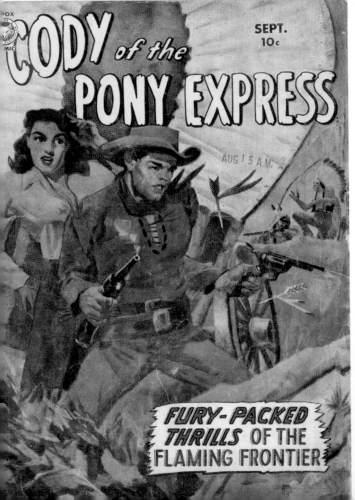

The Pony Express
was reborn in
fiction practically
the day after it died.
Occasionally there
was even a morsel
of truth in the tales.
TOP RIGHT: *(New York
Public Library);* TOP
LEFT: *(Courtesy of Peter
Hubbard)*

Western themes were popular in films during the 1950s and early '60s, and the Pony was along for the ride.

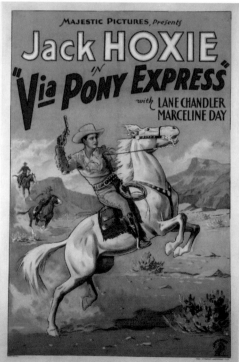

Today, the memory of the Pony Express is kept alive by enthusiasts and volunteers connected with the National Pony Express Association who stage "re-rides" every year; here local news people close in for a shot just before the ride takes off from Sacramento.
(Courtesy of the author)

A stamp from the 1940s on the eightieth anniversary of the service.

Horse and rider, caught in flight forever. The figure in Richard Bergen's sculpture is modeled after Jack Keetley, a rider on the section of the trail from Marysville to Big Sandy. The statue fills a square in Marysville, Kansas. *(Courtesy of the author)*

But Black had trouble finding any precedent that would allow Buchanan to march troops into a state just because people were talking about secession. He could protect public property, but that was it.

And if talk became action and the states seceded?

There were no legal precedents, no easy or even complicated answers based on the law as the United States had experienced it.

Buchanan tried working out his thoughts in a speech he would give in December. He was going to blame the North—hell, yeah, he was going to blame the North—for all the nullification and refusal to obey the law.

And he was going to urge the South to remain in the Union.

Because they would. It was logical. And it was just as logical to think, to know, that Lincoln and the Republicans would never, could never, use force to make them stay. The Republicans were a minority, and there was no law allowing them to keep the Union together; he'd had it researched.

UP IN NEW YORK, WILLIAM RUSSELL WENT BACK AND FORTH AMONG acquaintances, trying to raise the money he needed to stave off collapse. But the debt monster could not be satiated; not only was it difficult to find anyone willing to lend, but the bonds he had already used as collateral continued to sink in value.

Sell them all. Buy them back.

But then what?

His partners were already preparing for bankruptcy—Majors had assigned deeds of trust against several properties against debts he owed.

Friends who had helped with money in the past asked to be made whole, which was impossible. The country was on the verge of civil war. That was the real barrier—it made everything impossible. Bonds weren't worth the paper they were printed on. No one wanted to loan money against future promises; no one was confident in the future.

And yet the Pony was a success—the newspapers reported breathlessly the latest news. That part of the plan had worked.

It was just everything else that was going to hell.

DOWNHILL

The Sierra Nevada are part of a long row of mountains that range all the way down to Antarctica. The Sierra granite formed millions of years ago, around the time dinosaurs ruled the earth—it was Jurassic Park the world over, with herds of sauropods, the really huge plant eaters, ducking killer meat eaters like *Allosaurus* as they ate two hundred or more tons of food a day.

Uplifted by forces in the earth, the Sierra peaks ultimately reached some 14,505 feet in the United States. They were a little lower near Tahoe where the Pony crossed, roughly nine thousand at the highest. For the Pony riders, it was hard to find the exact peak along the trail. Yank's Station, Strawberry Station, Sugar Loaf House, Brockliss Bridge: they were all well up there, though the surrounding pines often blocked the view.

Yank's was a large inn, run by Lydia and Ephram "Yank" Clement, who'd bought it from George Douglas and Martin Smith. Douglas and Smith had built the station in 1851, during the height of the California Gold Rush. Yank and his wife had enough traffic to expand the building so that it totaled fourteen rooms across three stories. Their place was the center of a little hamlet that, besides a stable where the Pony's horses were kept, included a saloon, a blacksmith shop, and even a cooper's place.

Strawberry Station would have been the Pony's next stop. It allegedly earned its name not because of the fruit, but rather the habit of the owner—a certain Mr. Berry—to mix straw in with the hay he fed horses. (Hay is grown as forage or food for horses and cows; it has a higher nutritional value than straw, which has been shorn of the grain or seeds. The implication is that the owner was ripping off customers, so calling the place Strawberry Station wasn't a compliment.)

No such stories attached themselves to the next stop, Sugar Loaf—like pretty much every Sugarloaf in the country, named for a nearby mountain and its snow-covered head—or Brockliss Bridge. The bridge went across the American River, and while narrow and at the foot of a steep hill, provided easier access than the twisted paths below.

The county of El Dorado had paid for the bridge and charged a toll—but for the Pony, they cut a deal: one cent a month. Everyone in California wanted the mail to go through quickly and cheaply.

New roads were continually being cut through the Sierras, accommodating not only emigrants but also the silver that was coming out of Comstock, headed for Sacramento and San Francisco. There was a series of toll roads, a turnpike sponsored (but not properly funded) by the state legislature, and roads built by subscription. The road builders kept fighting fierce weather—snow mostly, but heavy spring rains as well as winter. They also had to deal with solid rock and steep grades. Traffic meant business, not only along the trail but down in Sacramento and San Francisco. Roads here meant traffic from all of the East, not just Tahoe or Salt Lake. The alternative route—through the southern deserts, from Santa Fe to Los Angeles—meant money for other people.

COMPARED WITH THE STOPS IN NEVADA AND UTAH, THE CALIFORNIA Pony and stagecoach stations were veritable palaces. Sportsman's Hall served as a home station, three stories high and with a stable that, at least by reputation, could accommodate as many as a thousand horses and mules. Warren "Sam" Hamilton had given the mochila here to Warren Upson on the very first ride, arriving from Sacramento in heavy rain only four hours and three minutes after setting out—a fantastic time for the sixtysome miles, even if he hadn't been riding uphill in the rain.

If you were riding west, you were going downhill—and you were riding toward gold, and ghosts, heading for a place called Hangtown.

PLACERVILLE

The official name, adopted by citizens in 1854 when they decided the third-largest city in the state of California deserved something a little more dignified, was Placerville.

The name came from placer mines—the term for mining in streambeds and open pits. While it's tempting to develop a fanciful English etymology along the lines of "this is the place to look for gold," the people who study word origins point out that "placer" was derived from the Spanish *placer*, which refers to the type of deposit that is mined: *alluvial* in Latin, a loose deposit washed or deposited by water. Gold found in placer mines has been eroded from its captive stone and grit by nature, leaving the nuggets on or near the surface. You pan for gold in a placer mine; the opposite is lode or hard rock mining, where you dig down into the earth and extract it from the rocks.

Sutter's Mill, the spot where gold was first discovered, was a short distance away from Placerville on the American River; soon after word spread of that discovery, ranchers dug up several thousand dollars' worth of gold from a dried-out bed that became the center of Dry Diggin's—an even earlier name for the town than Hangtown. (Dry Diggin's refers to how the area was mined: miners would dig up dry gravel and soil, then take it to the creek or a water source to be washed.)

Within a year, there were dozens and dozens of camps spread around the area. The city sprang up around, between, and among them—there were pit mines all around, including the main drag. Tents gave way to wooden structures, houses and stores.

Crime arrived before the law: in the winter of 1849, three men were accused of robbing and trying to kill one of the miners. A jury was convened; they were convicted, and then hanged. From there, the town took its most colorful and popular name: Hangtown.

—

THAT'S ONE VERSION. THERE ARE OTHERS.

Soon after the mining craze began, three friends visited a tent given over to drinking and gambling in the ramshackle settlement. They played for a while, until one of the men went bust. Not being a particularly good loser—and sure that his luck was about to turn—he and his companions decided a loan was order. There being no ATM handy, a gun was held to the saloon owner's head; in short order he turned over a bag of gold dust and the men played on.

The morning brought justice: the trio were run out of town by a majority of the camp.

Two of the gamblers decided to contest the banishment a few days later. They cornered some of the men who had kicked them out, and they whipped them for punishment. This didn't sit well with the rest of the town. The two were reapprehended, and this time given a more permanent sentence: they were hanged at the big oak tree near El Dorado Saloon, setting a precedent that would be repeated several times before more formal forms of justice arrived in the town.

FOR SHEER NUMBERS, THOUGH, THE STORY OF THE OWLS GANG CAN'T be beat. In this account, five gang members robbed a trading post but failed to make good their getaway. A jury was formed, and the sentence passed: thirty-nine lashes.

In the course of meting out the punishment, the vigilantes realized that three of the men were wanted for a nearby murder. The jury re-formed, and a verdict was rendered: the three were justly hanged, each by the neck.

The stories put the town's popular hanging tree at a slightly different location; it's not clear whether that means there were a lot of different hanging spots, or the tale simply moved from tree to tree. Nor will historians swear to any of the stories, not even the first. Whatever the exact details, vigilante justice was a fact of life in California, before and after statehood. The most famous of the organizations was the San

Francisco Committee of Vigilance, which was more powerful than the police or the government; they even chased William Tecumseh Sherman from his post as the state militia commander.

While the name Hangtown stuck to the growing burb, it does seem to have been an exaggeration; there are very few records of hangings after the first wave. Maybe they got the attention of potential thieves, for historians don't include it in the top places for necktie parties when making such lists. But ghosts seem to linger—even today, visitors to the town report strange goings on along Main Street: coins magically appearing, jukeboxes turning on by themselves, the scent of a lady's perfume drifting in the air . . . said to be wafting from a woman dressed entirely appropriately for the 1860s.

One story, a favorite of journalist and writer Linda Bottjer, concerns a dispute between two doctors who served the town around the time of the Pony. "Doc" Willis served the town from its tent days. He didn't have a degree, but by all accounts was a good doctor—when he was sober. Which wasn't often. By and by, a Dr. Hume showed up. Hume was a trained doctor, with a degree from Edinburgh, which he proudly displayed at his office.[11]

Some friends of Doc Willis stopped by Hume's practice for a consultation, which ended with them smashing his diploma. Hume didn't take that lightly, and in the end, he and Willis headed up to what is now Apple Hill to exchange their medical credentials—and fire at each other with pistols, as duels were not sanctioned within town limits.

Doc Hume proved the better shot—and his first official act as town doctor was to sign his former counterpart's death certificate.

Which may explain why many people report seeing an older man swaggering around the area with a whiskey bottle in his hand.[12]

But the most popular ghost sighting isn't actually a sighting at all—it's the sound of hoofbeats along the main drag, here and elsewhere on the trail nearby, at high noon, midnight, and all points in between.

SPIRITS OR NOT, PLACERVILLE THAT FALL OF 1860 WAS A BUSTLING CITY, with a telegraph as well as a sizable population. There was snow on the ground—it would measure three inches in a week's time, with much more to come—but that was nothing on this part of the route, at this time of the year. The Pony riders changed horses and rode on.[13] Sacramento, down the hill and across the plain, beckoned with a force even mightier than greed or justice:

The future.

A PLACE CALLED
TOMORROW

EL DORADO

The conquistador didn't *quite* understand: El Dorado, the gilded one, was a person, a god really, not a place.

But close enough: the important idea was gold, fortune, riches beyond measure. Enough to establish an empire.

More than enough reason to hack into the jungle and look for something that glitters.

The myth of *El Dorado*, a City of Gold somewhere in the hills and mountains of the New World, fired imaginations in the early sixteenth century and well beyond, first in Spain, then throughout the world. And if the *actual* City of Gold was never found, there were certainly plenty of gold deposits discovered in South America, more than enough to justify the financial expense of exploration and the spiritual expense of exploitation.

The history of hunting for gold in the United States was spotty until the California gold rush; immigrants' imaginations were fired by riches, for sure, but those riches were generally not found in rocks, and in many cases were more spiritual than material: Who can truly put a price on freedom, religious or otherwise?

The discovery of gold in California didn't change the American character, but it did tickle an important part. Not for nothing was the county where gold was first discovered in California called El Dorado. The part about curses that afflicted all who sought El Dorado never quite became as popular as the rest of the myth among Americans.

Nor were the actual hardships of those who lived in the camps ever as widely advertised as the riches.

The trail from Placerville down to Folsom Station and on toward Sacramento passed numerous mines, past, present, and future. Men dug the earth and moved soil, but really it was water that ruled. Washing shovelfuls of gravel in a creek a few feet away from where you dug was easy enough; truck hundreds of pounds of gravel a few hundred yards across a pair or three of hills to water and there had better be good reason. The early miners quickly realized it was easier to bring water to pay dirt than vice versa: wooden sluices ran up and down the hills on the slopes down to Sacramento, diverting water close to the spots where miners were digging.

With the easy gravel scraped away down to the bedrock, miners realized that more deposits of gravel could be mined below the upper layer of rock. Shovels and picks were slow and backbreaking; letting water do the work was far easier. Hydraulic mining, which put water to work, was erosion on steroids and at warp speed: fire-hose-like nozzles focused a stream of water rushing from a great height onto the earth, blowing away rock in minutes. Sluice boxes had to be constructed to grab and hold the rocks so they could be "processed."

Hard-rock mining, in this case digging out quartz containing gold, started a few years after the discovery at Sutter's Mill. Shafts were dug to intersect with veins in the rock, often from above and below, angling off a hillside. Rail tracks and lifts were laid to move the ore out of the mine. Sledgehammers broke the stone aboveground; loud machines powered by steam would break them down further so they could be washed and ground down by even louder machines, the gold pulverized from the rock holding it.

This was not an ecologically favorable process, not least of all because mercury was used in both placer and hard rock mining to make it easier to extract the gold from the rock holding it. Hills that a decade before had been covered with pines and populated by a food chain's worth of mammals were reduced to piles of rubble and thoroughly scrubbed rock.

Mining was hard work, above- and belowground. There were dangers all around, expected and unexpected. Finding a doctor to treat even a light infection could be difficult and expensive; even if you got treatment quickly, there was no guarantee you'd live. There were plenty of reasons to leave the minefields, and only one reason to stay: the possibility of striking it rich. But the longer one stayed, the less realistic that possibility became.

Gold fever had muted somewhat in the camps and hamlets that the Pony rider sprinted past on the last leg of his journey with the election messages. The fever was still there, but it was low grade. Fortunes could be made, or at least dreamed of, by mining, but the more reliable way to make a living was by serving the miners and the travelers who came over the mountains to the fertile valleys below. California, with nearly 380,000 people, was already larger than some states back east; it ranked twenty-sixth out of the forty-two states and territories included in the 1860 census. Its growth paled next to that of New York, where rapid industrialization and strife in Europe had helped increase the population by more than 800,000 in a decade. But California was on an upward curve. It had the highest percentage of "foreigners"—people who had not yet become citizens—in the country; the number of dwellings in the state had quadrupled, and there were fewer people in its households than anywhere else—an indication of youth as well as a lack of marriageable women (and men, perhaps) in the mining areas.

All these people created a huge demand for information and transportation—services that Russell, Majors, and Waddell could provide, through the Pony Express and their other companies. But the accelerating population also accelerated the future, which meant obsolescence for the Pony: something the riders were surely aware of, for they passed the engines of their demise as they rode down the slopes of the Sierra.

TELEGRAPH AND TRAIN

Riding out of Placerville, the rider passed near and at times under wires strung between the naked trunks of delimbed trees—telegraph poles, some of which had been planted only a few months before.

The telegraph itself had been born in the fevered, creative mind of Samuel B. Morse, an American painter who had developed his art and ideas on democracy in Europe as a young man. His skills with the brush made him excel as a portrait painter; his ideas about democracy led to works that celebrated democrats like Madison and the Marquis de Lafayette. He was working on a portrait of the latter in Washington in 1825 when a message arrived by horse messenger telling him his wife was sick but getting better; the next day a second message told him she had died. By the time he got home, she was already buried.

Another man might simply have sunk into grief; one with more stamina and the Calvinist bent that Morse shared might have thrown himself into work to escape it. Morse instead imagined a way for messages to move more quickly.

A demonstration of the wonders of electromagnetism a few years later showed him the way. In 1832, he patented his idea as a "recording telegraph," which translated bits of electromagnetic attraction into brief bursts of dots and dashes, a code that could be translated at either end into actual communication.

Morse had difficulties translating the idea into a commercial system. His initial idea either inspired others or was stolen by them—he thought the latter—and put to use in Great Britain on the Great Western Railroad before Morse could successfully exploit it. In the meantime, he developed a cheaper method, and by 1838 had a system that used one line and relays that conquered two problems at once: cost and distance.

He took his ideas to Congress, looking for funding for a telegraph system. He got Congress's usual response to anything brilliant that costs money: *Not today.*

Congress came around five years later. When an early attempt with underground wires didn't work out, Morse switched to poles. In 1844, he sent a telegraph from the Supreme Court chambers in Washington to a colleague in Baltimore exclaiming, "What hath God wrought!" and the world changed.

As obvious as the telegraph was, the path to commercial success proved far more twisted than the wires that created the magnetic impulses. Morse's life, invention, and companies entered a swirl of confrontations, legal and emotional, as he both tried to implement the telegraph and reap the financial rewards of doing so. But his personal trials aside, his idea thrived: telegraph lines were soon being erected all across the United States and the world.

By 1860, lines connected the major cities in the East, running out as far west as St. Joseph and St. Louis. By 1853—some sources say as early as 1849—San Francisco had a line from Point Lobos to Telegraph Hill to the center of the city, delivering news of arriving ships.[1] By the end of that year, a line connected San Francisco with Marysville, California, north on the Feather River, the major tributary of the Sacramento River.

Other lines were strung, some on trees, connecting California to Nevada. By the time of the presidential election of 1860, the Placerville Humboldt Company had connected Carson City and would soon reach Fort Churchill.

The ultimate goal was to stretch across the desert and Great Plains, connecting California with Missouri and from there the rest of the nation. Congress passed a bill authorizing the transcontinental route—the same one James Simpson had surveyed, and essentially the path the Pony Express took—in June 1860, awarding a contract to the only company that bid: Western Union, in the person of Hiram Sibley, an early Morse associate whose greatest genius was his ability to acquire and merge the various small companies operating local lines, consolidating finances and operations under the Morse system. Sibley created the Pacific Telegraph Company to construct the line out west; that firm and smaller California concerns were eventually merged with Western Union.

Electricity is faster than horses, and even though there were still a host of problems—lines could be cut by hostile forces, most especially those of nature, and initial transmission rates were fairly high—there was no doubt that telegraph was going to render the *express* portion of the Pony Express obsolete eventually. But the Pony had never been intended to last for very long. Even if there was a need for some messages—especially detailed ones, confidential transmissions, or financial notes—the Pony had been aimed at winning a regular mail contract for the parent stage service.

The future frowned on that as well, mostly in the person of Theodore Judah.

DONNER PASS AND THE TRAIN

Right around the time the Pony was recovering from the trouble with the Paiute bands around Pyramid Lake, a small band of engineers was climbing through the Sierra to Donner Pass. The head of the group was Theodore Judah, a civil engineer with a vision: the transcontinental railroad.

Judah had a rare quality for a civil engineer—rabid enthusiasm. And he was especially rabid when he talked about connecting the eastern and western ends of the United States with a railroad that ran to central California. Judah had already built a train line from Sacramento to Folsom, a twenty-three-mile route that brought travelers and goods from the foothills below the gold fields to the state capital, and from there to the world. But the line barely scratched his itch to connect the coasts.

There were two main barriers to his dream, at least if the connection was going to be made to Sacramento: money and a route across the Sierra Nevada. To solve the first, Judah had to figure out the second, and for a while it seemed as if getting through the mountains would be nearly impossible. While a man on a horse might be able to twist and turn his way up one grade and then another, a steam locomotive needed an easier grade and enough of a straightaway to build speed—

and then back off it. That did not describe the route the Pony Express and telegraph took, nor could such a route be mapped across most of the mountains, where double ridges meant uneconomical solutions.

Then in October 1860, scant weeks before the election, Judah heard about Donner Pass—not the tragedy, which was well known, but the fact that you could go through on a relatively straight line, climbing up and down only once. He inspected the area and saw immediately a straight line to the future. The train's path through the mountains was more complicated: there were four tunnels, miles of snow sheds, and a few walls to keep the earth from falling in on things. But the pass made it all possible.

All he needed was the money to build it.

THE LONELY LIFE OF A RIDER

Riding out of Louis Lepetit's station in Placerville, the Pony rider went down a steady grade, trotting past the largely naked hills to Pleasant Grove; another swap of the horse and he was off to Five Mile Station.

Sacramento was only forty-five miles from Placerville; the route took about four and a half hours. After the steep foothills, the ride from Pleasant Grove (today Folsom) to the city was relatively flat, bordering the American Fork. From July, the mail had often gone from Folsom to Sacramento by train, and vice versa, but today was not a day to chance delays because of train schedules, let alone breakdowns.[2]

William "Sam" Hamilton had ridden this stretch when the Pony service debuted in April, starting from the city at 2:15 in the morning. But the rider with the election message was Lucius Lodosky Hickok, who sat down and wrote his wife, Pruella, back in Wisconsin about his trip:

NORTH SAN JUAN NOV 18, 1860

My Dear Blessed wife I place my pen to paper once more to inform you how lonesome I am & of my health & other things in general first my health is good I am awful lonesome & grow so more every day. I want to see my family as bad as you can want to see me I know I wrote you on Oct 29 & sent you ten dollars & agreed to send you some more in 15 days but I have failed again but don't blame me for I could not get the bill of exchange in time. I will send it the fifth of Dec. I want you should write when you receive money from me every time for I have a receipt of the money & when you receive it I have to deliver it.

. . . I am still on the Pony Express yet & how long I shall stay there I don't know. I have had a pretty hard time of it through this Presidential Campaign.

. . . The Pony came through from St. Joseph on the Missouri river to Sacramento in six days & 16 hours & I rode 75 miles of it, 6 hours & 3 minutes. . . . I changed Ponies only 6 times.

What do you think of that?

We had Presidential news from the states on my trip . . .

Cal has gone for Lincoln. I voted for him.

You ought to see an election in Cal: the man that can drink the most liquor is the best fellow & then at night my god such a drunken set it is. Fighting, gambling & raving of all kinds.

I never want to see another in Cal nor don't believe I shall if I hold the mind.

I [am] now . . . home here in San Juan looking . . . to make money faster. At present [I] . . . go out with the Express twice a week; that takes me two days in all. The rest of the time I have to myself and it takes the rest of the week for me to get rested.

It is the hardest work that I ever done in my life. Think of me on every Thursday & Friday from the hours of six in the morning until the hours of 10 in the evening. Sometimes I have to wait for the return express. The longest I ever waited was 4 hours but it is seldom I have to wait any. . . .

Think of your husband riding a Pony at the rate of 12 miles an hour & on his back from 6 in the morning until 7 in the evening you bet it is hard work but I can make the most money at it yet but I am going to try to get into different business.[3]

Hickok, twenty-two, was extremely lonely; he was one of California's many recent transplants and hadn't had time to make many friends outside of work. He told his wife that he wanted to send for her soon. But that never have happened—according to the family, Lucius never returned, and in later years his wife altered the letter so that it appeared as if it had been sent right after Garfield's election twenty years later. By that time, Lucius had been dead some eight years.

CITY OF GOLD

Hickok sent his letter from North San Juan, one of the mining towns in the Sierra that had blossomed during the gold rush. He was living on a ranch about a mile from town, which was prosperous enough to have several brick buildings on its main street.

But it was a blip on the map compared with the city he rode to with the election news, Sacramento.

THE CITY WAS BORN FROM A SWINDLE. THE LAND WAS ORIGINALLY owned by John Sutter Jr. and his father, who had received it from Mexico thanks to John Sr.'s service against rebels in 1845. Gold had only just been discovered on John Sr.'s land farther north when Jr. arrived from Europe in 1848. Trained in a banking house, the twenty-two-year-old was appalled by the disorder at his father's ranch. Apparently not much of an organizer to begin with, Sr. found it impossible to keep any sort of help, good or bad, once news of the gold strike spread. Crops and cattle had been trampled by fortune hunters, and earlier debts threatened to send Sr. into bankruptcy, gold or no.

Jr. bought his father's property, which included the future Sacramento, along with fifteen hundred horses, fifty mules, six hundred cattle, and a schooner. A short time later, he began laying out a city at the intersection of the Sacramento and American Rivers. The rivers made travel inland from San Francisco relatively easy; the close proximity to the gold fields made for a natural nexus.

The city immediately boomed, with building lots that Sutter sold for $250 commanding a premium of two or three times that on resale almost immediately. But Sutter Jr. became ill just as things were taking off. Pressured to sell the land he still held, he eventually gave in at a bargain price to a group that included Sam Brannan, a Mormon merchant turned land speculator and quite a shark when it came to striking a deal. Brannan squeezed Jr. before finally agreeing to a price; Sutter signed the deal reluctantly, but never received a penny. He went south to Mexico, got better, returned, tried to collect his money, and got nowhere. Brannan, who became California's first millionaire, never did pay up, despite lawsuits and years of complaints by Jr.

In the first crush of the gold rush, Sacramento's most popular building material was canvas: tents sprang up everywhere. Gold coming down from the hills inflated the economy at a crazy pace: a man could earn $10 for a day's unskilled labor. But then he'd have to turn around and spend $16 for a barrel of flour and find someone to bake it for him.

Tent poles soon gave way to wooden planks and bricks. Thick foundations shored up two-story structures in the business area near the rivers. By 1860, Sacramento was the state capital, with all the accoutrements thereof: scores of hotels, a panoply of bars, and a colorful array of madams and their employees. (Most lived in the first ward, where official statistics claimed 28 percent of the female population was in the trade.[4]) More pedestrian—literally—were planked streets, which were served by over a dozen stage lines and more than twice that number of steamboats regularly docked at the riverfront—called the embarcadero. Chinatown extended along three blocks of I Street.

California was already a very competitive place, and a number of suitors—San Francisco, Oakland, San Jose—were trying to persuade the legislature to move the capital and its halo of prestige to their town. In 1860, Sacramento's city fathers pushed off the other bids by offering the state a large parcel of land on high ground over on Tenth and Twelfth Streets. The legislature subsequently approved a bill to build a capitol there for $500,000.

It ended up costing $2.6 million and took more than a decade to complete. No surprises there.

Nearly thirteen thousand and eight hundred people lived in Sacramento at the time of the election, making it the sixty-seventh-largest city in the country. That was a far cry from New York—population 813,669—and even well below San Francisco, which boasted nearly 57,000, making it the fifteenth-biggest in the country. But the city punched far above its weight when it came to innovation, and to financing that innovation: Sacramento was an early adopter of trains and the telegraph, and when Judah sought backing for the transcontinental railroad, he found it there.

SAYING SACRAMENTO WAS A PLACE OF CREATIVITY, WEALTH, AND RA-bid growth doesn't quite capture the scope of its soul, which included tenacity as well as invention. The best demonstration of what it was all about came the following year, when a flood devastated the downtown. A series of storms lasting forty-three days struck the entire state, ending a dry spell that stretched back years. Caught between the Sacramento and American Rivers, Sacramento was engulfed in ten feet of muddy water. On January 10, floodwaters rose a foot an hour, forcing the governor to commute to the capitol and his swearing-in ceremony by rowboat; he had to get in his house via a second-story window.

Houses floated away. Thousands of animals lost their lives. In a gesture toward the distant future and rock-concert benefits, musicians published sheet music dedicated to the city.

This was the second flood in the city in a little more than a decade; the first, though serious, was nothing compared with this.

Other cities might rebuild on high ground or on the other side of the river, giving up the battle with nature.

Sacramentans stayed in place, literally raising themselves up. The city fathers added eight feet or more to the downtown district, jacking up the buildings even while they kept doing business.

And they moved the river.

Not even God himself was going to prevent this city from meeting the future.

IN THE MOMENT OF THE MOMENT

The Pony's office was located in the B. F. Hastings Bank Building at 132 J Street, on the corner of Second Avenue. The building was one of the city's most important; besides the bank and the Pony Express, it housed the California Supreme Court, offices for the Alta Telegraph Company and the Sacramento Valley Railroad, and a Wells Fargo station.

William "Sam" Hamilton's arrival with the first mochila from the East on April 14 had been cause for a major celebration. According to the *Sacramento Bee*, a gunshot in the distance announced the Pony's approach at twenty-five past five that afternoon.[5] Church bells began to ring. An impromptu group of escorts joined the Pony somewhere between the city and Placerville; these thundered into view ahead of a tornado of dust. A brass band struck up a tune. Hamilton rode up with his horse and the mochila, dismounting with a flourish as he handed over the mail to the station keeper.

The arrival of the election news that November didn't rate a brass band. The letters for the local papers were quickly grabbed by the waiting correspondents; in the meantime, the packet of letters destined for San Francisco was separated from the local mail and handed off for the waiting steamer.

Given the momentous nature of the news the letters contained and the long journey they'd undertaken, their arrival was anticlimactic. But then most critical moments in history are like that. More attention is paid to artificial milestones and the symbols of change than the actual changes themselves.

And funny to say, it's most often those gestures, grand or even small, that we focus so much attention on.

Off in Illinois, Abraham Lincoln was working in the state capitol, reading letters from citizens around the country. They were filled with various forms of advice, encouragement, and complaints. One in particular struck him just as a portrait painter arrived to prepare his portrait for a gallery in Chicago.

"She complains of my ugliness," said Lincoln, holding out the letter. "It is allowed to be ugly in this world, but not as ugly as I am. She wishes me to put on false whiskers, to hide my horrible lantern face."

Lincoln asked the artist, G. P. A. Healy, if he might paint him with a beard. Healy declined. That day or perhaps a few later, Lincoln told his barber to put down the razor as he prepared to give him a shave.

Descriptions of a "wise-looking statesman" now tackling the handling of the nation's great problems followed as the whiskers grew in.[6]

REMAINS OF THE DAY

THIS JUST IN

On Thursday, November 15, the *Sacramento Daily Union* printed the story that had been delivered by the relay of Pony riders to Fort Churchill and its telegraph the day before. The closely set type hyperventilated with capital letters and exclamation points:

ARRIVAL OF THE PONY EXPRESS

⋆   ⋆   ⋆

Dates to November 7th, inclusive!
LINCOLN ELECTED PRESIDENT

⋆   ⋆   ⋆

Majority in New York 50,000!

⋆   ⋆   ⋆

Majority in Pennsylvania 50,000!

⋆   ⋆   ⋆

Majority in Massachusetts 70,000!

⋆   ⋆   ⋆

Majority in Ohio 30,000!

⋆   ⋆   ⋆

Majority in Maine, 25,000!

⋆   ⋆   ⋆

Majority in Vermont, 40,000!

⋆   ⋆   ⋆

Illinois, so far, 5,000!

*   *   *

OTHER NORTHERN STATES BY LARGELY INCREASED MAJORITIES!

*   *   *

All States South of Tennessee for Breckinridge!

*   *   *

VIRGINIA FOR BELL!

*   *   *

Fort Churchill, Nov. 14th—1:10 a.m.

The Pony Express, with dates from St. Louis to November 7th, has arrived.

St. Louis, Nov. 7th.—Lincoln is elected President.

New York city has given the fusion ticket twenty-eight thousand majority. The State has given about fifty thousand majority for Lincoln.

All six Union Congressmen elected the city.

Massachusetts, outside of Boston, as far as heard from, Lincoln has forty-five thousand majority.

The report continued with more specifics, rounded up from different states. By this time, the results from California didn't have to be repeated in the edition; they were already well known to the paper's readers. California was a Union state and went with Lincoln—though not by much. The Republican polled 38,733 votes, besting Douglas by less than a thousand. Breckinridge, the South's Democrat, trailed both men by only a few percentage points. John Bell, the antisecessionist former Whig running on the Constitutional Union Party line, finished a distant fourth.

The Pony's relay of the news in less than eight days was remarkable. But maybe more remarkable was the fact that it had taken the St. Louis correspondents less than a full day to gather the results from the major eastern states. Four years before, the *St. Louis Daily Missouri Republican*[1] had taken ten days to publish the election results from New York and other eastern states. Granted, they weren't particularly good sports about that election, in which their candidate, Frémont, lost—their first announcement of Buchanan as president was rather backhanded. But the 1856 election had been no less complicated and only a hair less critical.

SACRAMENTO WAS NOT THE FINAL STOP FOR ALL THE MAIL CARRIED BY the Pony, on that run or most others. Sacramento might have won the contest to be the state capital, but the largest city in the state, by far, was San Francisco, another hundred-plus miles away. Paddleboats plowing the winding Sacramento River connected the two cities; the record time in 1860 was a minute under five and a half hours, set some ten years before by the New York refugee *New World*. (She was an illegal refugee in every sense of the word—the ship and her captain had barely escaped the sheriff seeking to settle debts in New York harbor, sailing away all the way to San Francisco, where she had a long career carrying passengers and mail up and down the inland waters.)

Steamers usually took the mail back and forth; a Pony rider would board the ship, enjoy the ride, then gallop off to deliver the letters. Deliveries went as far as Oakland, on the far side of San Francisco; a rider would come off at Martinez, then ride up through the hills and down to the town. This was roughly a twenty-four-mile trip; riders would do it in under two hours, returning to catch another boat bound upriver to Sacramento.

DOOM

The end to William Russell's dream of a western empire and the Pony's part in it came suddenly a month and a half later, on Christmas Eve.

He'd known for weeks if not months that some end was inevitable, and yet it was still a shock. It came in the form of a US marshal, who knocked on the door shortly after a former aide to War Secretary Floyd had arrived to talk to him about the bonds—probably to warn him that the jig was up.

Russell was arrested and taken to Washington, suspected of having stolen hundreds of the thousands of dollars of bonds: $870,000 worth, to be exact.

After a few nights in jail, Russell's bail was reduced to a level his friends could afford. Released, he went back to New York to try to get his feet under him. In the meantime, Congress created a select committee to investigate not only the misuse of the bonds but the unauthorized acceptances. Russell appeared before the committee on January 11, 1861, and again on January 18, when he read a long statement into the record. The statement laid out the debts that the government owed the company and illustrated how the sums that it claimed he had purloined—over $2 million—were very much overstated. He argued that the company had been wronged, and that it was in a terrible position because the government had refused to pay its bills.

But he also admitted when questioned that he had accepted the bonds. Then again, since the committee had the receipt he'd given Bailey, it would have been difficult not to.

Memories in 1860 were apparently as poor as they are today, at least when questioned by congressional committees. What was different, however, was the speed with which the congressmen acted— the special committee issued a report lambasting Russell, Floyd, and Bailey on February 12. By then, Russell had been indicted, along with Bailey and Floyd, on four counts of conspiring to cheat, defraud, and impoverish the United States by stealing $870,000 in bonds from the Department of Interior. Russell was also indicted for larceny, receiving stolen property, and "abstraction"—a legal term for taking money that doesn't belong to you.

Russell potentially faced a long jail sentence. The trial would have been among the best attended in the city, even with the war on.

It never happened. Russell's lawyer filed a demurrer contesting the indictment, challenging it on the grounds that the bonds did not meet the statute's definition of "paper," regardless of what they were written on.

The judge agreed. All charges dismissed.

It was a technicality to beat all technicalities. Floyd's charges were dropped by the US attorney, who said he had no proof to make a case. Bailey disappeared; his charges, too, were eventually dropped.

HISTORIANS HAVE TENDED, WHEN TAKING UP THE ISSUE AT ALL, TO follow the Settles' judgment that Russell was telling the truth and pretty much the whole truth to the committee. While the Pony Express's most careful historians raise an eyebrow—or two—at some of the testimony, they present it at face value in their three books.

Maybe ours is a more cynical age, but the coincidence of Russell meeting Luke Lea on the train and his *happening* to know of a clerk who might have access to bonds seems like . . . ox dung. A cousin-in-law of the secretary of war just *happened* to work in a department where he has access to bonds but no actual authority over them?

The unexplained appearance of a former aide to the war secretary minutes before Russell's arrest—never fully explored by the committee—smacks of a cover-up, or at least an attempt. Such suspicions might be written off as the feverish workings of a twenty-first-century mind. But two other things happened that make it obvious we don't have the whole story:

- Russell was let off scot-free on a tenuous technicality; and
- his company was awarded part of the mail contract he had worked for months to get, albeit through Butterfield and Wells Fargo.

It's possible that in some way Russell, Majors & Waddell was considered too big to fail—that with a war looming the administration feared it might need all the freighting or stage capacity it could get. It's possible, too, that this was seen as the easiest way to get the contract over to Wells Fargo and Butterfield's Overland Mail, whose political connections presumably dwarfed even Russell's. Suspicious twenty-first-century minds don't have to work overtime to posit a conspiracy, which might include any of the following:

- Russell knew he couldn't pay off the acceptances and warned War Secretary Floyd, either directly or through an intermediary (Lea or someone else) that they would be presented.
- Floyd arranged for the bonds to be given, at least the first time.
- The bonds had been used in this way before.
- The charges were dismissed quickly to keep other people besides Russell from getting bruised.

None of that, though, is evident from the record.

The testimony before the committee states that there were no other acceptances issued by the War Department. That is hard to believe. Funding was an acute problem because of the way Congress did business on the budgets—and in fact was always a problem, stretching back to George Washington's time and the Revolution. But maybe Floyd, not credited for any innovation or thought of as a particularly sharp secretary of war, invented it.

There's no proof for any of this. The dismissal of the charges may have been a profound moment of legal jurisprudence. And the dismissal did not spare Russell from having to pay back what the government said he owed—their figures, not his.

AFTER THE CHARGES VAPORIZED, RUSSELL WENT BACK TO NEW YORK and wrote a long statement, trying to explain all that had happened; it was excerpted and commented on in the *New York Times* and picked up by papers across the country.[2]

He expressed regret for taking the second set of bonds, realizing that they did not belong to the Department of War.

> *There is no other transaction in the course of a long business life, in which I have had very large operations with a great variety of persons, upon which I cannot look with entire satisfactions.*
>
> *It was nevertheless a necessity brought on entirely by the failure of the Government to fulfill its engagements on the one hand, and its moral obligations on the other.*

I was dealing with a party exempt from prosecution and indifferent to the obligations of honor. Had my business been with one equal with myself, and alike amendable to law, none of the difficulties I have encountered would have occurred.[3]

In other words, two wrongs make a right. And it wasn't my fault.

By Russell's numbers, the government actually owed the company $161,548, when all was said and done.

It may very well have. But if so, it never paid up.

BUCHANAN'S SPEECH

President Buchanan delivered the message he'd been working on since the election on December 3. It was carefully considered and worded as forcefully as any he'd given, and as lame as a bit of statecraft could ever possibly be. With South Carolina in open rebellion and other Southern states heading for the exit, he claimed a president had no right to use force to back up his oath to preserve the Constitution.

He told Congress that they ought to hold a convention and fix the Constitution.

And if they didn't?

Well . . . Meh . . .

There's a reason we don't particularly remember Buchanan as an energetic and effective president, and that message is part of it. Even so, it was of a piece with the rest of his presidency.

CARRYING ON

Russell's arrest shocked the company, and the country. But the Pony kept riding.

On February 2, 1861, the Senate introduced a bill for the mail contract that Russell et al. had hoped to secure by starting the Express. The original terms were lower than he'd wanted: six-day mail service for $800,000 a year, delivered over a route to be determined ... which meant, in practice, either the Pony route or the southern Oxbow route favored by Overland—Butterfield et al.

There wasn't really a choice. On the same day that the bill was introduced, Texas representatives voted to leave the Union. The southern route was cut.

Russell had been talking with William B. Dinsmore, trying to reach some sort of agreement that would keep his company afloat. Dinsmore was president of Overland; he was also head of Adams Express—another transport company along the lines of American Express and Wells Fargo, which had worked out what was in effect a noncompete agreement with American Express allowing it to essentially control transport in the South.[4] The two men apparently came to an agreement and communicated it to their respective congressional contacts, because the Post Route Bill that ended up being approved moved the mail route to the central route—the one used by the Pony—provided $1 million per year for six-day delivery from Missouri to Placerville, and directed that the Pony Express would continue to run until the completion of the transcontinental telegraph.

What the bill passed March 2 did *not* do was award any money directly to Russell, Majors & Waddell. Even if the company had been in better financial shape, the cloud hanging over Russell would have nixed any possibility of a federal contract.

Exactly two weeks later, Russell and Dinsmore signed a contract agreeing that the mail would be routed over the Pony's line, with the responsibilities divided between their respective companies. Central Overland California & Pikes Peak Express would take the mail from Missouri to Salt Lake City; Overland would take it from Salt Lake to Placerville.[5]

The contract divided the US Post Office money roughly in half—$530,000 for Overland, $470,000 for Russell and his partners. But it also called for Russell, Majors, and Waddell to turn over 30 percent of their revenue from passenger and express service. Overland would appoint someone to oversee the entire line's operation, but

Russell et al. would share the costs. If things went sour, Dinsmore's company could take over the entire operation—from the stages to the ponies to every piece of rope—and charge Russell and partners $100,000 for the privilege.

It was the best contract he could manage, Russell told his partners in a private letter. If anything, they'd come out ahead of where they could have rightfully expected.

The contract was to go into effect July 1. Until that time, Wells Fargo was appointed "agent" for the Pony Express—the only overt mention of the company by Russell, even though its connections behind the scenes would have been visible to all the principals. Wells Fargo immediately began advertising the service, cutting the rate for delivering letters from $5 to $2, probably in an attempt to attract more business.

Wells Fargo's takeover of the Pony came with certain conditions clearly meant to cut losses. For one, the western terminus was moved to Placerville, lopping off roughly a rider's worth of expenses. The argument to do so was easy—stages could carry the mail in nearly the same amount of time. That argument could have been made at the start—but then there would have been little need for a Pony office in Sacramento, and none of the attendant publicity, which was a big part of the idea in the first place.

More important was the agreement put a stop-loss on the line: it would end as soon as the telegraph was completed from the East. It was a natural end in a way, since it was easy to make the argument that messages that had to be delivered quickly could go by telegraph.

Why keep the service going at all, when it was a clear money loser, and the number of messages that were being delivered the entire distance was rather small?

The contracts are silent, but the approaching war, or at least anxiety over its possibility, seems the likely answer. While no one knew how things would play out, it was clear enough that there would be a real rupture in the country. Communication between California and the eastern states was critical, and Washington would want to keep open a service like the Pony that had proved reliable despite Indian attacks and snowstorms.

A FEW HISTORIANS HAVE DEBATED THE EXACT ROLE OF WELLS FARGO in the last days of the Pony Express, with some arguing that it never had anything to do with the Pony. Waddell Smith, the great-grandson of William B. Waddell and an important historian and booster of the service's memory, wrote a pamphlet in 1966 attempting to completely divorce Wells Fargo from the enterprise. In Smith's view, Wells Fargo acted only as an agent of Russell, Majors & Waddell. But his account skimps on the obvious business relationships between the parties. Some of this may have been a reaction to claims by Wells Fargo that overstated the company's role in the Pony Express, which Smith and others undoubtedly saw as an instance of stolen valor. But just as it's clear that Russell, Majors, and Waddell succeeded in the herculean task of establishing and running the Pony, it's also clear that Wells Fargo and its related firms ended up with the mail route and the remains of the service, fairly or not. The company's strategy of working with alliances and semisubsidiaries—made possible by its deep pockets and started before Russell even thought of the Pony—was of a piece with its takeover.

The Pony was a David and Goliath story. In this case, though, Goliath won.[6]

CENTRAL OVERLAND CALIFORNIA & PIKES PEAK EXPRESS COMPANY signed a contract that March with Ben Holladay, a merchant and entrepreneur operating freight and stage transport in Utah. Holladay, who knew Majors well, had furnished credit to the company, supplying feed and stables as well as cash. The contract promised Holladay some $30,000 a year as payment for what he had advanced. But that was a small sum compared to what he was owed—$200,000. The more important aspect of the agreement was unstated—Holladay now had an important role in the company's future.

"BETTER ANGELS"

The Pony had one last shining moment, delivering the text of Lincoln's inaugural address, which he gave March 4, 1861; it was telegraphed west and then delivered overland by the Pony, promptly reported by all the newspapers along the route.

After saying that the Fugitive Slave Act remained in effect and would be enforced, Lincoln then said plainly that a minority—the South—could not overrule the majority, that slavery could not be extended to the North against the majority opinion.

Further, he said, there was no right to secede:

> Plainly the central idea of secession is the essence of anarchy. A majority held in restraint by constitutional checks and limitations, and always changing easily with deliberate changes of popular opinions and sentiments, is the only true sovereign of a free people. Whoever rejects it does of necessity fly to anarchy or to despotism. Unanimity is impossible. The rule of a minority, as a permanent arrangement, is wholly inadmissible; so that, rejecting the majority principle, anarchy or despotism in some form is all that is left.[7]

He suggested that a constitutional convention be held to settle the slavery issue; that horse had already galloped out of the barn. Nonetheless, he soldiered on, urging prudence rather than war.

> My countrymen, one and all, think calmly and well upon this whole subject. Nothing valuable can be lost by taking time. If there be an object to hurry any of you in hot haste to a step which you would never take deliberately, that object will be frustrated by taking time; but no good object can be frustrated by it. Such of you as are now dissatisfied still have the old Constitution unimpaired, and, on the sensitive point, the laws of your own framing under it; while the new Administration will have no immediate power, if it would, to change either. If it were admitted that you who are dissatisfied hold the right side in the dispute, there still is no single

good reason for precipitate action. Intelligence, patriotism, Christianity,
and a firm reliance on Him who has never yet forsaken this favored land
are still competent to adjust in the best way all our present difficulty.

In your hands, my dissatisfied fellow-countrymen, and not in mine,
is the momentous issue of civil war. The Government will not assail
you. You can have no conflict without being yourselves the aggressors.
You have no oath registered in heaven to destroy the Government, while
I shall have the most solemn one to "preserve, protect, and defend it."

Go ahead and secede, he was saying, and he would have no other
choice but to preserve the Union by force.

RUSSELL LEFT HIS WASHINGTON OFFICE SOON AFTER SIGNING THE CON-
tract with Dinsmore and went to New York; from there he headed
back to Missouri to meet with his partners and settle affairs. He
stopped in Missouri briefly, then continued on to Denver, where
he presided over a meeting of the board of directors for the Central
Overland California & Pikes Peak Express Company for the last time.
Majors and Waddell had already settled on a replacement as president: Bela M. Hughes, Ben Holladay's cousin and a St. Joe's banker.

Hughes, along with Wells Fargo and the Overland Stage, would
run the Pony until it closed.

MIRACULOUSLY, THE FINANCIAL TURMOIL IN THE CORPORATE OFFICES
did not noticeably affect the Pony's deliveries. Pony riders kept delivering the mail, despite Indian attacks, heavy weather, and probably
questions about whether they would be paid or not.

The crews working to erect the telegraph lines kept at it. Sioux
warriors cut part of the line that summer; they took some of the wire
and wore it as bracelets. Shortly after, they got sick—and when the
illness was blamed on the spirit of the wire, the attacks on it stopped.

Confederate forces took Lexington, Missouri, in September; Frémont,
commanding some thirty-eight thousand troops, reasserted control a
few days later, marching into the area and forcing a retreat. For the rest

of the war, Missouri would remain uneasily in Northern control, subject to guerrilla attacks but never successfully wrested from the North.

On October 24, 1861, the final telegraph connection between east and west was made at Salt Lake City. As per the contract, the Pony Express service was terminated. The *Sacramento Bee* ran its obituary:

> *Our little friend, the Pony, is to run no more. . . . Farewell and forever, thou staunch, wilderness-overcoming, swift-footed messenger. For the good thou has done we praise thee; and having run thy race, and accomplished all that was hoped for and expected, we can part with thy services without regret, because, and only because, in the progress of the age, in the advance of science and by the enterprise of capital, thou hast been superseded by a more subtle, active, but no more faithful, public service . . . Rest, then, in peace; for you have run thy race . . .*[8]

Some one hundred years later, Waddell F. Smith, the grandson of one of the founders, quoted from a notice that appeared in the October 26, 1861, edition of the *Sacramento Union*, summing up the service's achievements:

> *Through approximately eighteen months of variable weather, Indian disturbances, and almost insurmountable difficulties, the Express had faithfully discharged its responsibilities in such a manner as to win unstinted, unanimous praise. During that time 308 runs were made, covering a distance of 616,000 miles. On those runs, 34,753 letters were carried, with the loss of only one mochila. Of the total, 23,356 letters originated in California and 11,397 in the East. Estimated receipts were $91,404.00, of which the West supplied about two-thirds, or $60,844.*[9]

FAME IF NOT FORTUNE

The parent company struggled on, continuing to deliver the mail under the March 1861 contract. But it was deeply in debt, and in March

1862 Ben Holladay formally took over the entire operation. Two years later, he won a four-year mail contract; after expanding, he sold out to Wells Fargo in 1866. By then the Pony's riders had gone on to other things, some working for Wells Fargo, most either finding another line of work or joining the army.

But the Pony Express wasn't dead, at least not in spirit. After the war and a few years exiled from popular memory, it came roaring back, bigger than it ever was.

Interest in the West—an exotic place for most Americans on or near the eastern seaboard—met the boom in magazines and inexpensive novels after the Civil War. It was a perfect and profitable marriage. Ned Buntline and a score of similar writers traveled through the West, finding men who were already local heroes, enhancing their stories, and publishing them for a quick buck and massive public consumption.

The subjects had varied opinions of the process. Buntline went in search of Wild Bill Hickok, only to meet with something bordering on derision; the writer turned instead to Bill Cody—or so the legend goes.

Nonfiction tales—or at least *supposedly* nonfiction tales—were often followed by novels in which pretty much anything went. In Cody's case—the most extreme—a total of 557 novels by twenty authors have been counted; the king of Buffalo Bill fiction wasn't Buntline but rather Colonel Prentiss Ingraham, who was Buffalo Bill's own ghostwriter and is credited with more than 200 of them.[10]

Buffalo Bill gets a lot of credit for advertising the Pony Express, and he deserves it. Not only did he include vignettes in his Western shows, he recruited riders and others who had worked for the service and put them onstage with him. He even rescued Alexander Majors from obscurity, retrieving him from Denver, enlisting Ingraham to "help" write his autobiography, and paying Rand McNally to publish the book a year before Majors turned eighty.

Generous though he was, Cody would not have done any of this if the Pony had not already been held in high regard and was at least *somewhat* famous, if not quite at the level that it would be as Cody's shows gathered strength. The words *Pony Express* were synonymous not only with speed, but with adventure and rugged individualism— man against the elements and all that. Cody enhanced the legend, but he didn't invent it.

The stories riders told, both onstage and off, were recorded and locked into the nation's memory.

Which was not a problem until historians decided the Pony Express was a worthy topic for study. They naturally turned to the stories riders had told. The only problem was that many stories were easily shown to be inaccurate, or at least difficult to prove. What were originally seen as telling details of authenticity on closer inspection turned out to be sinkholes of error that put everything in doubt.

Cody is exhibit A, but there are plenty of other examples. Pony Bob—Bob Haslam—was part of Cody's Wild West Show, where among other things he spoke about his "role" in the Pyramid Indian War. He also told that story to Majors—or more accurately to the man who ghostwrote Majors's book, where it was included.

Neither are exactly marks indicating accuracy, but even putting that aside there are problems—like what to make of his claim that the ride on which he found the stations under attack took place eight months after the start of the Pony Express. That timeline puts them in the dead of winter, long after the war.

And when he talks of having a Spencer rifle—something many later writers repeated—does that make the entire story unbelievable?

There was a Pony Express, there was a Pyramid Indian War, there was a Bob Haslam—but did they intersect the way he says they did?

Most of the Pony's records have been lost over time, so it's difficult to find independent, documentary proof that Pony Bob even worked for the service, let alone in that area and at that time.

And no Robert Haslam appears anywhere on the census rolls from the Utah Territory.

But . . . there was a Robert *Hashlam* who was recorded by a census taker as living in Virginia City on August 26 when the taker did the survey. Hashlam is not only the right age—nineteen—for a rider, but also gave his occupation as Pony Express rider.[11]

Did the census taker get the name wrong? It's a reasonable guess, as anyone who's worked with the records can attest.

So probably he was a rider, in the right place and time. But did he take the ride he described over and over again?

There appear to be no newspaper accounts from that period describing it specifically. But there is a report in the *Sacramento Union* saying that two riders brought news of the burning of the station to the authorities.

Again, it's not proof, but it's at least suggestive. That's more than historians can say about a lot of other tales.[12]

Take another famous Pony rider: Uncle Nick, a.k.a. the White Indian, legal name Elijah Nicholas Wilson.

Uncle Nick was a bishop for the Mormon church, and while he had his troubles with some of the authorities over his practices—he liked tobacco; they didn't—he's generally regarded as an accurate source of tales from his youth, including the Pony Express. But those tales have plenty of discrepancies. The names of some of the people he connects with the Pony Express—Peter Neece, for example—are placed at the wrong stations. Some of the station names are slightly off or perhaps misplaced. And for what it's worth, he doesn't appear in the census, at least not under a name easily connected to his.

The discrepancies can be explained in many ways. Most obvious: he wrote his memoir long after the fact—which can be said for most if not all the first-person accounts we have of the service. In many cases, including Uncle Nick's, helpers, ghostwriters, and editors may have been responsible for inserting errors by interpreting or misinterpreting the original words or descriptions. Trying to put tangled memories into a proper timeline, taking the liberty to discuss weapons that weren't specifically mentioned, describing the general layout of stations rather than the specifics . . . there are plenty of ways to get things wrong.

Historians being historians, they are very careful in questioning his story. Here, for example, is a small piece of what Richard E. Fike and John W. Headley wrote in 1979 when questioning some of Uncle Nick's stories (it is included in a National Parks publication):

> Wilson states that as he lay in a small wash he raised his head a little and looked off towards the desert. Callao is in the desert, Six-Mile is up on the bench. . . . Laying in a wash at Six-Mile one can look toward the desert, but while lying in a wash at Willow Creek, by raising one's head a little, one probably cannot see more than ten feet. Later Wilson states "I saw a light shining between the logs in the back part of the house." The 1868 photograph from which Figure 28 was produced shows the Willow Springs Pony Express Station and the Wells Fargo and Company Stage building to be constructed of adobe, not logs. Cadastral plats made by the General Land Office show the Willow Springs stable across the road from the Kearney Ranch Hotel. If this skirmish happened at Willow Springs (Callao), why didn't these men go across the road and get help from Kearney or why didn't Wilson even mention Kearney? . . .
>
> The evidence presented here is not conclusive. Hopefully future investigations will end the controversy. . . .
>
> This paper has not been written to destroy any legends, but rather to present new facts and ask new questions which deal with the Pony Express Stations throughout the present State of Utah. The great epoch of the Pony Express is now over a hundred years old and unless every remaining thread of information is brought to light for other researchers, the full and true story may never be told.[13]

Unverifiable boasts are rampant in the oral tales—it seems like no rider ever spoke about his experience without claiming he rode the longest stretch or did it in the quickest time. (Length and endurance seem to be favored over speed as achievements.) But there's something about the Pony that pushed self-stroking into overdrive.

BRONCO CHARLIE AND OTHER LIARS OF THE PURPLE SAGE

In the annals of the Pony Express, the heroics of one man stand out.

Strike that—the heroics of one *boy* stand out. For Bronco Charlie (name at birth: Julius Mortimer Miller) started riding for the Pony when he was "eleven goin' on twelve."[14]

He was in Sacramento with his father soon after the service started, when what did he see coming down the street but a riderless horse with a bloodstained saddle. With the rider gone, apparently killed by Indians, Charlie volunteered to take the dead man's place. From then until the end of the service he rode with the best of them. He took the oath and received a Bible and a pistol in return. He knew the first man to ride very well; he had a friend—Billy Tate—who was killed by twelve Paiute Indians in an ambush after managing to kill seven.

He knew Bill Cody, too, riding in his show three seasons. He shook Abe Lincoln's hand in St. Joe. Bronco—he preferred to spell it Broncho—knew Sam Houston, Davy Crockett, Wild Bill. He'd been standing near Majors watching when the golden spike was hammered into place on the transcontinental railroad. He'd met Jesse James and kind of liked the fella. He'd killed at least one white guy, and a lot more Indians.

In later life, he found God at the Salvation Army and discovered the secret of life in a bottle: a shot of whiskey neat once a day kept him young.

Bronco Charlie became famous for his exploits and was regularly featured in shows and performances around the country. He was handy with a bullwhip, even into his old age—he could snatch a match from your mouth with it if you let him. When he died on January 15, 1955, at the age of 105, the newspapers declared that the last Pony Express man had passed on to the great trail in the sky.

They were right about that.

Bronco Charlie *was* a remarkable man, but not because he'd ridden for the Pony Express at age eleven—or any age. He was a remarkable tale teller, able to hold an audience rapt with a strong, clear voice and a master actor's sense of drama and pacing. He looked the part of a cowboy and had enough bona fides—he *was* really good with that bullwhip—to convince any doubter.

As long as they didn't know much about the Pony Express, that is.

Miller's story was debunked even during his lifetime by historians, people in Sacramento, and numerous writers, acquaintances, and folks who'd just read a book or two about the service. He would have been too young to have been hired, especially in Sacramento. A Pony Express rider being shot out of the saddle in the state capital—that would have made every newspaper in town, if not the entire state.

Bronco Charlie was the last man to steal the valor of Pony Express riders, but he was hardly alone. With the Pony Express becoming so well known and the exploits of its riders—real and imagined—more famous, men emerged from years of obscurity to claim a little piece of delayed stardom. Newspapers wrote stories about them; drinks were bought, parades were held.

Many deserved the accolades. Others didn't. But separating the two is extremely difficult, especially since most of the stories that riders told or have survived are far less detailed than Charlie's, and therefore harder to check out.

In fairness, it's often forgotten that there were several *other* express services, serving smaller routes overall but still presenting the same challenges for the riders. There was a fair bit of turnover in the desert portion of the Pony's route, and overall during winter. And there seem to have been a lot of substitute riders—despite what some histories say, it's clear from the testimony of legitimate riders that their relays were sometimes absent or even afraid to take the mochila.

Someone might have ridden for the "express," and not meant the Pony; someone might have ridden occasionally for the Pony, or one of its side shoots, and still considered himself a Pony man.

At least a few of the stolen glory stories tell about things that did happen; they just happened to other people. Or they happened to the person telling them; they just didn't happen while they were riding on the Pony Express.

All of this probably matters more to historians who are trying to be precise than to "civilians" who simply want to enjoy the tales. For a lot of us, "close enough" works for things other than grenades. On the other hand, the truth is the truth, and it's hard to really understand something if what you know is clogged up with things that aren't true.

Wherever you land on the problem of historical accuracy, nothing the liars of the purple sage—or their critics—said should take away the very real accomplishments of the Pony, its riders, and its owners.

END DAYS

By the time Overland Mail shut down the Pony Express, the Civil War had begun in earnest. A number of employees, riders especially, joined the army, a few as scouts, most as regular soldiers. They suffered a variety of fates, like everyone else in the country's most terrible war. When the conflict ended, they came home and resumed mostly quiet lives.

The exceptions are the ones we remember; Buffalo Bill Cody most of all. He was a teamster during the war, a private. Three years after the war ended, he rejoined the army as a scout. His exploits were real enough for him to earn a Medal of Honor; his fame warranted the attention of Ned Buntline, whose stories made Cody a national star. Cody took it from there, becoming an international sensation; his Wild West extravaganzas helped shape our perception not just of the West but also of the country, its development, and its essential values.

Wild Bill Hickok worked for the Union as a wagon master before being discharged in 1862; soon after he became a scout and maybe a spy. A tussle over a watch and unpaid gambling debts led to a shootout with Davis Tutt, a fellow gambler and rival beau, in Springfield, Missouri. The two men faced off in the street at a good distance and proceeded to draw on each other; Tutt missed, Hickok didn't.

Brought up on manslaughter charges, Hickok was acquitted, with a little help from the judge, who strongly implied that was the proper verdict. The gunfight, along with the earlier shooting at Rock Creek, became a sturdy part of Hickok's reputation, which grew exponentially when Colonel George Ward Nichols wrote about him in *Harper's New Monthly Magazine.*

Nichols's story shaded out the more despicable sides of Wild Bill's character and amped up the legendary, exaggerating these to the point that even Hickok was embarrassed. No matter: he racked up enough real-life, genuine achievements as marshal, scout, and sheriff over the next few years to outshine even the fiction Nichols had invented. After a short stint with Cody on the stage, Wild Bill went back to what he did best—gambling. It cost him his life: he was in Deadwood, South Dakota, on August 1, 1876, playing cards when a fellow gambler named Jack McCall walked up behind him and put a bullet through his head. It took two juries to convict McCall, but only a few minutes to hang him; they buried him with the noose around his neck.

The Pony Express superintendents had been chosen for their entrepreneurship and organizing abilities, and they continued to put those to good use after the end of the Pony. Bolivar Roberts moved to Salt Lake City and married; during the Indian wars that followed the Civil War he organized a company of scouts. He was a partner in a merchant firm, did contracting for the Central Pacific Railroad, and eventually established a wholesale and retail pharmacy with W. A. Nelden in Salt Lake City; collectors still prize their bottles.

Ben Ficklin joined the Confederate army and spent part of the war in England arranging for supplies. Back home in the South, he was sent to Washington to see if he could discuss what might happen to the rebel states after Lee's surrender; while there, Lincoln was assassinated. Ficklin was arrested, but eventually cleared of any connection to the conspiracy to assassinate the president.

After the war, he started a stagecoach business connecting Fort Smith, Arkansas, to California. A town grew up around the company headquarters; when he passed away in 1871, the townspeople named it Ben Ficklin.

Not far from Fort Concho in west-central Texas, it was an impressive city for a number of years; in 1875 it became the county seat of

Tom Green County. A flood in 1882 destroyed most of the town; the government moved to nearby San Angelo, where detractors claimed the saloons and houses of ill repute made a more congenial atmosphere for politicians.

Jack Slade didn't make out as well.

Slade moved to Virginia City in 1863, working as a freighter. He was respected well enough—or maybe just feared—to be named a member of the Vigilante Committee seeking to deal with local miscreants. Unfortunately, Slade's binary nature—polite and generous when sober, unreasonable polecat when drunk—had only gotten worse since the days of the Pony, and after rounding up the most serious disturbers of the peace, the committee was forced to look inside their own house.

What they saw wasn't pretty. Following one spree too many, the sheriff attempted to arrest Slade. Slade forced his way out of jail at gunpoint; he persuaded a judge not to prosecute him with the aid of a derringer pressed against His Honor's head.

Soon after, Slade was grabbed in the street, taken to corral, and hung high by popular demand. His wife, Maria Virginia, collected his body; planning to bury him back in Carlyle, Illinois, where he had been born, she made it only as far as Salt Lake City, Utah, where Jack now rests in plot B, block 4 of the Salt Lake Cemetery.

IN APRIL 1861, CHARLES BECKER STOPPED AT THREE CROSSINGS IN WYOming just after dawn. No one seemed to be waiting; worse, there wasn't a horse in sight. He rode off to the next stop, and after sending the mochila on, went back with a few other men to find out what had become of the keeper. They found him dead and scalped, the station ransacked.[15]

That event aside, Becker appreciated solitude riding the North Platte route. He went out to California, became a trader, then did some mining in Idaho. He was successful at one or the other or maybe both, doing well enough to put a stake down on a ranch in eastern Oregon. Invited to join President Warren G. Harding when he dedicated the Oregon Trail Highway in Blue Mountain, the pair struck up enough of a friendship for Harding to invite him on a trip to Alaska.

Thanks, but no thanks, said Becker, who by then was in his late eighties. *I have to go stack my hay.*

Becker passed away in 1925, ninety years old—some say ninety-one—still sharp by all accounts. And while he wasn't famous in the way that Bill Cody or Wild Bill were, there were those in town who remembered him—seventy-five years later, attendants still regularly found whiskey bottles lovingly placed atop his grave, an age-old tribute to the dead.

THE SMALL PACK OF MAIL STOLEN DURING THE PYRAMID LAKE WAR turned up in 1862. One of the surviving letters bears a stamp stating that it left San Francisco on July 24; a handwritten note across the envelope adds that it had been stolen by Indians in 1860.

How had they stolen it? No one now seems to have a definitive answer. Dead men tell no tales, nor does stolen mail.

It was the only pack of mail ever lost by the service.

THE BIG THREE

The collapse of their firm effectively ended William Waddell's career as an investor; he retreated to his Lexington, Missouri, home, deeding his home to his son to avoid losing it to creditors who might pursue him. The home and farm were raided several times during the war, and William lost a son when he was killed defending a slave. The family remained active Baptists, and the property passed eventually to the Lexington Baptist College, an all-women's school.

Waddell died on April Fool's Day, 1872, and is buried in Lexington.

Waddell was of Scotch descent, and descriptions of him tend toward the stereotype of a flinty Scotchman. Historians have tended to follow the Settles in describing him as a solid and calculating businessman; while this may be true, he certainly took chances when he thought he might profit—otherwise he never would have been involved in the enterprise to begin with. And while eventually they fell out, something about Russell and his optimism must have attracted him to form a partnership well before the Pony.

ALEXANDER MAJORS KEPT DOING WHAT HE DID BEST—FREIGHTING. HE hauled goods to the territories during the Civil War years, then moved to Utah in 1867. There he sold ties and telegraph poles to the railroad, looked for silver in the hills, and had a number of small enterprises until he wound up in Denver in the late 1880s. Somehow, he came to the attention of Buffalo Bill Cody.

Majors's book, *Seventy Years on the Frontier*, is a classic account not only of the Pony Express, but also of freighting and the Old West in general.

His life buoyed by Cody, Majors moved to Chicago, where he passed away on January 14, 1900.

DESPITE THE RUINOUS HIT TO HIS REPUTATION, RUSSELL REMAINED ACtive in the West for several years. His son John W. Russell remained secretary of Central Overland, but Russell himself was looking into other ventures. A few months after resigning as president of the company, he organized the Colorado and Pacific Wagon, Telegraph, and Railroad Company; soon after he formed the Clear Creek and Hot Sulphur Springs Wagon Road Company. The firms were to serve the Denver area, but his predictions for the area's progress proved too optimistic.

Back in New York, he tried his hand at brokerage. That didn't work well either.

In 1868, he applied for bankruptcy. The main creditor was the US government, which wanted payment on the $870,000 acceptances it held as collateral for the Indian bonds. Then there was another $467,909 worth of debt owed to several banks that held the war secretary's acceptances, which the feds would not pay. Throw in the rest of his debt, and Russell was nearly $2.5 million in the red.

He moved over to Broadway and eventually sold quack medicine to make ends meet. In 1872, he went back to Missouri and passed away at John Russell's home on September 10, 1872.

FUTURES PAST AND PRESENT

Theodore Judah returned to Sacramento after looking over the Donner Pass; over the next year and a half he would complete detailed surveys of the mountains and arrange for partners—who in the end would push him out. But it was Judah's plan for the transcontinental railroad that was essentially adopted by not only the Central Pacific Railroad but the federal government, whose financial backing for the project was critical for its completion.

The project was still years off when the war started, which Russell certainly would have understood from his dealings in Washington. Nonetheless, he and his partners understood the ultimate implications; this was clear not only from the inaugural Pony ride—which used both—but also from the way they negotiated their contract in St. Joe. This wasn't necessarily bad: had things gone well, not only for them but for the railroad and the country, they would have been sitting on a prime piece of real estate next to the best connection between California and Missouri. It would have been like owning the area around Grand Central Terminal in New York, or Union Station in Chicago, and arguably better, since there would be no competing lines west. And in the meantime, their mail contract would have provided the underpinnings for a stage network in the area served by the train. Transport would still be needed off the main line, and surely it would have grown from the network the Pony was supposed to have helped them build.

The Pony Express was unique, but it was not alone. There had been a myriad of expresses since the founding of the republic, plenty of them out west. Some of these services were highly reliable; some weren't. Almost none of the small ones lasted long. The work was either too intense or too irregular or both for an individual. The answer was consolidation and diversification. And no transportation company in California—no company in America, really—did that as well as the firm that ultimately was Russell, Majors & Waddell's main competition out west, Wells Fargo.

Wells Fargo, and the companies directly associated with it, especially American Express and Butterfield's Overland Mail, did everything Russell did, but better. They had a head start, and they were far better capitalized. But the model of their interwoven finances and alliances, the deep pockets of their banking business, and most of all, their aim at creating a monopoly in the areas they served so they could control pricing—that was something not only Russell but other nineteenth-century capitalists aimed at.

The men who ran Wells Fargo weren't infallible—Butterfield had to be kicked out of his mail company to keep it in operation. But today we use American Express cards rather than Pony Express credit cards for the basic reason that they succeeded and Russell, Majors & Waddell didn't. Maybe if there hadn't been a Mormon War, or a Civil War, if a deep-pocketed investor had appeared, if the government had actually paid its debts . . .

It's often said that the transcontinental telegraph killed the Pony Express. While the service did end the day the line was completed, that was by design; the Pony was always a short-term project.

It's also said—less often—that the railroad killed the Pony and its ilk. There's more truth to that, but again, people like Russell and his partners knew that day was coming; they all rode trains, Russell quite a lot. The idea was to sew up a monopoly before the transcontinental railroad came in. Then anyone who wanted to use the railroads—anyone who didn't live next to the tracks—would have to pay. Ditto the railroads, which is how it played out: they got hosed in the early competition for freight by the companies that controlled local freighting.

That's the nineteenth-century invention that often gets overlooked when discussing how much life changed then: monopolies. Not that they were new, exactly—medieval guilds were started to basically do the same thing: limit access to services so the people charging for those services benefited. But the monopolies of the nineteenth century did this on a scale never achieved before, for the benefit of a smaller group of people.

The Pony was part of that. But our memory of it has survived because it was far more. For us, the mystic chords of memory that Lincoln so memorably mentioned at the end of his inauguration address strike notes with deep roots. The tales, even those not entirely provable, are deep into who we want to be today and tomorrow.

The values that we see in the Pony riders are values we cherish, even if we've never been near a barn, let alone a horse: adventure, speed, determination, endurance. The values of the service itself: dependability against all odds, unflagging commitment to a mission— these are values we too want to emulate, whether or not we'd go to the extreme lengths of Pony Bob or the White Indian.

THE PONY AS A BUSINESS DIED AN IGNOBLE DEATH IN 1861, ITS PARENT company crushed under the weight of economic reality. But that was the body only; its spirit and soul lived on—and lives on today, embedded in America's culture and DNA.

Bill Cody brought the Pony back to life when he began featuring it in his Wild West shows in the latter half of the nineteenth century. The shows stirred memories—some real, some fanciful. Tales of the service and its riders, many stretching the truth, were spun in the great (though now mostly unappreciated) literary entertainments of the day, dime novels. Scribes following in the footsteps of Ned Buntline celebrated the exploits of Pony riders far and wide, often very wide, as titles such as *Fred Fearnot's Pony Express; or, a Rough Ride in Texas* attest.

After the turn of the century, the fictions began to give way to, or more accurately were supplemented by, actual histories. Arthur Chapman's in 1932 may represent a turning point, in which the taller tales were sifted out in favor of the verifiably awesome. Since then, myth-busting has become an almost mandatory part of the genre. But that has hardly dampened enthusiasm for books about the Pony Express—nor for the legends, true and otherwise, associated with it.

Hollywood has never worried much about the line between fact and fiction. When popular art and entertainment migrated from the printed word to the movie screen, the Pony Express was along for the ride. Historians as well as film critics might grimace at some of the plots. 1953's *The Pony Express*, which starred a pre-Moses Charleton Heston, has a plot described by the Internet Movie Database as "Buffalo Bill and Wild Bill Hickock work to establish the Pony Express and fight Indians and California separatists who seek to destroy it."

It's a lot of fun anyway.

Television has made its own history of the Pony Express, most notably in the series *Young Riders*, which aired from 1989 through 1992; it featured Stephen Baldwin as Buffalo Bill and Josh Brolin as Wild Bill Hickok. The riders and the service have ventured into countless other entertainments, often as tangents or color.

The raw ingredients of the Pony story—young men, horses, hardships, and danger—are potent bits for any narrative, whether in a rodeo ring or on the big screen. But there's more to the Pony Express's staying power than galloping horses and reckless young men. As important as Bill Cody and his shows were in keeping the memory of the service alive, I think it's likely that we'd remember it even without the great showman. The Pony is the perfect transport vehicle for the things we still value in America, and for the realities we as a nation continue to face: speed, courage, individualism . . . distance, time, and, yes, money. If the Pony riders were brave archetypes of the American spirit racing across the American heartland, Russell and his partners were surely nineteenth-century venture capitalists. The fact that they failed so spectacularly is itself thoroughly American. If you're going to fail, fail big.

IN THE SUMMER OF 2016, I TOOK A TRIP ACROSS THE PONY TRAIL, DRIV-ing and hiking—far more the former—over the path the service took.

At one point in Nevada, or maybe Utah, I detoured slightly and got lost. I was alone, it was the middle of a warm day, and I didn't know where I was or, for a short while, where the car was either.

Eventually, I found my way. I had no cell service and the GPS in the car also didn't work for some odd reason. But I knew if I drove in one direction—west, in this case—eventually I would find something like a road, and from that find another road, and eventually find my way to something I could either recognize or pretend I recognized, and get reoriented. Which is what happened.

Not long after I got back, I told that story to a friend. "Now you know how the riders felt, all alone on the desert," he told me.

But I didn't. Not at all.

What I felt was barely worse than coming out of the mall and not knowing where your car is. Because I knew that no matter what, if I kept going roughly the way I'd come, I would find civilization. I knew people would be waiting for me and contact authorities if I didn't turn up. I knew that in the worst case, whatever that might be, I could find help, either by someone passing or a cell signal.

Pony riders had none of that. They lived with the reality that at any moment they might be completely on their own, without any hope of help, utterly dependent on themselves in the harshest environment possible.

That was a reality not just for the riders, but for everyone involved in the service, and pretty much everyone on the frontier at one time or another. Living with that reality—embracing it—made them who they were.

It didn't make them better than us; we live in different times, with different challenges. But it does make their lives worthy of study and, at their best, emulation. The Pony flashed briefly across the American landscape, a strike of lightning in a sky often dark with danger and ambiguity. In its history, real and sometimes imagined, we see ourselves as we'd like to be: brave, resourceful, racing against nature and all manner of dangers, with determination in our hearts and a smile on our faces.

ACKNOWLEDGMENTS

Every writer owes a great debt to those who came before him, and that is certainly true in my case; previous stories and studies of the Pony were a foundation I've tried to build on. Even more important, directly and indirectly, were the efforts of the thousands of people who have worked to keep the Pony alive, from museum guides to park rangers, amateur historians to storytellers, volunteers and (generally underpaid) staffers. I was privileged to meet a good number of these people during my research, and I owe them a debt of gratitude that can never be repaid.

Working on the book during the summer of 2016, I retraced the Pony's route, stopping at literally dozens of museums and parks along the old route, often without advance notice. My trip was possible only because of the hard work by a literal army of volunteers as well as state and federal workers, including the National Park Service, the Pony Express Trail Association, the Oregon-California Trails Association, and the National Pony Express Association, who have labored for over a century to mark and preserve the route, its various artifacts, and indeed its memory. To say that the people I pestered for information were forthcoming and helpful would be to understate the kindness and assistance they gave so enthusiastically.

Since I can't name them all, let me mention a few who will not appear in other works, and who are unlikely to get media attention anywhere for their quiet but critical contributions to our historical heritage. There was Tom Butler, at the desk of the Lexington Museum in Missouri, who kindly spent several hours showing me artifacts collected over the years; I could have stayed another week and not managed to hear everything he knows. There was Jill at the Marysville Pony Station, who opened some of the darkened corners of the exhibit one early morning; the ranger at Hollenberg in Kansas, who stayed after closing; Dana at St. Joe's Museum, who took time from other duties; Ranger Phil in Sacramento, who kept pointing out sources . . . the list truly is endless. And I can't begin to give proper props to the "re-riders" and members of the National Pony Express Association, whose enthusiasm for history and hard work have not only kept the Pony alive, but won over a new generation of enthusiasts to ensure it will not be forgotten.

More formally, my wife, Debra Scacciaferro, contributed countless hours of research to the project. Thanks to the librarians at the New York Public Library, the Mid-Hudson Library System, and California for their assistance. Thanks also to Dave Robinson and his wife for the personal connection to some of the surviving descendants of the Pony family.

Special thanks goes to the great team at William Morrow. A lot of writers have great editors supporting them, but I can't think of another writer who can brag that he had a New York City editor travel three thousand miles to help him do research in the middle of Wyoming—as my editor, Peter Hubbard, did. Peter even camped out on the trail, or close to it; the man lives his books.

Others at William Morrow who have helped along the way include Nick Amphlett; Andrea Molitor; cover designer Owen Corrigan; and copy editor Laurie McGee, who had many helpful suggestions as well as finding and correcting many embarrassing errors. Thanks also to Anna Maria Allessi and her team on the audio side. And of course the incomparable Sharyn Rosenbloom and the publicity and marketing staff, Amelia Wood, and the video team at Book Studio 16. Gratitude to Morrow's publisher, Liate Stehlik, and deputy publisher, Lynn Grady.

Tracing the trail by car and foot, I was left in awe of the vast distance the Pony riders covered. It's no wonder, really, that their accomplishment is now the stuff of legend. I only hope that I have helped in a small way to keep that legend alive.

SUNDRY AND OTHER

APPENDIX

THE PLEDGE

Every book on the Pony Express, without exception, has quoted the oath that Majors made his employees take. This one is no different.

It should probably be mentioned—though it rarely is—that the oath was originally meant for men on the ox trains, and while there is evidence that Pony riders did take it, it's not like records were kept indicating that every single rider, let alone every employee, did. And there's plenty of testimony from Richard Burton, and others, that at least some of the provisions—cussing most prominently—were more observed in the breach.

It's somewhat picturesque to imagine someone like Jack Slade taking the oath; you can almost see him spitting a wad of tobacco out between phrases and toasting the conclusion with a bottle of Julesburg's best. But it's an integral part of Pony lore, and there were plenty of Pony riders who took it seriously:

> I _____, do hereby swear, before the great and Living God, that during my engagement, and while I am an employee of Russel, Majors & Waddell, I will, under no circumstances, use profane language; that I will drink no intoxicating liquors; that I will not quarrel or fight with any other employee of the firm, and that in every respect I will conduct myself honestly, be faithful to my duties, and so direct all my acts as to win the confidence of my employers. So help me God.

RIDERS

Because the Pony's records have been lost to posterity, and because of the occasionally haphazard way replacement riders were found and used, a definitive list of exactly who rode for the service can never be compiled.

Which doesn't mean people haven't tried.

The following is a list of everyone who has been listed as a rider by at least one reliable compiler—either a museum or a historian. To help readers envision where the locations of the Pony Express stations were, present-day state names are used. Names with an asterisk appear on only one or two lists and are considered by some to be suspect; names with two asterisks are generally regarded as unlikely to have been riders, but still appear on lists. A few cases seem to be alternative names and duplicates, but it's difficult at this point to know which is the correct one.

*Anderson, Andrew Ole Mormon rider, seventeen, in Howard Egan's division in Utah.

*Anderson, J. W. Possible rider out of Ruby Valley Station, Nevada, listed on 1860 census as twenty-nine-year-old mail carrier.

Anson, John

Anton

Avis, Henry Rode from Mud Springs, Nebraska, to Horseshoe Station, Wyoming. He was on the historic run to deliver Lincoln's inaugural address. Said to have doubled his run to Deer Creek (Wyoming) for a $300 bonus when other riders refused to ride because of Indian troubles.

Babbit, Rodney

Ball, Lafayette W.

Banks, S. W. Lafayette

Barnell, James W.

Baughn, Jim "Boston"

Baughn, Melville Rode from St. Joseph to Seneca (Kansas). Later became a horse thief and outlaw, hung for his crimes.

Beardsley, Marve

*Beatley, James (Foote) (James Bentley) Listed as James Bentley on 1860 census as living at Smith's Hotel in Seneca with other Pony Express riders in Nemaha County, Kansas.

Becker, Charles Rider from Plante's Station on the Sweetwater River (Wyoming) to Rocky Ridge, then along North Platte from Deer Creek to Red Buttes.

Bedford, Thomas Jefferson On April 23, 1861, hired as an emergency rider to meet a Pony Express rider who missed the steamer in Sacramento. His route went through Pacheco, Walnut Creek, and Lafayette to Oakland, where he delivered the mail to another steamer bound for San Francisco.

*Bigelow, Asher Rider out of Seneca Station, listed in the 1860 census taken at Smith's Hotel in Kansas.

Billman, Charles Henry (Hy) Rode from Salt Lake City to Willow Springs, Utah, with Rush Valley, Nevada, as his home station. He was twenty-one.

Bills, G. R.

"Black Sam"

Black, Thomas

"Black Tom"

Boulton, William Rider between Seneca and Marysville in Kansas.

Brandenburger, John

Brink, James W ("Doc," "Dock") Believed to have been a rider on the westbound first run in Nebraska from Rock Creek Station to 32 Mile Creek Station. One of five riders buried in St. Joseph, Missouri, at Mount Auburn Cemetery. Brink was present when Wild Bill Hickok killed David McCanles.

Brown, Hugh

Brown, James

Bucklin, James

Burnett, John or David

Bush, Ed

Butterfield, Henry Possible rider out of Ruby Valley Station, Nevada, listed in the 1860 census as twenty-year-old mail carrier.

Campbell, William Rider from Fort Kearny to Big Sandy, Nebraska. The National Pony Express Association also has him on the Nebraska route between Valley Station and Box Elder (Cottonwood Springs).

*Carlen, James H. (Carlin) Possible rider out of Ruby Valley Station, Nevada, listed on 1860 census as twenty-year-old mail carrier.

*Carlton, Gustavas Possible rider out of Ruby Valley Station, Nevada, listed on 1860 census as twenty-nine-year-old mail carrier.

Carlyle, Alexander (Carlisle, Carlistle) Rider out of St. Joseph; said to have contracted tuberculosis and had to give up the job. Some say he was the first rider out of St. Joe.

Carr, William

Carrigan, William

Carson

Carter, James

Casey, Michael Rider from Julesburg, Colorado, to Mud Springs, Nebraska.

Cates, William A. His route included Cottonwood Springs (Deer Creek Station) west to Horseshoe Station, Wyoming. One of first riders to be hired, staying until the end, he carried Lincoln's inaugural address.

Cayton, Francis M

Clark, Jimmy (James)

Clark, John

Clarke, Richard W (Deadwood Dick)

Cleve, Richard (Cleave) One of the early riders who stayed to the end of the Pony Express, his route ran west from Fort Kearny to Cottonwood Springs, Nebraska.

Cliff, Charles— Shared a route between St. Joseph, Missouri, and Seneca, Kansas, with his brother Gustavas. One of five Pony Express riders buried in St. Joseph, at Mount Mora Cemetery.

Cliff, Gustavas (Gus) Shared a route between St. Joseph, Missouri, and Seneca, Kansas, with his brother Charles Cliff. They bunked at Smith's Hotel.

**Cody, William Frederick (Buffalo Bill)

Cole, Buck

Combo, James ("Sawed-Off Jim")

Corbett, Bill

Covington, Edward

Cowan, James

Crawford, Jack

*Cumbo, James

Danley, James

Dean, Louis

Dennis, James William "Will" Rider from Egan Canyon to Ruby Valley Station, Nevada, listed on 1860 census as twenty-two-year-old mail carrier.

Derrick, Frank

Diffenbacher, Alex

Dobson, Thomas Rode between Ruby Valley, Nevada, and Deep Creek, Utah, in the spring of 1860; Pacific Springs, Wyoming, and Salt Lake City, Utah, in 1861.

Dodge, J.

Donovan, Joseph

Donvan, Tom

Dorrington, W. E.

Downs, Calvin

Drumheller, Daniel M.

Dunlap, James E.

Eckels, William

Egan, Major Howard Division superintendent for the Pony Express, he also carried the first eastbound mochila in Utah from Rush Valley Station to Salt Lake City in a sleet storm on April 7, 1860.

Egan, Richard Erasmus ("Ras") Son of Major Howard Egan, as a Pony rider he carried first westbound mochila in Utah out of Salt Lake City to Rush Valley.

Elliot, Thomas J.

Ellis, J. K. (Jack)

Enos, Charles

Fair, George

Faust, H. J. Listed in a newspaper as being the first eastbound rider to carry the mail in Nevada from Jacob's Station to Ruby Valley.

*Faylor, Josiah Albert Lived at Willow Springs Station in Utah with his English wife, written about by Richard Burton. It was said he had icicles in his red beard when coming in from his rides in the winter.

Fisher, John (Fischer) Credited as the first eastbound rider to carry the mochila from Simpson's Springs to Camp Floyd in Utah.

Fisher, William Frederick (Billy) Carried first eastbound mochila in Nevada from Ruby Valley to Egan's Station. Delivered the Lincoln inaugural address.

Flynn, Thomas Rider between Genoa and the Carson Sink in Nevada. In 1861, he continued to Dry Creek, where the station was under Indian attack.

Foreman, Jimmie

Fry, Johnny (Johnnie, Johny Fry) Believed to be the first rider to leave St. Joe. Rode between St. Joseph, Missouri, and Seneca, Kansas, until May 1861.

*William Fulkerson

Fuller, Abraham Maple (Abram)

Gardner, George ("Irish")

Gentry, James Listed in news article as the first rider eastbound of the Pony Express to make the run from Schell Creek, Nevada, to Deep Creek, Utah.

*Gilson, James Rider in Utah Territory.

Gilson, Samuel H. Brother to James. Both served as riders in Utah Territory.

Gleason, James

*Gould, Frank Rider in both Kansas and Nebraska Territories.

Grady, Thomas "Irish Tom"

Hall, Martin

Hall, Parley

Hall, Sam

*Hamilton, Billy

*Hamilton, Samuel

*Hamilton, William (Sam) Rider for Roberts Creek, Nevada, to Sacramento, California. Credited for taking first mochila off the boat at Sacramento and carrying the first westbound mail from Placerville to Sacramento where he and his horse boarded the *Antelope* steamboat bound for San Francisco.

*James "Bean" Hamilton Rider between St. Joseph, Missouri, and Seneca, Kansas.

Harder, George

Hardy

Haslam, Robert (Pony Bob) First route: Deep Creek, Utah, to Ruby Valley, Nevada. Second route in Nevada, Buckland's to Friday's Station near Lake Tahoe.

Hawkins, Theodore (Thee)

Haws, Sam

Helvey, Frank Substitute rider between Marysville, Kansas, and Big Sandy, Nebraska.

Hensel, Levi

Hickman, Bill (William)

*Hickok, Lucius Ludosky Rider in California; delivered Lincoln's inaugural address.

Higginbotham, Charles

Hogan, Martin

Huntington, Clark (Allen)

Huntington, Let (Lester, Lee) An "L. Huntington" was credited with making the first eastbound run from Deep Creek Station in Utah to Simpson's Springs Station.

Huntington, Lou L. Huntington was credited with making the first eastbound run from Deep Creek Station in Utah to Simpson's Springs Station.

Irish Jim

James, William Rider in 1861 from Simpson Park in Nevada to Cold Springs, a sixty-mile trip crossing two mountain ridges, which he finished in six hours, switching between five California mustangs.

*Jay, David Robert Hired to ride from Seneca, Kansas, to Big Sandy, Nebraska; later Big Sandy to Fort Kearny, occasionally all the way to Julesburg, Colorado.

Jenkins, William D.

Jennings (Bob) A substitute rider and hunter who provided meat for eastern Wyoming stations.

Jobe, Samuel S. Rider between Horseshoe Station, Wyoming, past Chimney Rock, Nebraska, ending in Julesburg, Colorado.

Jones, William Rider, possibly on the section that crossed the Kansas-Nebraska border.

*Kates, William

Keetley, Jack H. Rider for the entire eighteen months of Pony Express from Seneca, Kansas, to Big Sandy, Nebraska. Claimed he rode three-hundred-plus miles from Big Sandy to Elwood Station (in Kansas across the river from St. Joseph) and back to Seneca Station in twenty-four hours, eating "lunch" as he rode.

Kelley, Hiram Loomis Rider in Nebraska Territory, between Mud Springs Station and Fort Laramie (Wyoming).

Kelley, Jay G. (Kelly) Initially hired to help build many of the stations in Nevada, he was a rider and assistant station keeper under James McNaughton at Sand Springs.

*Kelley, Merrit P.

Kelley, Mike Rider from Sacramento to Roberts Creek, Nevada.

King, Thomas Owen Rider from Bear River, Wyoming, through Echo Canyon in Utah to Weber Station. Later rode sections between Salt Lake City, Utah, and Ham's Fork, Wyoming.

King, Tony

Koerner, John Phillip Substitute rider out of St. Joseph, Missouri. One of five Pony Express riders buried in St. Joseph, at Ashland Cemetery.

La Mont, Harry Rider for area around Rock Creek, Nebraska Territory; later between South Pass and Fort Bridger, Wyoming.

*Landon, Thomas Rider, thirty-six years old, for the Seneca station in Kansas.

Larzelere, Charles Substitute rider for Johnny Fry.

Lawson, William

*Lenhart, James (Madison) Rider during the winter of 1860–61 on the route from Pacific House to Strawberry Valley, California.

Leonard, George

Little, George Edwin

Lytle, N. N.

Macaulas, Sye (Silas McAulas on census) Possible rider out of Ruby Valley Station, Nevada, listed on 1860 census as twenty-two-year-old mail carrier.

*Malcom, Joseph Rider in 1861 with route through Wasatch Mountains in Utah.

Martin, Robert

Maxfield, Elijah Rider in Nebraska Territory.

Maze, Montgomery Twenty-five-year-old station keeper at Sand Springs Station, Nevada; later a rider from Friday's Station at Lake Tahoe to Reese River Station in Nevada. Discharged for shooting station keeper H. Trumbo in the hip at Smith's Creek Station.

McCain, Emmet Rider connected with Carson Sink in Nevada.

McCall, J. G. (Jay) Rider connected with Carson Sink Station in Nevada.

McCarty, Charlie

McDonald, James

McEneaney, Pat (McEnamey, McEnearrny, McEneammy) Rider 1860 from Fremont Springs, Nebraska, to Julesburg, Colorado.

McLaughlin, David

McNaughton, William

Meacona, Lorenzo

Mellen, J. P.

Mifflin, Howard

**Miller, Charlie B. (Bronco Charlie) Alleged rider from Placerville, California, to Carson City, Nevada; pretty much everyone agrees he was not a real rider.

Moore, James One of first riders hired by A. E. Lewis out of St. Joseph. On June 8, 1860, he was credited with riding 140 miles from Midway Station, Nebraska, to Julesburg, Colorado, then subbing for a rider who had been killed the day before, returning to Midway Station in fourteen hours and forty-six minutes, averaging eighteen miles per hour.

*John Mufsey Rider out of Cottonwood Station (also known as the Hollenberg Station) in Hanover, Kansas.

Murphy, Jeramiah H. Rider stationed at Fort Bridger in Wyoming.

Myrick, Newton

*Obershaw, Paul Possible rider out of Ruby Valley Station, Nevada, listed on 1860 census as twenty-one-year-old mail carrier.

Orr, Matthew Stationmaster at Deep Creek, Utah, and substitute rider. Brother of Robert Orr.

Orr, Robert Rider on routes near Deep Creek Station in Utah. Brother of Matthew Orr. Their mother owned a store frequented by freight drivers and Pony Express riders.

Pace, Thad

Packard, G.

Page, William Rider between Salt Lake City and Fort Bridger, Wyoming.

Parr, Dick

Paul, John

Paxton, Joe ("Mochila Joe") Rider in the Colorado and Nebraska region around Julesburg to Mud Springs. He is said to have rescued rider W. S. Tough, half-frozen in a blizzard near Mud Springs Station, unable to deliver the mail.

Perkins, George Washington ("Wash") Rider, age twenty-four, from Egan Canyon Station to Ruby Valley Station in Nevada.

Perkins, Josh (Joseph on census) Listed as the first rider to carry the mail out of Ruby Valley Station to Schell Creek Station, Nevada; listed on 1860 census as seventeen-year-old mail carrier.

*Pollinger, Edward Twenty-two-year-old rider from Seneca Station in Kansas, staying at Smith's Hotel during 1860 census.

Pridham, William Rider connected to Smith's Creek Station in Nevada.

Ranahan, Thomas J. ("Irish Tommy," "Happy Tom") Substitute rider and stagecoach driver between Pacific Springs and Green River in Wyoming.

Rand, Theodore ("Little Yank")

Randall, James

Reynolds, Charles Alexander

Reynolds, Thomas J.

Richards, William Minor Station keeper at Cottonwood Springs in Nebraska, rider between Cottonwood Springs and Alkali Lake. Married the sister of pony rider Jack Keetley.

Richardson, H.

*Richardson, Johnson William Although some sources list him as one of first riders hired by A. E. Lewis out of St. Joseph, the biographical information available indicates he would have been only nine at the time. A Johnson Richardson is connected to Carson Sink Station in Nevada; it's not clear whether this is the same rider.

*Sewel, Ridley Rider, age thirty-two, for Seneca Station in Kansas. He appears on July 1860 census listings as staying at Smith's Hotel.

Riles, Bartholomew (Riley)

Rinehart, Jonathon (Rinhart, Rynehart)

Rising, Don C. One of the first riders hired by A. E. Lewis, he rode in Kansas between Granada Station and Marysville, and later from Big Sandy to Fort Kearny. His father, Noble, was station keeper of Log Chain Station in Kansas.

Roff, Harry Loren (Harvey) California rider. Some credit him with being the first eastbound rider out of Sacramento, but others credit William "Sam" Hamilton.

Ruffin, C. H.

Rush, Edward

*Rutsel, John Possible rider out of Ruby Valley Station, Nevada, listed on 1860 census as twenty-five-year-old mail carrier.

*Ryan, Thomas Listed as rider out of Marysville, Kansas, but may have only brought mail into Marysville to be delivered by the Pony Express.

Sanders, Robert

Scovell, George Rider from Roberts Creek Station in Nevada east to Ruby Valley, believed to have carried the first eastbound mail.

Seerbeck, John (Seebeck)

Selman, Jack

Serish, Joseph

Shanks, James (James Dock, Doc)

Sinclair, John

*Smethurst, George Rider for three months in the Reese River, Utah, region.

Spurr, George

Sterling, Edward ("Sandy") Rider between St. Joseph, Missouri, and Fort Kearny, Nebraska, and stationmaster at Rock Creek (Nebraska) and Log Chain (Kansas) stations.

Streeper, William Henry ("Black Bill") Rider, twenty-two, between Ruby Valley and Smith's Creek in Nevada.

Strickland, Robert C. (Stricklen) Rider in Nebraska Territory between Horse Creek and Diamond Springs.

Strohm, William

Sugget, John W.

*Talcott, George Possible rider out of Ruby Valley Station, Nevada, listed on 1860 census as twenty-nine-year-old mail carrier.

Tate, William (Billy)

*Taylor, Josiah

Thacher, George (Thatcher, George Washington) Rider in Utah from Salt Lake City to Camp Floyd.

Thomas, J. J.

Thompson, Bill

Thompson, Charles Peck ("Cyclone Charlie") Substitute rider for Johnny Fry for one month. One of five Pony Express riders buried in St. Joseph, at Mount Auburn Cemetery.

Thompson, James M.

Tough, Elias Littleton (listed as Elias Tough Littleton in a 1935 issue of *Pony Express Courier*) The Tough brothers, Elias and William, were both Pony Express riders in Nebraska.

Tough, William Sloan Rode in western Nebraska, possibly at Mud Springs Station.

Towne, George

Trotter, Bill

Tuckett, Henry Rider on Howard Egan's division west of Salt Lake City; helped to restore operations along the line after Indian attacks.

Upson, Warren ("Boston") Credited by a Sacramento paper as the first rider to carry mail eastward from Sportsman's Hall Station in California to Friday's Station at Lake Tahoe.

Van Blaricon, William Edgon ("Pony Ned")

Vickery, Bill

Wade, John B. Rider for various routes in Wyoming, possibly Fort Laramie, Wyoming, to Salt Lake City, Utah. Said to have been captured by Indians for two years at age eight.

Wallace, Henry

*Waller Jun, A. B. Possible rider out of Ruby Valley Station, Nevada, listed on 1860 census as twenty-two-year-old mail carrier.

Weaver, Cap

Westcott, Daniel (Don Wescott)

Whalen, Michael M. (Whelan) Rider for two months in spring of 1861 between Salt Lake City west to Camp Floyd. One of five Pony Express riders buried in St. Joseph, at Ashland Cemetery.

Wheat, Charles Orson (George)

"Whipsaw"

William, James

Willis, H. C. (Wills)

*Willson, Thomas Thornhill The only rider identified as having ridden from Atchison, Kansas, to Seneca; mail was moved from Atchison because of rebel activity during the fall of 1861.

Wilson, Elijah Nicholas (Uncle Nick) Rider between Schell Creek, Nevada, and Deep Creek, Utah, in fall of 1860; later rode in Nevada from Carson Sink to Fort Churchill. His autobiography is *The White Indian Boy: The Story of Uncle Nick Among the Shoshones*.

*Wines, Ira Relief rider, worked as horse herder at Egan Station in Nevada for stagecoach company.

Wintle, Joseph Barney (Joseph E.) Rider from April 1860 to early 1861 in Nevada; later from Fort Kearny to Cottonwood Springs Station in Nebraska. He carried news of Lincoln's election.

Worley, Henry

Worthington, James

Wright, George

Wright, Mose (Amos, Morse) Rider, twenty-one, from Ruby Valley to Carson City, west of Salt Lake City. Learned Shoshone language as a kid. British writer Sir Richard Burton wrote that Wright helped him improve his Shoshone vocabulary during his stay at Ruby Valley Station in Nevada on October 7, 1861.

Zowgaltz, Jose (Zowglat, Zowgalty, Zogwalt)

STATIONS EAST TO WEST

The following list was compiled from various sources including National Park Service guides and maps, the National Pony Express website, the Legends of America website, *City of the Saints* by Richard F. Burton, and *The Saga of the Pony Express* by Joseph J. DiCerto.

Station names with an asterisk are listed on the National Parks Service map of the Pony Express National Historic Trail.

SUPERINTENDENTS

Benjamin Ficklin. Pony Express route superintendent, in charge of the entire route. He resigned in July 1860 under extreme pressure from Russell.

James Erwen Bromley. Division superintendent of the route between Horseshoe Station in Wyoming and Salt Lake City, Utah.

Major Howard Egan. Division superintendent of the route between Salt Lake City, Utah Territory, and Roberts Creek, Nevada. Station keeper at Deep Creek Station in Utah, his family ranch. Also substituted as Pony Express rider, carrying the first eastbound mail into Salt Lake City.

A. E. Lewis. Division superintendent from St. Joseph to Fort Kearny.

Bolivar Roberts. Division superintendent of the route between Roberts Creek, Nevada, and Sacramento, California.

Joseph Alfred "Jack" Slade. Division superintendent between Fort Kearny, Nebraska, to Horseshoe Station in Wyoming.

DIVISION ONE—ST. JOSEPH, MISSOURI, TO FORT KEARNY, NEBRASKA

A. E. Lewis, division superintendent

- *St. Joseph, MO. Eastern terminus for the Pony Express.
  - Pikes Peak Stables held up to two hundred horses.
  - Pony Express General Office was in the Patee House.
- Elwood Station, KS. Livery stable located on the west bank of the Missouri River. Late-night riders from the West could leave their horse to take the mail by rowboat across the river to St. Joseph.
- Cottonwood Springs (Thompson's Ranch, Johnson's Ranch), KS. Relay station on the southern fork of the Pottawatomie Trail, requiring the rider to ford Peter's Creek. Abandoned for the newer Troy relay station on the northern branch of the trail.
- Troy, KS. Relay station with a barn for five horses near the adjacent hotel owned by Leonard Smith.
- Cold Springs Rock Station (Syracuse Station, Lewis Station), KS. Relay station (also served as freight and stagecoach station) on the Pottawatomie Road at the Cold Spring Branch of Wolf River. Located in tiny hamlet of Syracuse, which no longer exists.
- *Kennekuk Station, KS. Relay station in a bustling town of one hundred, some thirty-five miles south of St. Joseph, boasting two churches and two hotels.
  - Tom Perry, station keeper
- Kickapoo (Goteschall) Station, KS. Relay station, located on Delaware Creek on the Kickapoo Indian Reservation.
  - Noble H. Rising, station keeper
  - W. W. Letson, station keeper or assistant
- *Log Chain Station, KS. Relay station and overland stagecoach

stop, log house, and seventy-foot barn built by Noble H. Rising, near Locknane's Creek.

- **Noble H. Rising,** station keeper
- **Seneca, KS.** Smith's Hotel and restaurant, an elegant building on corner of Fourth and Main Streets, became a home station in July 1860.
  - **John E. Smith,** listed as postmaster and proprietor of Smith's Hotel, where Pony Express riders stayed. It's unclear if he was a station keeper.
  - **Captain Levi Hensel,** blacksmith stationed there, who shod horses for the Pony Express and stage lines, from Kennekuk, KS, to Big Sandy, NE.
- **Ash Point, KS.** Laramie Creek relay station, in the tiny settlement of Ash Point, on a branch of the California Road.
  - **"Uncle John" O'Laughlin,** who sold whiskey from his general store, might have been the station keeper.
- ***Guittards Station, KS.** Relay station and stagecoach stop, with a barn for twenty-four horses, operated by the George Guittard family. Sir John Burton describes it as unusually clean and the food "fresh and good."
  - **Xavier Guittard,** station keeper
- ***Marysville Station, KS.** Large stone house and livery station on the banks of the Big Blue River functioned as both relay and sometimes home station for the stagecoach and Pony Express. Today it is known as Pony Express Home Station No. 1, used as a museum, including the original stone barn of 1859.
- ***Cottonwood (Hollenberg Station), KS.** This six-room Pony Express home station, near Cottonwood Creek, was the largest station in Kansas, with a barn for a hundred horses. It's now a National Historic Landmark.
  - **Gerat H. Hollenberg,** station keeper
- **Rock House Station, NE.** Isolated relay station in Jefferson County, Nebraska Territory, in a section of wasteland.[1]
- ***Rock Creek Station, NE.** Small relay station near Fairbury, rented

from David McCanles, who built and ran a toll bridge across the creek.

- Edward "Sandy" Sterling, station keeper and relief rider
- Horace Wellman, station keeper
- **Virginia City (Graysons, Whiskey Run Station), NE.** Relay station located four miles north of Fairbury, in Jefferson County.[2]
- **Big Sandy, NE.** Home station and stagecoach inn, three miles east of Alexandria in Jefferson County.
  - Daniel Patterson, first station keeper and building owner
  - Asa and John Latham, later station keepers
- **Millersville (Thompson Station), NE.** Relay station located two miles north of Hebron in Thayer County.
  - George B. Thompson, station keeper
- **Kiowa Station, NE.** Relay station ten miles northwest of Hebron, serving Pony Express riders and express stagecoaches.
  - Jim Douglas, station keeper
- ***Oak Creek (Little Blue Station), NE.** Small relay station near Oak, Nebraska, on the Little Blue River.
  - Al Holladay, station keeper in 1861
- ***Liberty Farm, NE.** Stagecoach and home station, near Deweese in Clay County.
  - James Lemmons, first station keeper
  - Charles "Chas" Emory, later station keeper
- **Spring Ranch (Lone Tree Station), NE.** A large road ranch located some four miles from Deweese, served as a stagecoach stop, and may have been a relay station for the Pony Express.
- ***32 Mile Creek (Dinner Station), NE.** A long, one-story relay and stagecoach station, about six miles southeast of Hastings in Indian territory.
  - George A. Comstock, station keeper
- ***Sand Hill (Summit Station), NE.** Remote relay station, a mile or so south of Kenesaw near Summit Springs; vulnerable to Indian raids.
- **Hook's Station, NE.** A home station in the vicinity of Fort Kearny,

known also as Dogtown, Valley City, Kearney, or Hinshaw's Ranch at various times.

- M. H. Hook, station keeper
- *Kearny, NE. Relay station in Kearney County, about two miles from Fort Kearny.
  - Richard Ellsworth, station tender at Fort Kearny

DIVISION TWO—FORT KEARNY, NE, TO HORSESHOE CREEK, WY

Joseph Alfred "Jack" Slade, division superintendent

- Platte Station (Seventeen Mile Station), NE. Relay station and stagecoach stop, some five miles southeast of Odessa.
- Craig's Station (Garden Station), NE. Relay station, some six miles southwest of Elm Creek, in Phelps County.
- *Plum Creek Station, NE. Log cabin relay station about ten miles southeast of Lexington, near Fort McPherson, and the site of Indian raids.
- *Willow Island Station (Willow Bend), NE. An adobe house, stables, and a general store made up this relay station six miles southeast of Cozad.
- Midway Station (Cold Water Station), NE. Four miles south of Gothenburg, this relay station was situated midway on the stagecoach route between Atchison, Kansas, and Denver, Colorado.
- *Gilman's Station, NE. Relay station in Lincoln County, exact location unknown.
  - Mr. Gilman, station keeper
- Sam Machette's Station (Machette Station), NE. Log cabin moved and reassembled in Ehmen Park, Gothenburg; now a Pony Express museum. Some historians question whether it was an official station.
- Cottonwood Springs Station (Box Elder), NE. Relay station two miles west of Fort McPherson.
  - John North, station keeper
  - Mr. Boyer, station keeper
- Cold Springs Station, NE. Relay station roughly two miles south

and a mile west of North Platte. A marker is located on U.S. 85, 1.5 miles south from the junction of U.S. 26.

- **Fremont Springs Station, NE.** Home station and stage stop near Hershey, Nebraska. Described by Sir Richard Burton in 1860.
- **Dansey's Station (Elkhorn, O'Fallon's Bluff), NE.** Relay station located southwest of Sutherland, NE, and west of O'Fallon's Bluff. It was four hundred miles from St. Joseph, Missouri, and deep in Indian country.
- **Alkali Lake Station (Pikes Peak Station), NE.** Possible relay station two miles southwest of Paxton.
- **Gill's Station (Sand Hill Station), NE.** Relay station just south of Ogallala.
- ***Diamond Springs Station, NE.** Rely station one mile west of Brule, NE, built overlooking the South Platte River, where the trail turns mountainous just over the border in Colorado.
- **Frontz Station (South Platte Station), CO.** Relay station possibly located a mile or two east of Julesburg in Sedgwick County.
- ***Julesburg Station, CO.** Home station and stage stop in a large frontier town, named after French Canadian trader Jules Beni.
  - **George Chrisman,** station keeper
- **Nine Mile Station (Lodge Pole), NE.** Relay station two miles southeast of Chappell, NE.
- **Pole Creek #2 Station, NE.** Relay station of uncertain location.
- ***Pole Creek #3 Station, NE.** Relay station on the north side of Lodgepole Creek, on the old St. George Cattle Ranch, about three and one-half miles east of Sidney, Cheyenne County.
- **Midway Station, NE.** Possible relay station near Gurley, NE.
- ***Mud Springs Station, NE.** Home station and stage station located five and half miles north of Dalton, NE. Described by Sir Richard Burton in 1860 as a primitive sod hut with a timber roof and no door.
  - **James McArdle,** station keeper
- **Courthouse Rock Station, NE.** A relay station some five miles south of Bridgeport at Pumpkin Seed Crossing, near the ledge known as Courthouse Rock.

- **Chimney Rock Station, NE.** Relay station in unknown location near the famous Chimney Rock formation.
- ***Ficklin's Springs Station, NE.** Relay station a mile west of Melbeta, NE, in Scotts Bluff County, named for Pony Express Superintendent Benjamin F. Ficklin.
- **Scott's Bluff Station, NE.** Home station near site of Fort Mitchell.
- **Horse Creek Station, NE.** Relay station on west bank of Horse Creek, two miles northeast of Lyman, in Scotts Bluff County.
- **Spring Ranch Station (Cold Springs Station), WY.** First relay station in Wyoming, two miles southeast of Torrington. From here, the mountainous terrain included forests, deep ravines, and high plateaus.
- **Bordeaux Station, WY.** Relay station.
- ***Fort Laramie Station, WY.** Home station located within the Fort Laramie National Historic Site at 965 Gray Rocks Road in Fort Laramie.
  - **Seth Ward,** station keeper
- **Sand Point Station (Nine Mile Station, Star Station), WY.** Relay station, now marked by a white site marker just north of Register Cliff near Guernsey, Wyoming, on Route US-26.
- **Cottonwood Station (Bitter Cottonwood Creek Camp), WY.** A Mormon pioneer camp and Pony Express relay station west of Guernsey.
- **Horseshoe Station, WY.** Home station. Historians believe Jack Slade lived here.

DIVISION THREE—HORSESHOE, WY TO SALT LAKE CITY, UTAH

James Erwen Bromley, division superintendent

- **Elkhorn Station, WY.** Relay station, exact location unknown.
- **La Bonte, WY.** Relay station with a primitive dried brush enclosure.
- **Bed Tick, WY.** Possible relay station, unknown location.
- **La Prele (Lapierelle, La Prelle), WY.** Relay station, unknown location.

- **Box Elder, WY.** Relay station, exact location unknown.
  - **John North**, station keeper (according to June 1860 US Census)
  - **Wheeler**, station keeper
- **Deer Creek Station, WY.** Relay or home station in Glenrock, WY, burned in 1866.
- **Little Muddy Creek Station (Muddy Creek), WY.** Possible relay stone station about six miles west of Glenrock, marked by a Pony Express marker.
- **Bridger Station, WY.** Relay station.
- **Platte Bridge Station, WY.** Relay station in Casper, WY, later used by Fort Caspar, now part of the Fort Caspar Museum.
  - **Louis Guenot**, station keeper
- ***Red Butte Station, WY.** Relay station near Red Butte escarpment, about five miles west of the North Platte River.
- ***Willow Springs, WY.** Relay station located by the first spring of potable water west of Casper.
- **Horse Creek Station (Greasewood Creek, Sage Creek), WY.** Relay and stagecoach station located about seventeen miles from Willow Springs on County Road 319/Oregon Trail Road.
- **Sweetwater Station, WY.** Relay station near Independence Rock, with a shack and horse shed for a quick change of horse. Abandoned before the service ended.
- **Devil's Gate, WY.** May have been an alternate relay station used instead of Sweetwater Station, located near Devil's Gate rock formation, a deep, narrow fifteen-hundred-foot gorge carved out by the Sweetwater River.
- **Split Rock (Plante's Station), WY.** Relay station near the geological notch in the mountain pass, east of Jeffrey City, WY.
  - **Mr. Plante**, station keeper
- ***Three Crossings Station, WY.** Home station near the Sweetwater River, south of the Gas Hills and north of the Green Mountains. The name referred to the tight bends in the river nearby, which required three separate crossings.
  - **Mr. Moore**, Mormon station keeper.

- **Ice Slough Station, WY.** Relay station nine and a half miles west of Jeffrey City, near a bog where underground water remained frozen well into the summer months, providing ice and cold water for travelers.
- **Warm Springs Station, WY.** Relay station near Sulphur Creek.
- ***Rocky Ridge Station (St. Mary's Station), WY.** Relay station, or possibly home station.
  - **William "Bill" A. Reid,** station keeper
- **Rock Creek Station, WY.** Relay or possibly home station.
- **South Pass Station.** Relay station near a twenty-mile-wide gap in the Rocky Mountains, now a National Historic landmark on WY-Rt 28 near South Pass City.
- ***Pacific Springs Station, WY.** Relay station just west of the Continental Divide, exact location unknown.
- ***Dry Sandy Station, WY.** Relay station.
- ***Little Sandy Station, WY.** Relay station near a popular fording place toward Fort Bridger, on WY-Rt 28 in Farson.
- ***Big Sandy Station, WY.** Relay station burned by Indians in 1862, just south of Big Sandy crossing on US-191 in Farson, WY.
- ***Big Timber Station (Big Bend), WY.** Relay station.
- **Green River Station, WY.** Home station, where three English women served food and offered lodging to Pony Riders and stage passengers.
- **Michael Martin's Station, WY.** Relay station.
- **Ham's Fork Station, WY.** Relay station stood just south of the river in Granger, WY. A Pony Express stone marker stands a half mile away from the original site, near the Granger Stagecoach Station, built in 1862.
  - **David Lewis,** Scottish station keeper
- ***Church Buttes Station, WY.** Relay station near the geological formation of Church Buttes.
- ***Fort Bridger (Millersville Station), WY.** Relay station and trading post on the Oregon and California Trails, where Fort Bridger Historic Park is now located.
  - **Mr. Holmes,** station keeper

- Muddy Creek Station, WY. Relay station or possibly a home station.
- Quaking Asp Station, WY. Relay station.
- *Bear River Station, WY. Relay station, located near Bear River State Park in Evanston, WY.
  - Mr. Myers, station keeper
- *Needle Rock Station, UT. Relay station near Needle Rock, just west of Yellow Creek in hilly country.
- Echo Canyon Station, UT. Relay station consisting of a long, low log cabin at the foot of the canyon.
  - James Laird, station keeper
- Halfway Station (Daniel's Station, Emery Station), UT. Relay station in a bleak terrain.
  - Mr. Daniels, station keeper
- *Weber Station, UT. Division superintendent James Bromley ran his business from the stone building that housed a general store, inn, saloon, jail, and blacksmith shop.
  - James E. Bromley, station keeper
- East Canyon (Henefer Station, Heneferville Station), UT. Relay station near Dixie Hollow.
  - Mr. Bauchmann, station keeper
  - James McDonald, station keeper
- Wheaton Springs Station, UT. Relay station, exact location unknown.
- Mountain Dell Station, UT. Relay station.
  - Ephraim Hanks, station keeper
- *Salt Lake House, Salt Lake City UT. Home station considered one of the most prosperous and well run by Sir Richard Burton, Mark Twain, and others who stayed there.
  - A. B. Miller, station keeper

DIVISION FOUR—SALT LAKE CITY, UT TO ROBERT'S CREEK, NV

Major Howard Egan, division superintendent

- *Trader's Rest Station (Traveler's Rest), UT. Relay station.
- Rockwell's Station, UT. Relay station at Hot Springs Brewery

Hotel. The station keeper had been the personal bodyguard to the Mormon leader Brigham Young and was the territorial marshal.

- **Porter Rockwell,** station keeper
- **Absalom Smith,** assistant station keeper

- **Joe's Dugout Station, UT.** South of Great Salt Lake, this relay station was on barren land, with water delivered from Utah Lake, which was sold for 25 cents a bucket. The two-room brick building had a log barn and a small dugout home for the helper.
  - **Joe Dorton,** station keeper

- ***Camp Floyd (Stagecoach Inn, Fairfield Station, Carson's Inn), UT.** Carson's Inn served as stagecoach and Pony Express station, possibly adjacent to the fort known as Camp Floyd (later renamed Fort Crittenden.) At the time, it had a population of seven thousand, including soldiers, but was abandoned and destroyed at the start of the Civil War.
  - **John Carson,** station keeper

- ***Faust's Station (East Rush Valley Station), UT.** Home station in a barren landscape, it was also used to raise horses for the Pony Express.
  - **Henry Jacob Faust,** station keeper

- ***Point Lookout Station, UT.** Relay station overlooking a rocky desert, with the trail going through miles of sand and alkali dirt.
  - **Mr. Jackson,** station keeper

- ***Simpson's Springs Station, UT.** One of the few relay stations with good drinking water from the springs.
  - **George Dewers,** station keeper

- **Riverbed Station, UT.** Large relay station built in a dry riverbed; so remote, station keepers didn't stay long.
  - **George Wright,** station keeper
  - **William F. Hosiepool,** station keeper
  - **Oscar Quinn,** station keeper

- ***Dugway Station, UT.** Sod house relay station with an adobe chimney, a wooden front door, and no well. Water had to be hauled in barrels from Simpson's Springs.
  - **William Riley,** station keeper, killed with his crew in an Indian ambush massacre as they ate breakfast, unarmed, in the dugout.

- **Black Rock Station, UT.** Relay station about fourteen miles west of Dugway Station.
- ***Fish Springs Station, UT.** Home station situated on a natural pond filled with fish and wild waterfowl.
  - **Mr. Smith,** station keeper
- ***Boyd's Station, UT.** Relay station dug into the side of a hill.
  - **Bid Boyd,** station keeper
- ***Willow Springs Station, UT.** Primitive relay station in Callao.
- **Willow Creek Station, UT.** Primitive relay station.
  - **Pete Joyce,** station keeper
  - **Peter Neece,** station keeper
- ***Cañon Station (Canyon Station), UT.** Primitive relay station.
- ***Deep Creek Station (Ibapah Station), UT.** One of the biggest home stations in the territory, with a brick house, large barn, and corral. It raised grain, cattle, and sheep to provide food and feed for other stations in the division.
  - **Howard Ransom Egan,** station keeper, son of Superintendent Major Howard Egan.
  - **Mathew Orr,** station keeper or assistant
  - **Harrison Sevier,** station keeper or assistant
- **Eight Mile Station (Prairie Gate Station), NV.** Primitive relay station built a few months after the Pony Express started.
- ***Antelope Springs Station, NV.** Primitive relay station burned down by Paiute warriors a few months after it opened.
- ***Spring Valley Station, NV.** Alternate station built toward the end of the Pony Express.
  - **Constant Dubail,** station keeper (also at Schell Creek Station)
  - **Reynal,** station keeper
- ***Schell Creek Station, NV.** Home station located near Schellbourne, NV, seven miles east of US-Rt. 93.
  - **Constant Dubail,** station keeper (also at Spring Valley Station)
- ***Egan Canyon Station, NV.** Relay station burned by Paiute warriors in the fall of 1860, rebuilt and attacked several more times.
  - **Mike Holton,** station keeper

- Albert Armstrong, station keeper
- Henry Woodville Wilson, station keeper
- Henry Wilson, station keeper
- Butte Station (Bates Station, Robbers Roost), NV. Primitive sandstone, wood, and mud-plastered relay station, burned by Paiute warriors, then rebuilt.
  - Mr. Thomas, station keeper
- Mountain Springs Station, NV. Primitive relay station.
  - Lafayette (Bolly) Bolwinkle, station keeper (also at Dry Creek Station)
- Ruby Valley, NV. Relay station operated by William "Uncle Billy" Rogers and Frederick W. Hurst, situated on rich soil with plenty of potable water. It provided food and hay for other stations.
  - Frederick W. Hurst, station keeper
  - Charles C. Hawley, station keeper or assistant
  - William Sherman, mail station keeper
  - George Wolf, station or stock tender
  - William Young, station or stock tender
- Jacob's Well, NV. Relay station opened in October 1860, in Huntington Valley, on the spot where General Frederick Jacobs had dug a well.
- *Diamond Springs Station, NV. Relay station northwest of Eureka in the Diamond Mountains, with crystal clear springs.
  - William Francis Cox, station keeper
- *Sulphur Springs Station, NV. Relay station, rebuilt in July 1861.
- *Roberts Creek Station, NV. Home station that was attacked by Paiute warriors and partially rebuilt.
  - Mose Wright, station keeper

DIVISION FIVE—ROBERTS CREEK, NV, TO SAN FRANCISCO, CA
Bolivar Roberts, division superintendent
- *Grubb's Well Station (Camp Station), NV. Relay station built in July 1861, halfway between Roberts Creek Station and Dry Creek.

- ***Dry Creek Station, NV.** Probably a home station, it was attacked by Paiute warriors.
  - **John Applegate,** station keeper killed by Indians on May 21, 1860.
  - **Ralph Rosier,** station hand. With Applegate, Rosier was shot and scalped by Indians while preparing breakfast.
  - **Colonel Totten,** station keeper
  - **Lafayette (Bolly) Bolwinkle,** station keeper (also at Mountain Springs Station)
- **Simpson Park Station, NV.** Relay station burned in an attack, later rebuilt.
  - **Alcott, James "Jack,"** station keeper killed by Indians in June 1860
- **Reese River Station, NV.** Relay station burned by Paiute warriors, then rebuilt as an adobe house.
  - **George Washington Jacobs,** station keeper
- **Dry Wells Station (Mount Airy), NV.** Relay station built in 1861 in the Shoshone Mountains.
- **Smith's Creek Station, NV.** Home station in the Desatoya Mountains.
  - **H. Trumbo,** station keeper who shot and wounded rider Montgomery Maze
- **Edwards Creek Station, NV.** Relay station.
- ***Cold Springs Station, NV.** Roofless stone home station located on a hill, later moved to a lower elevation. The first wooden structure was burned down by Paiute warriors.
  - **James McNaughton,** station keeper (also worked at Sand Springs Station)
  - **John Williams,** station keeper who was killed on duty
- **Middlegate Station (Middlecreek Station), NV.** Relay station ten miles west of Cold Springs Station on US-50.
- ***Sand Springs Station, NV.** Roofless, primitive relay station with foul water near the foot of Sand Mountain on the southern split of the Pony Express trail.

- Montgomery Maze, station keeper, later rider
- James McNaughton, station keeper (also worked at Cold Springs Station)
- **Sand Hill Station, NV.** Primitive relay station.
- **Carson Sink Station, NV.** Adobe construction relay station with potable water.
  - J. G. Kelly, assistant station keeper and rider
- **Williams Station (Honey Lake Station), NV.** Relay station where the incident that began the Pyramid Lake War took place.
  - J. O. Williams, station keeper
- **Desert Station (Hooten Wells Station).** Relay station.
- ***Buckland's Station, NV.** Home station at Samuel Buckland's ranch and trading post. After the Pyramid Lake War, an adobe fort was built on the shore of Carson River and later used for a home station.
  - **Samuel S. Buckland,** station owner
  - **W. C. Marley,** station keeper
- **Fort Churchill Station, NV.** Fort built following the Pyramid Lake War. Used as a home station in the final months of the Pony Express.
  - **Captain F. F. Flint,** stationmaster
- **Miller's Station (Reed's Station), NV.** Relay station thirty miles east of Carson City.
- **Dayton Station (Spafford Hall), NV.** Relay station. Today its rock wall still stands on West Main Street, Dayton.
- ***Carson City (Carson Station), NV.** Home station.
- ***Old Mormon's Station (Genoa Station), NV.** Home station marked by granite monument on the west side of Main Street in Genoa, Nevada's first permanent settlement.
- ***Friday's Station, NV.** Home station in Lake Tahoe. It consisted of a large log cabin, hotel, dining room, kitchen, storeroom, woodshed, large stable, and hay barns.
  - **Martin K. "Friday" Burke,** station keeper
  - **James Washington Small,** station keeper

CALIFORNIA

- *Woodfords Station (Hope Valley), CA. Relay station that was soon bypassed on a shorter route.
- Fountain Place Station, CA. Relay station in Garrett Washington Fountain's log cabin.
- *Yank's Station, CA. Large relay station originally built as a three-story, fourteen-room hotel for stagecoaches, with a large stable and corral. Located in today's town of Myers.
  - Ephraim "Yank" and wife, Lydia Clement, station keepers
- *Strawberry Station, CA. Relay station on the site of a hotel
  - Mr. Berry, station keeper
- Webster's Station (Sugar Loaf House), CA. Relay station in the vicinity of Sugar Loaf Mountain.
- Moore's Station (Moss Station), CA. Relay station.
- *Sportsman's Hall, CA. Home station, one of the most comfortable, run by two brothers, just twelve miles from Placerville.
  - John and James Blair, station keepers
- *Placerville Station (Hangtown Station), CA. Relay station, with a telegraph office to transmit telegrams sent by Pony Express.
  - Louis Lepetit, station keeper
- El Dorado, CA. Relay station on the White Rock Road of the original southern route.
- *Mormon Tavern Station (Sunrise House), CA. Relay station on the southern White Rock Road route.
- *Fifteen Mile Station, CA. Relay station on the southern White Rock Road route.
- Pleasant Grove Station (Duroc Station), CA. Relay station on the Green Valley Road on the northern route.
- *Folsom Station, CA. Relay stop on the northern Green Valley Road route. Mail was taken from here to Sacramento by train beginning in July 1860.
- *Five Mile Station (Mills Station), CA. Relay station five miles from Sacramento.

- ***Sacramento, CA.** Home station and office in the BF Hastings Building.
- **Benicia, Martinez, and Oakland Stations, CA.** Relay stations used if a rider missed the San Francisco–bound steamer and had to be sent by horse to the next ferry port.

THE SCHEDULE

Starting from St. Joseph's and riding west during good weather, Pony riders were expected to make the following posts on this schedule:

Marysville—12 hours
Fort Kearny—34
Fort Laramie—80
Fort Bridger—108
Salt Lake City—124
Carson City—188
Placerville—226
Sacramento—234
San Francisco—240

The schedule was lengthened to fifteen days that December, according to the *Daily Alta* in Sacramento. Judging from postmarks, the service went faster east to west, generally by about a day. While the schedule was for ten days, most trips took a little longer.

TIMELINE

Major events in American and Pony history:

1753—Benjamin Franklin of Philadelphia and William Hunter of Williamsburg, Virginia, are appointed as joint postmasters for the American colonies. They establish a series of post roads from Maine to Florida, and from New York to Canada. Post riders on horseback were the first contractors to carry mail between post offices. For the first time, riders carried mail at night to speed service between Philadelphia and New York.

1773—The first stagecoach delivery of semiweekly mail between Portsmouth, New Hampshire, and Boston, Massachusetts.

1775—The Second Continental Congress appoints a postmaster general. He's paid one thousand dollars a year, can hire deputy postmasters, and creates a line of post offices from Falmouth, New England, to Savannah, Georgia.

1803—The Louisiana Purchase doubles the size of US territory.

1807—Robert Fulton's steamboat, the *Clermont*, makes a successful run from New York City to Albany. By 1809, he has steamboats on six major rivers and the Chesapeake Bay.

1812—Fur trader Robert Stuart discovers South Pass, the key path through the Continental Divide.

1836—Missionaries Marcus and Narcissa Whitman head a group that uses wagons to travel the Oregon Trail, settling in modern-day Washington State. They are the first of many to use wagons across the trail.

1839—John Sutter Sr. establishes Sutter's Fort in California.

1844—Samuel Morse demonstrates a long-distance telegraph.

1848—Gold is discovered in California. By the following year, some three hundred thousand prospectors arrive in search of gold. The US Post Office Department pays two steamship companies to carry mail from New York to California.

1850—Sacramento is incorporated the same year that California becomes the thirty-first state. The city becomes a major distribution point for agricultural and commercial goods.

1852—Twenty different telegraph companies connect major towns on both US coasts by stringing twenty-three thousand miles of wire. But because of difficult terrain and sparse population, the Great Plains and Rocky Mountains have no wired communication.

1853—First telegraph office in St. Joseph, Missouri, opens March 4, receiving its first message: details of President Benjamin F. Pierce's inauguration.

1854—William Russell, Alexander Majors, and William Waddell join forces to create a freighting company. The company is the largest freighting service in the West, with a monopoly on transporting army supplies.

1857—Russell, Majors, and Waddell sustain heavy financial losses from damages to wagons and stations during the Mormon War.

1859—When gold is discovered at Pikes Peak, Russell starts a passenger service to Denver. Trying to win a mail contract over the central route to California, he proposes the Pony Express.

April 1860—The Pony Express launches April 3, 1860, from St. Joseph, Missouri, and Sacramento, California. Riders arrive on time April 14 in both cities.

May–June 1860—The Pyramid Lake War disrupts the Pony Express. Attacks on stations cost the firm $70,000. (The number of human casualties among the firm, possibly ranging from one to more than a dozen, is a matter of debate.) Harassment by Indian bands along the Pony line continues even after the war ends.

June 1860—The federal government agrees to subsidize a telegraph line connecting the West Coast to the East.

November 1860—Lincoln is elected. The Pony delivers the news in record time.

December 20, 1860—South Carolina secedes from the Union.

December 24, 1860—William Russell is arrested on suspicion of embezzlement for taking $870,000 worth of bonds from the Indian Trust Fund to use as collateral against loans.

January 1861—Russell appears before a select congressional committee investigating the case. He is indicted on criminal charges related to the theft, but the charges are quickly dropped.

March 1861—With the southern mail and stage routes cut off by the South, a new mail contract is let to the Overland Mail Company. Russell, Majors, and Waddell share the eastern portion of the route.

April 12, 1861—South Carolina troops attack Fort Sumter. President Lincoln declares a state of war.

April 1861—Wells Fargo acts as an "agent" of the Pony Express. Russell resigns as president of the company.

July 1861—The Overland Mail Company, affiliated with Wells Fargo, takes over the western half of the Pony Express route.

October 1861 The telegraph line from Missouri to California is completed. The Pony Express closes.

REENACTORS

If Buffalo Bill Cody did more than anyone to keep the memory of the Pony alive at the end of the nineteenth century, today's National Pony Express Association is doing just as much, and with an equal amount of enthusiasm and gusto.

Each summer, the group holds a "Re-Ride," re-creating the Pony's famous trail as they ride horses from St. Joseph to Sacramento—or vice versa—in ten days. Braving the weather and traffic rather than Indian raiders, the volunteer riders and their mounts keep to the same schedule the Pony did, winning nearly as much acclaim as they pause—very briefly—in small towns along the way to greet well-wishers and journalists in their quest to keep the Pony alive.

The re-creations are fun events; spectators occasionally dress in period costumes to cheer the riders on. Ceremonies at the beginning and end attract crowds of all ages, but the most valued audience members are clearly the kids, many of whom are learning about the service and even the Old West for the first time.

Dressed in the flannel shirts and jean trousers typically worn back in the day, riders carry replica mochilas with letters just like in 1860. There are a few concessions to the present, however—progress is tracked with a GPS unit, and of course there is a website: http://na tionalponyexpress.org, and a Facebook page: https://www.facebook .com/expressrider. There's also a support team that moves along with the ride, and volunteers on foot talk about the service's history with bystanders while they wait for the mochila—and sometimes for hours afterward. It's a hands-on—or maybe stirrups-on—way to learn about history while having a bit of fun at the same time.

Among its other projects, the group has a lesson plan for teachers that is available through its website.

SOURCES

IN GENERAL

It has to be said that many of the sources, primary as well as secondary, for information about the Pony Express are a glorious but hopeless tangle of reminiscences, guesses, and suppositions, many of which don't agree and can't be verified or cross-checked. Many tales and supposed facts, like where a station may have been, are in dispute. There are plenty of times when anyone delving into the Pony's history can only shrug and hope for the best. It's far easier to get lost in the conflicting accounts than it is when following the actual trail—and I speak from experience on both counts.

In trying to sort things out, I've tried to avoid any very obvious or really embarrassing errors, but I'm sure I've made both.

In the summer of 2016 I took a trip retracing the Pony trail from Sacramento to St. Joseph. Along the way I stopped at countless small museums, national parks, and a few private homes, gathering information and generally being an annoyance to anyone with the slightest knowledge about the service. That trip was invaluable, not just for gathering information, but to comprehend the enormity of the task Russell, Majors, and Waddell undertook, and the achievements of their riders. I found archival material in many of these places, and it helped shape and in many cases reshape my understanding of the service.

In planning that trip, the National Park Service's guides, maps from the Bureau of Land Management, and websites maintained by local historical and dedicated Pony Express organizations were essential. William E. Hill's *The Pony Express Trail: Yesterday and Today* (Caldwell, ID: Canton Press, 2010) was another important guide.

I still got lost, but I would have been far worse off without them.

Newspaper archives with stories on the Pony itself and with information from the Pony were helpful, especially the California Digital Newspaper Collection and the State Historical Society of Missouri's Missouri Digital Newspaper Project, both of which can be accessed online.

Raymond and Mary Lund Settle deserve more than a mere mention as historians of the Pony Express, Russell, Majors & Waddell, and the Old West in general. Working in the 1950s and 1960s at a time when people were thrilling to (mostly inaccurate) stories of the West, the pair worked diligently to separate fact from fiction. In some ways, they were on the vanguard of the movement that corrected many wrong conceptions. They also celebrated many of the legends, acknowledging that these often spoke the truth in ways mere facts could not.

Three books by the Settles are essential to any work on the Pony Express, including this one:

The Story of the Pony Express (London: Redwood Burn Limited Trowbridge & Esher: 1955) This is the British edition of *The Story of the Pony Express*; it has an index, which the American version does not.
War Drums and Wagon Wheels: The Story of Russell, Majors and Waddell (Lincoln: University of Nebraska Press, 1966)
Empire on Wheels (Stanford, CA: Stanford University Press, 1949)
As mentioned, William E. Hill's *The Pony Express Trail* was also valuable throughout, especially while traveling.

When in doubt about the times of some of the trips, I've accepted the statistics compiled by Richard C. Frajola, George J. Kramer, and Steven C. Walske in *The Pony Express: A Postal History* (New York: The Philatelic Foundation, 2005) as the final authority.

Some additional notes are included in the following sections.

CHAPTER ONE

Information on the arrangements for the special election run, including information about the telegraph lines, was carried in several newspapers at the time, including the *Sacramento Daily Union*'s November 15, 1860, edition. A summary and additional sources are included in Anthony Godfrey's *Historic Resource Study, Pony Express National Historic Trail*, August 1994, available online at https://archive.org/details/historicresource00godf.

If the Pony Express Company kept records of who took which ride, they've been lost in the treacherous trod of history. But Johnny Fry was the "lead" rider on the leg from St. Jo's west for the longest period of time, and years later he was the man most residents remembered when speaking about the Pony Express—so much so that he was credited with having taken the first mail run, which he probably didn't make.

He did handle all the important runs after the first two months until almost the end of the service, including the one carrying Lincoln's inaugural address, which we have some evidence for. Given that, it seems highly likely that he took this run.

My description of Fry is drawn from photographs printed in Jacqueline Lewin Marilyn Taylor, *On the Winds of Destiny: A Biographical Look at Pony Express Riders* (St. Joseph, MO: Platte Purchase Publishers, 2002); anecdotes and other information come from Arthur Chapman, *The Pony Express: The Record of a Romantic Adventure in Business* (New York: G. P. Putnam's, 1932), and, of course, the Settles. I should mention that there is considerable disagreement over the spelling of both his first and last names. I have used the most common rendering for both.

CHAPTER TWO

Most of the biographical information in this chapter is drawn from the Settles and Alexander Majors, *Seventy Years on the Frontier* (Lincoln: University of Nebraska Press, 1989). The mail information comes largely from *War Drums and Wagon Wheels*. Also helpful was J. M. Guinn's "Early Postal Service of California," *Annual Publication of the Historical Society of Southern California and Pioneer Register, Los Angeles* 4, no. 1 (1897): 18–26.

CHAPTER THREE

The information on Guittard comes from the National Park Service. The station was located on what is now private farmland. (It's not there anymore; I looked.) Some of the information on Benjamin Ficklin comes from the VMI archives, http://www.vmi.edu/archives/genealogy-biography-alumni/featured-historical-biographies/ben-ficklin-pony-express-pioneer/.

Besides the sources listed below for Hickok, general readers might like to start by perusing some websites like http://www.kansasheritage.org/gunfighters/JBH.html.

Kit Carson had zero to do with the Pony, but if you're interested in him, check out David Remley, *Kit Carson: The Life of an American Border Man* (Norman: University of Oklahoma Press, 2011). But before that, read Carson's "autobiography," even though it's not. That can be found online at https://archive.org/details/thelifeandadvent16274gut.

CHAPTER FOUR

Among the sources used for Colt, the man and the weapons, was R. L. Wilson's *Colt, An American Legend* (New York: Abbeville Press, 1985). This is the official history of Colt firearms.

CHAPTER FIVE

As far as I can tell the best detailed breakdown of Russell et al.'s finances was published by Raymond W. and Mary Lund Settle in *War Drums and Wagon*

Wheels. Given Russell's many other deals and visions, we're missing a lot, but the Settles did a phenomenal job with the available data. While I think some of their conclusions regarding culpability in the bond scandal are generous to a fault, there's no way this chapter could have been written without having read their book first.

Other important sources include the congressional report on the bond scandal: United States Congress House Select Committee on the Fraudulent Abstraction of Bonds from the Interior Dept. Abstracted Indian Trust Bonds Report [and Supplemental Report] (Washington, 1861), and *George Root and Russell K. Hickman's Pikes Peak Express Companies Part III—The Platte Route* (available at http://www.kancoll.org/khq/1945/45_8_roothickman.htm), and LeRoy R. Hafen, *The Overland Mail: 1849–1869* (Cleveland: Arthur H. Clark, 1926).

CHAPTER SIX

My main sources for the Slade-Reni feud are Thomas Dimsdale, *The Vigilantes of Montana* (London: Endeavor Press, 2016), Arthur Chapman, *The Pony Express*, and the Settles, *The Story of the Pony Express*. There are many different variations.

Chapman has his account from William Campbell. Everyone else seems to rely on Dimsdale.

Twain's description is in *Rough Riders*.

CHAPTER SEVEN

Sources for this chapter include Cody's autobiographies, most especially *The Life of Hon. William F. Cody, Known as Buffalo Bill the Famous Hunter, Scout and Guide. An Autobiography* (Hartford, CT: Frank E. Bliss, 1879). Retrieved from http://codyarchive.org/texts/wfc.bks00007.html.

Among Cody's biographers, Robert A. Carver's *Buffalo Bill Cody: The Man behind the Legend* (New York: John Wiley & Sons, 2000) was most important for me. My thoughts on Cody's importance to the Pony Express in our national memory were seeded by Christopher Corbett, *Orphans Preferred: The Twisted Truth and Lasting Legend of the Pony Express* (New York: Broadway Books, 2003).

Majors's autobiography, *Seventy Years on the Frontier*, was also useful, though it's not cited in the chapter and its details relating to Cody are suspect.

For Judson, a.k.a. Ned Buntline (and the era in which he fits), I relied heavily on *The House of Beadle and Adams*, a project of the Northern Illinois University Libraries, DeKalb, Illinois, whose website is here: http://www.ulib.niu.edu/badndp/bibindex.html.

And of course Buntline's book, *Buffalo Bill and His Adventures in the West* (New York: J.S. Ogilvie and Company, 1886).

CHAPTER EIGHT

Russell's testimony before Congress after the scandal broke is my main source—which I do take with a grain of salt.

A "chance" meeting with Lea seems almost too good to be true, but there's no evidence to the contrary, and aside from perhaps protecting Lea, there was little reason for Russell to lie about that aspect of the affair.

The question of whether Lea proposed the "solution" to the problem of the maturing acceptances without any sort of consideration—such as a kickback—seems never to have been raised, at least not in print. But come on. The congressional committee clearly suspected there was more involved, going out of its way to note how uncooperative Lea was, something that can't be completely put off to politics.

If his bank was holding acceptances, and if he had helped place some, then his motivations for "helping" Russell solve the problem had to at least include the fact that he wanted his own reputation protected . . . and his positions made whole.

Most historians won't go even that far, not even the Settles, who laid out the situation most thoroughly in *War Drums and Wagon Wheels* without implying he was a crook. So maybe I'm just a twenty-first-century cynic.

The chapter is based primarily on the congressional report and *War Drums and Wagon Wheels*.

CHAPTER NINE

My understanding of Fort Laramie and its history began with *Fort Laramie Park History, 1834–1977*, by Merrill J. Mattes (Rocky Mountain Regional Office, National Park Service, U.S. Department of the Interior, 1980). This can also be found online at https://www.nps.gov/parkhistory/online_books/fola/history/contents.htm.

Lincoln's day-by-day doings are based primarily on Harold Holzer, *Lincoln: President-Elect*, (New York: Simon & Schuster, 2009). For what James Buchanan—a vastly understudied president—was doing, Philip S. Klein's biography, *President Buchanan* (Newtown, CT: American Political Biography Press, 1995), was invaluable.

My main source for the material on Bridger was Grace Raymond Hebard and E.A. Brininstool, *Jim Bridger, "The Grand Old Man of the Rockies"* (Cleveland: Arthur H. Clark Company, 1922).

CHAPTER TEN

Among my sources for the section on Joseph Smith, I found the Joseph Smith Papers (available online at http://www.josephsmithpapers.org/) invaluable.

Matthew Bowman's *The Mormon People* (New York: Random House, 2012) is a short, very accessible book that places the faith in the context of its time; it's a great introduction.

The Pony Express in Utah, by Patrick Hearty and Dr. Joseph Hatch (Charleston: Arcadia Publishing, 2015), contains many useful photos as well as details about the service in Utah.

Much of the Egan material comes from *Pioneering the West, 1846 to 1878: Major Howard Egan's diary: also thrilling experiences of pre-frontier life among Indians, their traits, civil and savage, and part of autobiography, inter-related to his father's—* that is the whole and official title as originally published. It's by Howard R. Egan, edited, compiled, and connected in nearly chronological order by Wm. M. Egan, published by the Howard R. Egan estate in 1917 and available at https://archive.org/details/pioneeringwest1800eganrich.

The White Indian section is primarily based on *The White Indian Boy and its sequel The Return of the White Indian* (Salt Lake City: University of Utah Press, 2005) by Elijah Nicholas Wilson and his son, Charles A. Wilson, originally published in 1895. (You can also find a version of just the first book here: https://archive.org/stream/whiteindianboy00wilsrich.)

CHAPTER ELEVEN

Besides the ever-caustic Richard Burton and the always entertaining Mark Twain, my description of Carson City relies on the *J. Lamson Diary* by James Lamson, collected by the California Historical Society (Manuscript Collection, Vault MS 39). Lamson was in the area a few months before the election letter carried by the Pony passed through. I learned about the diary first from Barbara Lekisch, *Embracing Scenes about Lakes Tahoe & Donner, Painters, Illustrators & Artists 1855–1915* (Lafayette, CA: Great West Books, 2003), in which I found some wonderful images as well.

CHAPTER TWELVE

The sources for the creation myths included *Handbook of North American Indians, Volume 11: Great Basin* by Warren L. D'Azevedo, William C. Sturtevant, (US Independent Agencies and Commissions, 1986).

For general information about the Northern Paiute and the Pyramid Lake War, I found Ferol Egan's *Sand in a Whirlwind: The Paiute Indian War of 1860* (New York: Doubleday, 1972) most useful. Some have noted that Egan's book makes use of invented or imagined dialogue, and by necessity it does not include the side of the men at the station. My interpretation of events may be somewhat different from Egan's.

Another important source was *Sarah Winnemucca* by Sally Zanjani (Lincoln:

Bison Books, 2004), a meticulous accounting of the life of a Paiute woman who lived with William Ormsy's family around the time of the war. Sarah later worked as an interpreter and was an important advocate for Native American rights, lecturing and writing a book on her life.

Also critical was *Northern Paiute and Western Shoshone Land Use in Northern Nevada: A Class I Ethnographic/Ethnohistoric Overview* by Ginny Begston, published by the US Department of the Interior, 2003.

A Nevada historian, writer, and outdoorsman, Dennis Cassinelli, keeps a likely blog at https://denniscassinelli.com and it was there that I found information on Smith's Creek Station, which I would have missed entirely on my own (https://denniscassinelli.com/series/pony-express-stations/).

CHAPTER THIRTEEN

For information on the Donner Party, I turned first to *Desperate Passage* by Ethan Rarick (New York: Oxford University Press, 2009).

The discussion of what the South wanted is developed in eminently readable depth in James McPherson's indispensable book on the *Civil War, Battle Cry of Freedom* (New York: Oxford University Press, 1988). See chapter 8, but read the whole thing.

Linda J. Bottjer kindly shared the story of the dueling doctors during an interview. As a journalist and author, she describes herself as "respectful" regarding the spirits that may inhabit the area, and more a gatherer of stories and information, rather than being a psychic.

CHAPTER FOURTEEN

There are endless sources about El Dorado, including what is seen as the earliest formulation of the Spanish myth—written in 1636 but not actually published until 1859—*Conquista i descubrimiento del nuevo reino de Granada de las Indias Occidentales del mar oceano, i fundacion de la ciudad de Santa Fe de Bogota* (El Carnero de Bogata) by Juan Rodriguez Freyle.

That's written in Spanish; English translations are hard to find. But for a flavor in English, *The Conquest of New Granada, Being the Life of Gonzalo Jimenez de Quesada* by R. B. Cunninghame Graham (New York: Houghton Mifflin, 1922) brings the reader closer to the mind-set of nineteenth-century Americans than more modern books do. It's also available on line at https://archive.org/details/conquestofnewgra00cunn.

The data about California's population comes from the 1860 US Census, which is available online at http://www2.census.gov/prod2/decennial/documents/1860a-02.pdf.

It's fascinating reading. Seriously.

One of my leads to the early history of the telegraph was *Guide to the Western Union Telegraph Company Records* by Robert Harding and Alison Oswald (Washington, DC: Archives Center, National Museum of American History, 1986). Alice L. Bates, "The History of the Telegraph in California," *Annual Publication of the Historical Society of Southern California* 9, no. 3 (1914), provided critical data.

Some of the hanging stories come from C. W. Guthrie and Bart Smith, *The Pony Express, an Illustrated History* (Guilford, CT: TwoDot, 2010.)

The story of Lincoln's whiskers here is drawn from Harold Holzer's account in *Lincoln: President-Elect*. There are, of course, many different variations of what has become an important part of the Lincoln legend.

CHAPTER FIFTEEN

My main sources for Russell's arrest are, again, the congressional report, and the Settles' *War Drums and Wagon Wheels*.

My reading of the committee report differs from the Settles', perhaps because I am living in a more cynical time. Still, it seems to me that the witnesses—Russell included—were purposefully evasive, an impression in keeping with the quick dismissal of the charges. Who else knew about the acceptances and the bonds? Why was a former secretary who supposedly no longer worked for Floyd enlisted as a messenger? . . . There are many questions and few answers.

My brief description of Bronco Charlie's claims is based on his write-up in the Glens Falls cemetery (he's in plot 6, lot 22), as well as Corbett's *Orphans Preferred*.

Besides the sources below for Hickok, I found Joseph G. Rosa, "George Ward Nichols and the Legend of Wild Bill Hickok," *Arizona and the West* 19, no. 2 (1977) extremely helpful. The retrieval data is from JSTOR: http://www.jstor.org/stable/40168620.

Information on Roberts's pharmacy is from the family history notes and *Proceedings of the National Wholesale Druggists' Association* (Indianapolis: Hollenbeck Press, 1905).

My sources for Charles Becker were Marie Pinney's "Charles Becker, Pony Express Rider and Oregon Pioneer," *Oregon Historical Quarterly* 67, no. 3 (1966), http://www.jstor.org/stable/20612929, and "A Whiskey Bottle Left on the Grave a Toast to the Past," *The Seattle Times*, August 27, 2000, http://community.seattletimes.nwsource.com/archive/?date=20000827&slug=4039077.

NOTES

CHAPTER 1: GO!

1. To explain my dates: The story in the *Sacramento Daily Union* with these results indicates that the message was sent November 7 from St. Louis. It's not clear exactly when the message was sent, but the dateline is 1:10 a.m. Lincoln went to bed after midnight November 6 confident of victory; he was congratulated the next morning (November 7) at ten. As for the date from St. Jo's: the extant cover for a letter detailing the results sent from St. Joseph has a stamped date of November 8 (see Frajola, Kramer, and Walske, *The Pony Express, A Postal History*).

2. This land belonged ostensibly to Native Americans, as had everything else, but would soon be taken over or greatly reduced—as had everything else. The largest "unorganized territories" were in the areas north of Texas—modern-day Oklahoma—and west of Minnesota, which had become a state in 1858.

3. Various sources say Lincoln received only twelve votes in the city or county. But the results given by the *Liberty Tribune* on December 14, 1860, and rechecked against county records by the Missouri Division of the Sons of Confederate Veterans give the following results: Lincoln, 452; Breckenridge, 614; Douglas, 1,626; Bell, 1,287. This was actually a good showing for Lincoln in Missouri. For results, see http://www.missouridivision-scv .org/election.htm.

4. As I go on to explain, this is admittedly a contrarian point of view. Christopher Corbett provides all of the arguments against in *Orphans Preferred*, p. 184. The letter was first included in full in William Visscher, *Truthful History*, which of course is not necessarily truthful. Corbett has a delightful account of the supposed colonel cum historian in his book (chapter 11: "The Colonel and His Thrilling and Truthful History").

5. Settle and Settle, *The Story of the Pony Express*, p. 46. They did hedge their bets, mentioning that Fry was another leading contender and adding Carlyle as well. Their selection was based on work by Louise Platt Hauck, who found the report in old newspaper clippings.

6. Root and Connelley, *The Overland Stage to California: Personal Reminiscences*, p. 117. Root claims that there were even more expensive shipments of government papers, though he did not see these personally. A good portion of the

book relating to the Pony is clearly based on less-than-reliable sources—not that can't be said of all, including this one.

7.   Based on the averages during this period; I'm using the numbers from Frajola et al., *The Pony Express: A Postal History*. Eastbound numbers were always higher; during the same October to December 1860 period I'm using here, there was an average of 120 letters per trip.

8.   Root and Connelley, *The Overland Stage to California*, p. 117.

9.   The cover is reproduced in Frajola et al., *The Pony Express: A Postal History*. The authors believe that the company's stage carried that particular letter from Julesburg to Denver, where the results were published November 12.

CHAPTER 2: MONEY, AMBITION, AND OTHER COMPLICATIONS

1.   This was the first Continental Bank building; the later one, occupied in 1932 and now considered a historical skyscraper, still stands at 30 Broad Street, a short distance away.

2.   Raymond and Mary Settle, the reigning authorities on the Pony Express, state this in *The Story of the Pony Express* (New York: W. Foulsham & Co., 1955) and elsewhere. William Eaton Russell does not appear on existing lists of the commanders; see, for example, the list of units at http://www.archives.gov/research/military/war-of-1812/1812-discharge-certificates/units-subunits.html#leg. This may be because he had died at some point in the battle, or his first name is listed differently (there are several Russells), or simply due to gaps in the record keeping . . . Or maybe the family legend was wrong and he wasn't there.

3.   Based on a family genealogy. There are gaps in the record, and the year of her death listed before the birth of two of the children there. No dates are given on her gravestone.

4.   Alexander Majors, *Seventy Years on the Frontier*, ebook location 954–955.

5.   Majors, *Seventy Years*, location 955.

6.   The order of the names probably reflects who was closer to the day-to-day affairs in which place. Note that Russell doesn't take front stage.

7.   The Settles theorize that the contributions were actually made in terms of merchandise on the part of Russell and Waddell, and oxen and wagons on the part of Majors.

8.   It was a $20 note—See Whitfield, *Kansas Paper Money: An Illustrated History, 1854–1935*, p. 56. Waddell was on a fifty.

9.   How much more depended on where and when they were working. In Louisiana, one of the highest-paying areas in the South, you could earn $17 a month in 1860 (*Trends in the American Economy in the Nineteenth Century*, The Conference on Research in Income and Wealth, Princeton University Press,

1960, table, p. 453.) Wages on the frontier could be higher due to the scarcity of laborers; in California near active gold mines, the general inflation greatly boosted pay—and the cost of living.

10. Settle and Settle, *War Drums and Wagon Wheels*, note on p. 83.

CHAPTER 3: BLEEDING KANSAS, BLEEDING MEN

1. According to the story that Arthur Chapman was told for *The Pony Express*, at least. The way Chapman tells it (p. 214) would make it seem that Johnny stopped and had breakfast before continuing, which would be unlikely if the ferry was running.

2. Quoted in Corbett, *Orphans Preferred*, ebook location 1475.

3. Chapman, *The Pony Express*, p. 228.

4. A successor was built in the 1880s at Main and Fourth; depending on the source, this was either the original location of Smith's Hotel, or a few blocks away. (An old photograph seems to indicate the former, but others disagree.) The building currently houses a small museum.

5. By some accounts, there was a home station at the now-vanished town of Kenneku, which can be found as a farm crossroads in Grasshopper, Kansas. While there certainly could have been a transfer there, it seems too close to the stations east and west to be considered a full-blown home station.

6. Wilson, *The White Indian Boy*, p. 141.

7. The figure includes soldiers.

8. All quotes from the speech are taken from *Collected Works of Abraham Lincoln*, edited by Roy P. Blaser, and reproduced at https://www.nps.gov/liho/learn/historyculture/cooperunionaddress.htm.

9. See Louis Barry, editor, *Albert D. Richardson's Letters on the Pike's Peak Gold Region Written to the Editor of the Lawrence Republican, May 22–August 25, 1860* and Albert D. Richardson, *The Secret Service, the Field, the Dungeon, and the Escape*. Both collected at http://www.gutenberg.org/ebooks/44865.

CHAPTER 4: OF COLTS AND CRANKS

1. In the interest of full disclosure: Spencer had the design in hand by 1859. Giving prototypes to the most famous fast-mail delivery service in the world would have won him plenty of publicity, and surely made it easier to sell the gun to Lincoln if not the army. But if he'd done that, we'd expect laudatory stories in the press. Most likely, people confused what was a popular gun after the war with what were either more ordinary weapons—or guns that didn't exist at all.

2. According to the Levi Strauss & Co.'s official history, the rivet was not added to the jeans and patented until later; the patent was granted May 20, 1873.

3. The numbers come from *The Plains Across: The Overland Emigrants on the Trans-Mississippi West, 1840–60*, by John D. Unruh Jr. Chart, p. 120.

4. Root and Connelley, *The Overland Stage to California*, p. 193. It's not clear from the way Root tells the story whether this happened on the trail or at his ranch.

5. See Burton, *City of the Saints*, p. 28.

6. Burton, *City of the Saints*, p. 29.

7. Burton, *City of the Saints*, p. 66.

8. Burton, *City of the Saints*, p. 5.

9. Burton, *City of the Saints*, p. 5. I especially appreciate the use of quotes around "lady."

10. Burton, *City of the Saints*, p. 170. "Ichabod" appears to be a name Burton appropriated as a general stand-in for the rider; it brings to mind the character in Washington Irving's short story "The Legend of Sleepy Hollow."

11. Burton, "Notes on Scalping," *Anthropological Review* II (1864), pp. 49–52.

12. Mark Twain, *Roughing It*, pp. 70–71 (1872 edition published by American Publishing Company), http://www.gutenberg.org/ebooks/3177.

CHAPTER 5: THREAT OF DISSOLUTION

1. Without getting too deep, American Express and Wells Fargo were started as joint stock associations; while shares could be traded like corporations, members took on personal liability as in a partnership. Among other things, stock associations were not subject to state regulations that grant the right to incorporate.

2. Technically, a stamp would do, but in practice the envelopes were usually used.

3. Philip L. Fradkin estimates the service yielded a total profit of $46,000 in 1859 (*Stagecoach*, p. 25), but also notes that it was netting $15,000 a month, which would compute far higher.

4. Why *Oxbow*? That's what the newspapers called it, supposedly because it looked like one. And what is an oxbow? An oxbow is the piece of wood that connects the oxen's yokes so that they are paired up. Webster compares it to a misshapen U, but it's more like an extremely fat W that's been taken out back and flattened against a pair of rocks. My metaphor may be inexact, but so was the original—the route looked more like a shallow semicircle than anything else. You can get the basic shape by drawing a line from St. Louis to El Paso to LA and up to San Francisco . . . though if you see an oxbow in that you might want to check your eyes for astigmatism.

5. Barry, *Richardson's Letters*, no. 17.

6. Gwin's position on slavery is questioned by some historians. My interpre-

tation is based on Gerald Stanley, "Senator William Gwin: Moderate or Racist?" *California Historical Quarterly* 50, no. 3 (1971): 243–255. Stanley's case is persuasive.

7. Gwin did try to avert secession—the following March, he briefly acted as a go-between with the Confederacy, only to quit when he realized there would be no compromise that left slavery intact.

8. The number is from *War Drums and Wagon Wheels*, p. 113. It's based on 500 horses at an average of $175 per horse.

9. The five-hundred-pieces-of-mail figure was used by the company when Wells Fargo was about to take over. See appendix C in *War Drums and Wagon Wheels* for the analysis. The number was fairly realistic, as the actual receipts bear out.

10. *The Evening Post*, November 9, 1860. Available at http://nyshistoricnews papers.org/lccn/sn83030390/1860–11–09/ed-1/seq-1/. This was William Cullen Bryant's paper and as such was a strong Lincoln supporter. Gist resigned his office in December on the same day leaders of the Southern states met to decide to secede; he was followed by Francis Wilkinson Pickens.

11. The first New York law set children born as slaves free, but not until they were young adults. A law in 1817 declared everyone free . . . in ten years. According to the US Census, there were no longer slaves in New York by 1840.

12. The property requirement amounted to $250, a significant sum for a laborer.

CHAPTER 6: ROUGH MEN

1. The spot of the home station near Fort Kearny has been lost. While there is an historical marker on the approximate location of Dobytown a short distance from the fort, historians continue to quibble over the station's exact location. As there were no GPS locators at the time of the Pony Express, the matter seems unlikely to be resolved.

2. Hill, in the *Pony Express Trail Yesterday and Today*, calculates the total distance as 280 miles and gives the speed as over 18 miles an hour (p. 114). Possible, but . . .

3. While there are some debates, I'm using Raymond and Mary Settle's divisions and locations from *The Story of the Pony Express*, pp. 34–37.

4. Mark Twain, *Roughing It*, chapter 9. Archived here: http://www.gutenberg.org/files/31.

5. Mark Twain, *Roughing It*, chapter 10. Archived here: http://www.gutenberg.org/files/31.

6. This information and much of what follows is from Nebraskastudies.org, as well as museum displays in the area. See http://www.nebraskastudies.org/0500/frameset_reset.html?http://www.nebraskastudies.org/0500/stories/0501_0108.html.

7. The population figures are compiled at http://www.neded.org/files/re search/stathand/bsect5a.htm.

8. There is considerable debate among historians about the exact location of the Chimney Rock Pony station; it was somewhere between the actual rocks and the river, but where exactly is lost to history. Today the formation is a National Historic Site.

9. Chapman, *The Pony Express*, pp. 227–228.

10. Chapman, *The Pony Express*, p. 229.

CHAPTER 7: BUFFALO BILL

1. *Democratic Platform*, September 28, 1854 (also quoted in Robert A. Carter, *Buffalo Bill Cody* [New York: John Wiley and Sons], p. 20). The background of the newspaper is from William Nelson, *Notes Toward a History of the American Newspaper* (New York: Charles F. Heartman, 1918), p. 126.

2. *The Life of Hon. William F. Cody Known as Buffalo Bill the Famous Hunter, Scout and Guide* (Hartford, CT: Frank E. Bliss, 1879), p. 91. Retrieved from: http://codyarchive.org/texts/wfc.bks00007.html. The rest of this section and the next are based mostly on chapters 8 to 9 in the book, pp. 103 to 118. I'm liberally paraphrasing.

3. Larry McMurtry, *The Colonel and Little Missie* (New York: Simon & Schuster, 2005), p. 49.

4. This is all on Cody's word; most historians accept it, but as with anything from Cody, its veracity is not guaranteed.

5. The alternative version would give credit to a different scout, Luther North. The officers at McPherson who'd witnessed the battle back the version that has Cody doing the killing. Killing Tall Bull had little to do with the medal; rather, Cody was cited for his work finding the Indians and getting the army into position for a victory.

6. Robert A. Carter, *Buffalo Bill Cody: The Man Behind the Legend* (New York: John Wiley & Sons, 2000), p. 178.

CHAPTER 8: UNBONDED

1. The bonds were also hypothecated—Bailey removed the coupons or interest payments, which made them worth less but presumably would keep them from being missed, since the coupons could be redeemed on schedule.

CHAPTER 9: THE GREAT DIVIDE

1. For more information on the Wyoming cattle boom and bust, start here: http://www.wyohistory.org/essays/wyoming-cattle-boom.

2. La Ramee is reputed to have been the first white trapper in the Wyoming

and Idaho areas. At a time when large companies were vying for control of the fur trade, he led a group of independent trappers who eschewed the corporate connections. While on an expedition in 1821, he disappeared in the area of the Laramie River. His death remains a mystery, and one that that has given rise to many theories and rumors, from accident to foul play and back again.

3. I would guess that is an error, but clearly the post was tiny.

4. The description is from Alfred Jacob Miller, an artist who accompanied the Scottish Sir William Drummond Stewart on a trip in 1837. Stewart is the subject of *Men in Eden: William Drummond Stewart and Same-Sex Desire in the Rocky Mountain Fur Trade*, written by William Benemann and published by the University of Nebraska Press; the book has a unique perspective on the fur trade and gay history.

5. History books give the conflict a grand name: the Battle of Ash Hollow, or alternatively, the Battle of Blue Water Creek. More accurate is the Harney Massacre, named after the army brigadier general who presided over it.

6. Burton, *City of the Saints*, p. 92.

7. Such is the testimony of Dimsdale in *The Vigilantes of Montana* (location 2829 in the ebook). Presumably he had no reason to be kind, but others have called her fat, and Burton was his customary caustic self, labeling her a hermaphrodite, which would not have been a compliment.

8. There are plenty of stories of riders being offered bonuses to take extra segments or ride through extraordinary danger, but $300 is far and away the highest bonus ever mentioned. At six months' salary, it's a bit hard to credit. This is sometimes listed as one of the longest rides undertaken in the service, claimed to be at 220 miles. It may have been the longest, but even allowing for detours, it doesn't reach 200 miles.

9. The descriptions here based on Pinney, "Charles Becker." Becker posed with President Warren Harding years later with one of the letters he carried.

10. The *Augusta*, rechristened as the USS *Augusta*, was purchased by the North during the war; she served gallantly.

11. The army had used the area for encampments since the 1840s; in 1861 it assigned a unit to guard Guinard's bridge, by that point considered a strategic crossing. In 1862, the soldiers began building Fort Caspar on the site, incorporating the trading post and buildings.

12. Tom Rea, *Devil's Gate: Owning the Land, Owning the Story* (Norman: University of Okalahoma Press, 2013), p. 76. Rea's larger point in citing the story (among others) is that much of the history of Native Americans and whites who intermarried with them has been lost, often because it was invisible to many whites or inconvenient to the stories whites wanted to tell.

13. There are no statistics covering childbirth on the trail, and few relating to the nation in general at that time. The Census of 1900 reported a death rate for infants one year and younger of 4,605 per 100,000, or a death rate of about 4.5 percent.

14. Quoted in William A. Bowen, *The Willamette Valley: Migration and Settlement on the Oregon Frontier* (Seattle: University of Washington Press, 1978), p. 73.

15. He did not literally say that, but that was the ultimate meaning of his questions, since if he used force, people would surely die.

16. Raymond and Mary Settle, *The Story of the Pony Express*, p. 112.

CHAPTER 10: SAINTS

1. *History, circa Summer 1832*, The Joseph Smith Papers, accessed via http://www.josephsmithpapers.org/paper-summary/history-circa-summer-1832/3. Smith wrote two other accounts, slightly different.

2. Bowman, *The Mormon People*, p. 60.

3. See Richard W. Sadler and Claudia S. Sadler, "Augustine Spencer: Nauvoo Gentile, Joseph Smith Antagonist," *Mormon Historical Studies* 12, no. 2 (Fall 2011).

4. Among those who came to Utah were a small number of black slaves. See James B. Christensen, "Negro Slavery in the Utah Territory," *The Phylon Quarterly* 18, no. 3 (1957): 298–305.

5. Christensen, "Negro Slavery," pp. 298–305.

6. C. Mark Hamilton, *Nineteenth Century Mormon Architecture and City Planning* (New York: Oxford University Press, 1995), pp. 15–17.

7. See Majors, *Seven Years on the Frontier*, location 883.

8. Burton, *City of the Saints*, p. 197.

9. Edward W. Tullidge, *History of Salt Lake City* (Salt Lake City: Star Printing Company, 1886), p. 247. (Tullidge is credited as the publisher rather than the author in the book, but city minutes reveal that he wrote it.)

According to Burton, regular mail could take as little as ten days by stage, if the weather was good; stagecoach passengers generally took about twenty-one days to make the trip. Private wagons—"ambulances"—would take about forty days, traveling at an easier pace.

10. Majors, *Seven Years on the Frontier*, location 805.

11. Given the history of the church and of American attitudes, the fateful decision Young and the other leaders made to join the North in the Civil War is surprising. Mormon attitudes toward slavery were certainly critical, but a realpolitick movement that declared the territory independent of both would have been a complicated development for the North in 1861.

12. Most sources say they are following Burton and put the end of the district

before Roberts Creek station. But I think that's based on a misread of Burton; he intended Roberts Creek Station to be the first station in Roberts's district. Or it may be a misinterpretation of the names—his description can also be applied to another station a little farther west. The problem is compounded by differences of opinion over what was the last station before Roberts Creek; the route here seems to have evolved over time, possibly due to Indian troubles. And then there's the fact that Egan's son, who rode this section, refers to Ruby Valley as the main station in this area, which *could* be interpreted as meaning it was the endpoint of his territory. This is the sort of debate that drives some Pony researchers to drink, and others to party.

13. Or he and a bunch of friends went out to seek gold; accounts vary.

14. Kenneth L. Cannon II, "Mountain Common Law: The Extralegal Punishment of Seducers in Early Utah," *Utah Historical Quarterly* 51, no. 4 (Fall 1983). (Also at http://digitallibrary.utah.gov/awweb/main.jsp?flag=browse&smd=1&awdid=1 and excerpted here: mormonpolygamydocuments.org/wp-content/uploads/2014/12/JS0257.doc)

15. Howard R. Egan, *Pioneering The West, 1846 to 1878* (Richmond, UT: Howard R. Egan Estate, 1917), p. 42. I'm not quite quoting.

16. Egan, *Pioneering the West*, p. 218. This incident is often reported as having happened to a Pony Express rider, but though the original text is a bit confusing, it appears to have occurred in 1862 on a smaller line.

17. Egan, *Pioneering the West*, p. 219.

18. The story is in Egan, *Pioneering the West*, p. 281. The timing of the mails runs is somewhat suspicious, since at most there were two runs per week. But it's a good story.

19. Egan, *Pioneering the West*, p. 281.

20. Egan, *Pioneering the West*, p. 226. The incident occurred before there was a station at Egan Canyon

21. Wilson, *The White Indian Boy*, p. 137.

22. Census data retrieved through Ancestry.com. Don McConnell first used the census data in a report for the www.xphomestation.com website page on riders. The discrepancies, and the fact that Wilson did not mention the soldiers, raises questions about how accurate his account is.

The census was taken around the time of the Pyramid Lake Indian War, at which point Wilson may have been farther west, according to the rough timeline he sets out in the book. "Elijah Wilson" does not appear to be listed anywhere in the Utah Territory; on the other hand, the last name is extremely common, and it's possible that he appears under a different first name. And then there's the question of how likely someone who calls himself the White Indian is going to give his name to a government official. Ultimately, like a lot of the stories about Pony riders, Wilson's account has to be either taken partly on faith or rejected on the same basis.

Regarding the number of riders at the station: it's either the work party or employees sheltering because of the war.

23. Wilson, *The White Indian Boy*, p. 141.

24. Raymond and Mary Settle date this incident in June, during the Paiute War. It's not dated in Wilson's book.

25. Wilson said "Willow Creek" rather than Wilson Springs. Some believe that there was a station on Six Mile Creek which was called Willow Creek and cite Wilson's text as evidence. It seems more likely that he used the wrong or another name for Willow Springs. On the other hand, it's possible he's referring to a station abandoned because of Indian trouble.

26. Burton, *City of the Saints*, p. 147.

27. Wilson, *White Indian Boy*, p. 144. The rest of the account is paraphrased from his version.

28. Wilson, *White Indian Boy*, p. 145.

CHAPTER 11: SAND AND SILVER

1. Twain, *Roughing It*, chapter 20.

2. William Prows is sometimes credited with this discovery. For a thorough debunking of that claim, see Will Bagley's commentary on Abner Blackburn's diary in *Frontiersman*, edited by Will Bagley, pp. 132–136.

3. See the account of Peter Orr, John's brother, and Bagley's gloss in *Frontiersman*, p. 160.

4. The figures come from Grant H. Smith, *The History of the Comstock Lode 1850–1920* (Reno: University of Nevada Press, 1974), p. 9.

5. The number is from Smith, *History of the Comstock Lode*, table, p. 292. Other histories put the number over $300 million. Calculating the "actual" value is tricky because of devaluation of silver during the nineteenth century.

6. Simpson's letter is quoted in Chapman, *The Pony Express*, pp. 129–130.

7. Burton, *City of the Saints*, p. 470.

8. Burton, *City of the Saints*, p. 471.

9. Twain, *Roughing It*, chapter XXL.

10. At least by later standards, there was not a lot of local news in country papers during the first half of the nineteenth century. If you wanted gossip, it was much easier to go down to the general store, the post office, or the saloon and get your fill.

11. The story is variously known as "The Notorious Jumping Frog of Calaveras County" and "The Celebrated Jumping Frog of Calaveras County."

12. Klein, *President Buchanan*, p. 355.

13. *Sacramento Daily Union*, November 15, 1860, California Digital Newspaper Collection.

14. Presumably there were others for other newspapers, along with some "regular" mail picked up along the way.

15. Buckland ran a toll bridge as well as a small inn at his home; it cost $2 to take a wagon across, twenty-five cents if you were walking. Buckland later bought some of the buildings from the fort, including (possibly) the building used for the Pony station.

16. The fort never seems to have held close to its capacity. Its defenses were never tested—the army abandoned it in 1869, selling off the buildings for $750.

17. Sources generally call the ride 190 miles long, but unless Haslam got lost . . .

CHAPTER 12: INDIAN WARS

1. Burton, *City of the Saints*, p. 481.

2. Burton, *City of the Saints*, p. 481.

3. Egan, *Sand in a Whirlwind*, p. 92. Egan quotes Winnemucca, who said this in *Life Among the Paiutes, Wrongs and Their Claims*. Without knowing the condition of the gun or the horse, it's impossible to judge the actual value of the deal. The number five was a number of special significance to the Paiute, and sometimes is used in tales for its symbolic value, so it's very possible that the details here are not specific . . . a.k.a. wrong.

4. This was reported in the *Sacramento Union*, May 9, 1860. The two names given—J. B. Bartoles and J. H. Smith—do not appear on any list of riders.

5. Technically, the service was completely suspended for only one week, since it still accepted mail in St. Jo's; only the westward run from June 24 was officially canceled. Mail postmarked May 20 in St. Jo took thirty-six days to reach San Francisco, arriving June 25, as did the next three runs. Eastbound, there was no service between June 9 and July 7. There were many shorter disruptions in the weeks that followed, but the service still ran.

6. Raymond and Mary Settle, *The Story of the Pony Express*, p. 127.

7. Majors, *Seventy Years*, pp. 190–191. Also quoted in Settle and Settle, *Saddles and Spurs*, pp. 99–100.

8. Majors, *Seventy Years*, p. 192.

9. The Settles date this in September (*Story of the Pony Express*, p. 130), but it is undated in Wilson's own account. The delays in service that it implies are no help in dating it, as there were enough delays and gaps in the record to cover any period from May to the fall.

10. It's not clear where Cedar Wells station was, but that's the name Wilson gives. The story is collected in *The White Indian Boy*, p. 147, and later in a com-

pilation published by the *Deseret News* called *The Children's Friend*, vol. 17, see pp. 282–283.

11. Eight Mile Station was also called Prairie Gate. It has never been definitively located, though the best theories are that it was on Gosiute Indian land. This is one of the many Pony Express stories that is highly suspect, though the majority of historians seem to accept it.

12. Some historians contend that Bolivar was not a Mormon, but the family histories indicate he was. Burton was correct in saying that there were far fewer Mormons in the district Bolivar oversaw than in, say, Salt Lake. See: https://family search.org/photos/artifacts/12726508; and Ancestry.com. Utah, Our Pioneer Heritage [database online]. Provo, UT, USA: Ancestry.com Operations Inc, 1998.

    Original data: International Society, Daughters of Utah Pioneers. *Our Pioneer Heritage* (Salt Lake City: Infobases, 1996). Published under license. All rights reserved.

13. I've changed the logistics of the way the story is often told so that it makes sense.

14. Or "Chessy," as the name is often given elsewhere. The station is identified in Wilson's book as Thousand Wells on the Overland Trail, though which trail—Central, which was the Pony's trail, or Southern, isn't specified. Thousand Wells is not a known Pony Express stop. It's not clear how this murder, which is pretty well documented, ended up associated with the Pony Express. Possibly the station Cherry operated was actually Smith's Creek and called Thousand Wells by a witness at the trial or Cherry himself.

15. The count is from the database at DeathPenaltyUSA.org. Carr is inexplicably listed as having been hanged in 1862, and I've added him to the count here.

16. An *Outline of Capital Punishment in Nevada*, Nevada State Library, Archives and Public Records. While hanging was the general punishment for murder— by legal courts as well as "informal" or vigilante ones—it wasn't the only one: banishment was just as common a punishment, especially along the trail among emigrants—though it could be argued that in many cases that amounted to an even crueler death sentence.

CHAPTER 13: STORMS

1.   *Sacramento Daily*, October 3, 1860.

2.   The site later became a hotel, served temporarily as the legislature's meeting place, and then became a prison—undoubtedly there's a connection there, or at least a progression.

3.   Information on the lawsuit comes from *History of Nevada*, chapter 5, (1881), accessible here: http://files.usgwarchives.net/nv/statewide/history/1881/histo ryo/chapterv8gms.txt. Most sources believe that Reese originally built Mormon

Station; he had filed a land claim earlier that covers the ground. But Chorpenning claimed he built the station. Chorpenning, incidentally, sued the government for compensation on those contracts because of losses to Indians—possibly the reason he was in financial straits to begin with—and eventually was rewarded a total of $443,000 in damages by Congress. But he never received the money. His claims declared that he had lost sixteen men and three hundred horses and mules, along with other property. See "The Case of George Chorpenning vs. The United States."

4. Descriptions of this run are hopelessly tangled, but the conditions themselves are entirely believable. Unfortunately, not much is known about Upson, who must have been among the most resolute riders.

5. Egan, *Pioneering the West*, p. 248.

6. Egan, *Pioneering the West*, p. 248.

7. This story is in Egan, *Pioneering the West*, p. 248. It calls Floyd Cedar Fort and then equates it with Fort Crittenden, which may lead some to think of the later Arizona fort. But the description matches the Utah area.

8. This run is often said to have taken seven days and seventeen hours; it's also often said that it covered the entire distance. Arthur Chapman, however, calculated it from the newspaper reports, and I think his calculations can't be argued with. See Chapman, *Pony Express*, pp. 222–223.

9. Chapman, *Pony Express*, p, 221.

10. Quoted in Klein, *President James Buchanan*, p. 359. Buchanan's manuscript dates the president's review of the questions as November 17, 1860.

11. The University of Edinburgh has one of the oldest and most prestigious medical colleges in the world, and presumably that was where the degree was from. However, there was an Edenborough Medical College in North Carolina open around the same time; its history is far shorter and very sketchy. See William S. Powell's article on North Carolina's medical schools, collected here: https://www.ncpedia.org/medical-schools.

12. There are a host of other stories connected with the area. See Linda J. Bottjer's *Gold Rush Ghosts of Placerville* (Charleston: Haunted America, 2014). Better yet, take one of the tours the author offers in Placerville; for more information: https://www.facebook.com/ghosttoursofplacerville.

13. At this point, Placerville was only a stop to change horses. The following July it became the western terminus.

CHAPTER 14: A PLACE CALLED TOMORROW

1. Alice Bates, "The History of the Telegraph in California." *Annual Publication of the Historical Society of Southern California 9*, no. 3 (1914): 181–187. Other sources date the first telegraph line in San Francisco to 1849.

2. It's not clear how often the train took the mail. While state historical markers declare that Folsom was the Pony's end point from July 1860 onward, there's ample evidence that at least some of the trips, including this one, were done by horse. One possibility is that a horse might have been used only for special occasions such as this one, or if the mail arrived at the station when the train wasn't available, such as the middle of the night. The train in question was owned by the Sacramento Valley Railroad, which has its own important place in history, perhaps most notably as a sort of inspiration for the transcontinental railroad. The line had started regular runs between Sacramento and Folosm in 1856.

3. The letter is collected at http://www.xphomestation.com/frm-riders.html. I've cleaned up some of the spelling and punctuation.

4. Cindy Baker, "Sacramento's Sophisticated Ladies: Prostitution in 1860," Sacramento Historical Society, *Golden Notes*, 41, no. 2 (Summer 1995). Available online at http://www.sachistoricalsociety.org/wp-content/uploads/2013/09/GN_V41No2_Summer1995_Prostitution_red.pdf.

5. Quoted in Hill, *The Pony Express Trail: Yesterday and Today*, pp. 259–260.

6. Holzer, *Lincoln President-Elect*, p. 85. "Wise-looking statesman" is Holzer's own phrase.

CHAPTER 15: REMAINS OF THE DAY

1. *St. Louis Daily Missouri Republican*, November 7–15, 1856. Editions retrieved through the State Historical Society of Missouri website.

2. "The Indian Bonds Defence of W.H. Russell," *New York Times*, April 2, 1861, p. 4.

3. The entire statement is printed as "Apendix D" in Settle, *War Drums and Wagon Wheels*, pp. 231–241.

4. Adams had an extensive network along the East Coast as well. For more on the relationship between American Express and Adams Express, see Peter Z. Grossman, *American Express: The People Who Built the Great Financial Empire* (New York: Crown, 1987).

5. Overland subsequently arranged with the Pioneer Stage Company (another company loosely associated with Wells Fargo) to handle a good portion of the line, running from Carson City through Virginia City and on to Placerville.

6. Smith lays out his argument in the pamphlet *Pony Express versus Wells Fargo Express*, published by Pony Express History and Art Gallery, San Rafael, California, 1966. The pamphlet quotes from the Settles, *The Story of the Pony Express*; they use language a notch less strident to make a similar case. W. Turrentine Jackson dismantles the argument in "A New Look at Wells Fargo, Stage-Coaches and the Pony Express," *California Historical Society Quarterly* 45, no. 4 (1966): 291–

324, http://www.jstor.org/stable/25154156, though a look at the contracts and correspondence is convincing on their face. No one, including Waddell Smith, has suggested that Wells Fargo actively sought to hurt the company.

7. Lincoln's address is available in many places, including the Presidency Project website: http://www.presidency.ucsb.edu/ws/index.php?pid=25818.

8. Quoted by Waddell F. Smith in *The Story of the Pony Express* (San Rafael, CA: Pony Express History and Art Gallery, 1964), p. 90.

9. Smith, *The Story of the Pony Express*, p. 91. The section is actually a reprint of an article by Raymond Settle published in the *Utah Historical Quarterly*, April 1959.The quote appears in many other sources.

10. Jeremy Agnew, *The Creation of the Cowboy Hero* (Jefferson, NC: McFarland & Company, 2015), pp. 47–38.

11. Census records were retrieved through FamilySearch.org: https://family search.org/ark:/61903/3:1:33S7–9BS8–9PSV?i=49&wc=QZ2C-WR%3A158943 6327%2C1589436499%2C1589436548%3Fcc%3D1473181&cc=1473181.

12. Based on the census records and the newspaper reports, I think the rough outlines of Pony Bob's story are true: that he did ride for the Pony at that time, and he was one of the people who brought news of the attacks. But it's clear that many of the other details he tells of his time in the Pony (which I haven't put in the book) are mistaken. Now, whether that was his fault or the fault of others recording it, innocent confusion, or out-and-out lies . . .

13. Excerpted from a National Parks brochure, which can be found online at https://www.nps.gov/parkhistory/online_books/blm/ut/2/sec2e.htm. The essay was originally published in *The Pony Express Stations of Utah in Historical Perspective*, by Richard E. Fike and John W. Headley, 1979, Bureau of Land Management, Utah, Cultural Resources Series, Monograph 2. Unlike Pony Bob's accounts, I think Uncle Nick was pretty much full of it most of the time when talking about the Pony Express. But mine is a minority view.

14. Charlie Miller and Gladys Shaw Erskine, *Broncho Charlie: A Saga of the Saddle* (London: G. G. Harrap, 1935), p. 48.

15. The story is from Pinney, "Charles Becker," pp. 212–256. See http://www.jstor.org/stable/20612929. Like most Pony stories, the details are confusing; while the outline of the tale may be true, some of the particulars, like the name of the keeper—Smith—are probably confused or misremembered.

SUNDRY AND OTHER: APPENDIX

1. Rock House Station is listed by Joseph DiCerto in *The Saga of the Pony Express*, p. 206. However, it does not seem to be listed elsewhere.

2. Virginia City is listed by DiCerto in *Saga of the Pony Express*, p. 206. It does not seem to be listed elsewhere.

SELECT BIBLIOGRAPHY

BOOKS

Bagley, Will. *Across the Plains, Mountains, and Deserts: A Bibliography of the Oregon-California Trail.* Salt Lake City: Prairie Dog Press. 2014, https://www.nps.gov/oreg/learn/historyculture/upload/NPS-HRS-Biblio-Master-February2014_WillBagley.pdf.

Beck, Warren A. and Ynez D. Haase. *Historical Atlas of the American West.* Norman: University of Oklahoma Press, 1989.

Biggs, Donald C. *The Pony Express: Creation of the Legend.* Privately printed in San Francisco, 1956.

Blackburn, Abner. *Frontiersman: Abner Blackburn's Narrative.* Edited by Will Bagley. Salt Lake City: University of Utah Press.

Bottjer, Linda J. *Gold Rush Ghosts of Placerville, Coloma & Georgetown (Haunted America).* Charleston: The History Press, 2014.

Bowman, Matthew. *The Mormon People: The Making of an American Faith.* New York: Random House, 2012.

Bradley, Glenn D. *The Story of the Pony Express: An Account of the Most Remarkable Mail Service Ever in Existence, and Its Place in History.* Chicago: A.C. McClurg & Co. 1913.

Brands, H. W. *The Age of Gold: The California Gold Rush and the New American Dream.* New York: Doubleday, 2002.

Buntline, Ned. *Buffalo Bill and His Adventures in the West.* J.S. Ogilvie and Company, 1886.

Bushman, Claudia Lauper and Richard Lyman Bushman. *Building the Kingdom: A History of Mormons in America.* New York: Oxford University Press, 1999, 2001.

Bushman, Richard Lyman. *Mormonism: A Very Short Introduction.* New York: Oxford University Press, 2008.

Burton, Richard F. *The City of the Saints.* New York: Alfred A. Knopf, 1963.

Carter, Robert A. *Buffalo Bill Cody: The Man Behind the Legend.* New York: John Wiley & Sons, 2000.

Chapman, Arthur. *The Pony Express.* New York: G.P. Putnam's Sons, 1932.

Conard, Howard L., editor, *The Encyclopedia of the History of Missouri.* New York: Southern History Company, 1901.

Cooper, Edward S. *Traitors: The Secession Period, November 1860–July 1861.* Rosemont Publishing and Printing Corporation, 2008.

Corbett, Christopher. *Orphans Preferred: The Twisted Truth and Lasting Legend of the Pony Express*. New York: Broadway Books, 2003.

D'Azevedo, Warren L. and William C. Sturtevant. *Handbook of North American Indians, Volume 11: Great Basin*. U.S. Independent Agencies and Commissions, 1986.

Denton, Sally. *American Massacre: The Tragedy at Mountain Meadows, September 1857*. New York: Alfred A. Knopf, 2003.

DiCerto, Joseph J. *The Saga of the Pony Express*. Missoula: Mountain Press Publishing Company, 2002.

Dimsdale, Thomas. *The Vigilantes of Montana, 1920*. (Arcadia Ebooks edition, 2016).

Duncan, R. S. *A History of the Baptists in Missouri*. St. Louis: Scammel, 1882.

Eagan, Ferol. *Sand in a Whirlwind: The Paiute Indian War of 1860*. Reprint. Reno: University of Nevada Press, 1985.

Egan, Howard Ransom. *Pioneering the West*. Skelton Publishing Company, 1917.

Fradkin, Philip L. *Stagecoach: Wells Fargo and the American West*. New York: Simon & Schuster, 2002.

Frajola, Richard C., George J. Kramer, and Steven C. Walske. *The Pony Express: A Postal History*. New York: The Philatelic Foundation, 2005.

Givens, Terryl L. *The Viper on the Hearth: Mormons, Myths and the Construction of the Heresy*. New York: Oxford University Press, 1997, 2013.

Godfrey, Anthony Ph.D. *Historic Resource Study, Pony Express National Historic Trail*. Washington: U.S. Dept. of the Interior, 1994.

Grossman, Peter Z. *American Express: The People Who Built the Great Financial Empire*. Beard Books, 1987.

Guthrie, C. W. *The Pony Express: An Illustrated History*. Guilford, CT: Globe Pequot Press, 2010.

Hafen, LeRoy Reuben. *The Overland Mail, 1849–1869: Promoter of Settlement, Precursor of Railroads*. Cleveland, A.H. Clark Company, 1929. Reprinted by University of Oklahoma Press, 2004.

Hamlin, Herb S., editor, et al. *The Pony Express (A Collection of Miscellaneous Stories, Memories, Etc., Originally Published as a Monthly Newsletter)*. Placerville, California: The Pony Express Museum.

Haven, Charles T. and Frank A. Belden. *A History of The Colt Revolver and the Other Arms Made by Colt's Patent Fire Arms Manufacturing Company from 1836 to 1940*. New York: Bonanza Books, 1978.

Hawgood, John A. *America's Western Frontiers: The Exploration and Settlement of the Trans-Mississippi West*. New York: Alfred A Knopf, 1967.

Hearty, Patrick and Hatch, Joseph. *The Pony Express in Utah*. Charleston, SC: Arcadia Publishing, 2015.

Hebard, Grace Raymond, and Brininstool, E. A. *Jim Bridger, Grand Old Man of the Rockies.* Arthur H. Clark Company, 1922.

Hill, William E. *The Pony Express Trail: Yesterday and Today.* Caldwell: Caxton Press, 2010.

Hinckle, Warren and Fredric Hobbs. *The Richest Place on Earth: The Story of Virginia City, Nevada, and the Heyday of the Comstock Lode.* Boston: Houghton Mifflin Company, 1978.

Holliday, J. S. *The World Rushed In: The California Gold Rush Experience.* New York: Simon and Schuster. 1981.

Holzer, Harold. *Lincoln President-Elect: Abraham Lincoln and the Great Secession Winter, 1860–1861.* New York: Simon & Schuster, 2008.

Hopkins, Sarah. *Winnemucca, Life Among the Piutes.* New York: G.P. Putnam's Sons, 1883.

Hosley, William. *Colt: The Making of an American Legend.* Amherst: University of Massachusetts Press, 1996.

Kenderdine, Thaddeus S. *California As I Saw It: First-Person Narratives of California's Early Years, 1849–1897.* Newtown, PA, Doylestown Publishing Company, 1898. (Digitized on American Memory, http://hdl.loc.gov/loc.gdc/calbk.164.)

Klein, Philip S. *President James Buchanan: A Biography.* Newton: American Political Biography Press, 1962.

Kohler, Carl. *A History of Costume.* Reprinted by Dover Publications, 1963.

Lekisch, Barbara. *Embracing Scenes about Lakes Tahoe & Donner: Painters, Illustrators & Sketch Artists.* Great West Books, 2003.

Lewin, Jacqueline and Marilyn Taylor. *On the Winds of Destiny: A Biographical Look at Pony Express Riders.* St. Joseph: St. Joseph Museums, 2002.

Logan, Sheridan A. *Old Saint Jo: Gateway to the West, 1799–1932.* John Sublett Logan Foundation, 1979.

Long, Clarence D. *Wages and Earnings in the United States, 1860–1890.* National Bureau of Economic Research. Princeton University Press, 1960, pp 69–93. (Digitized at www.nber.org/books/long60-1.)

Majors, Alexander. *Seventy Years on the Frontier: Memoirs of a Lifetime on the Frontier.* Reprinted by University of Nevada Press, 1991.

Mattes, Merrill J. *Fort Laramie Park History, 1834–1977.* Washington, DC: US Department of the Interior, 1980.

McCartney, Laton. *Across the Great Divide: Robert Stuart and the Discovery of the Oregon Trail.* New York: Free Press, 2003.

McCormick, John S. *Salt Lake City: The Gathering Place.* Woodland Hills, CA: Windsor Publications, 1980.

McMurtry, Larry. *The Colonel and Little Missie: Buffalo Bill, Annie Oakley, and the Beginnings of Stardom in America.* New York: Simon & Schuster, 2005.

McPherson, James M. *Battle Cry of Freedom: The Civil War Era*. New York: Oxford University Press, 1988.

Meeker, Ezra, and Driggs, Howard R. *Ox-Team Days on the Oregon Trail*. New York: World Book Company, 1927.

Miller, Rev. George. *Missouri's Memorable Decade, 1860–1870: An Historical Sketch*. Columbia: Press of E. W. Stephens, 1898. (Missouriana Digital Text Collection).

Moody, Ralph. *Riders of the Pony Express*. Boston: Houghton Mifflin, 1948. Reprint, Lincoln: University of Nebraska Press, 2004.

Mossman, Isaac Van Dorsey. *A Pony Expressman's Recollections*. Champoeg Press, 1955.

O'Connor, Richard. *Wild Bill Hickok*. New York: Konecky & Konecky, 1959.

Petersen, Jesse G. *A Route for the Overland Stage: James H. Simpson's 1859 Trail Across the Great Basin*. Logan: Utah State, 2008.

Rarick, Ethan. *Desperate Passage: The Donner Party's Perilous Journey West*. New York: Oxford University Press, 2008.

Richardson, Albert A. *The Secret Service, the Field, the Dungeon, and the Escape*. Hartford, CT: American Publishing Company, 1865 (Project Gutenberg, February 10, 2014).

Richards, Leonard L. *The California Gold Rush and the Coming of the Civil War*. New York: Alfred A. Knopf, 2007.

Roberts, Brian. *American Alchemy: The California Gold Rush and Middle-Class Culture*. Chapel Hill: University of North Carolina Press, 2000.

Root, Frank A., and Connelley, William Elsey. *The Overland Stage to California—Personal Reminiscences and Authentic History*. Topeka, KS: Crane & Company, 1901.

Rosa, Joseph G. *The Life and Adventures of James Butler Hickok*. Norman: University of Oklahoma Press, 1964.

———. *The West of Wild Bill Hickok*. Norman: University of Oklahoma Press, 1982.

———. *The Taming of the West: Age of the Gunfighter: Men and Weapons on the Frontier, 1840–1900*. New York: Salamander Books, Ltd, 1993.

———. *Wild Bill Hickok: The Man and His Myth*. Lawrence: University Press of Kansas, 1996.

Scott, Edward B. *The Saga of Lake Tahoe: A Complete Documentation of Lake Tahoe's Development Over the Last One Hundred Years*, vol. 1. Tahoe: Sierra-Tahoe Publishing Company, 1957.

Selcer, Richard F. *Civil War America, 1850 to 1875*. Infobase Publishing, 2014.

Serven, James E. *Colt Firearms, 1836–1960*. Santa Ana: Serven Books, 1954.

Settle, Raymond W. and Mary Lund Settle. *Empire on Wheels*. Stanford: Stanford University Press, 1949.

———. *Saddles and Spurs: The Pony Express Saga*. Lincoln: University of Nebraska Press, 1955.

———. *War Drums and Wagon Wheels: The Story of Russell, Majors and Waddell*. Lincoln: University of Nebraska Press, 1966.

Silverman, Kenneth. *Lightning Man: The Accursed Life of Samuel F.B. Morse*. New York: Random House.

Simpson, Capt. J. H.. *Report of explorations across the great basin of the territory of Utah for a direct wagon route from Camp Floyd to Genoa, in Carson Valley*. Washington, DC: Government Printing Office, 1859. (This is the same Simpson as the next entry.)

Simpson, Lt. Col. James H. *Change of Route West from Omaha, Nebraska Territory*. Washington, DC: Government Printing Office, 1865.

Smith, Joseph. *The Book of Mormon*. Project Guttenberg ebook, 2008.

Smith, Waddell F. *The Story of the Pony Express*. San Rafael: Pony Express and Art Gallery, 1960.

———. *Pony Express versus Wells Fargo Express, or Hoof Prints That Cannot Be Eroded by Time*. San Rafael: Pony Express and Art Gallery. 1966.

Snodgrass, Mary Ellen. *The Civil War Era and Reconstruction: An Encyclopedia of Social, Political, Cultural and Economic History*. Routledge, 2011 (e-book 2015).

Stampp, Kenneth M. *America in 1857: A Nation on the Brink*. New York and Oxford: Oxford University Press, 1990.

Stevens, Walter B. *Lincoln and Missouri*. Columbia: The State Historical Society of Missouri, 1916. (Missouriana Digital Text Collection)

Thompson, John. *America's Historic Trails*. National Geographic Society, 2001.

Twain, Mark. *Roughing It*. Hartford: The American Publishing Company, 1903.

Victor, Orville J. *Southern Rebellion and the War for the Union*. New York: James D. Torrey, 1862.

Visscher, William Lightfoot. *A Thrilling and Truthful History of the Pony Express; or, Blazing the Westward Way, and Other Sketches and Incidents of Those Stirring Times*. Chicago: Rand, McNally & Co., 1908.

Warren, Louis S. *Buffalo Bill's America: William Cody and the Wild West Shows*. New York, Alfred A. Knopf, 2005.

Whitfield, Steve. *Kansas Paper Money: An Illustrated History, 1854–1935*. McFarland, 2010.

Wilkerson, Lyn. *Slow Travels: California and Nevada*. Cado Publications: 2010.

Wilson, Elijah Nicholas and Charles A. Wilson. *"The White Indian Boy," and Its Sequel, "The Return of the White Indian."* Reprinted by University of Utah Press, 2005.

Wilson, Michael R. *Legal Executions in the Western Territories, 1847–1911*. Jefferson, NC: McFarland & Company, 2010.

Wilson, Robert Lawrence. *Colt: An American Legend*. Sesquicentennial Edition. New York: Abbeville Publishing Group, 1985.

Zanjani, Sally. *Sarah Winnemucca*. Lincoln: University of Nebraska Press, 2001.

(No author listed.) *History of Lafayette County, Mo.* St. Louis: Missouri Historical Company, 1881.

(No author listed.) *History of Nevada with Illustrations and Biographical Sketches of Its Prominent Men and Pioneers*. Oakland, CA: Thompson & West, 1881.

ARTICLES AND DOCUMENTS

Ahnert, Gerald T. "The Construction of the Butterfield Overland Mail Company Line in California." California Parks & Recreation: 2013. https://www.parks.ca.gov/pages/22491/files/construction_of_butterfield_overland_mail_company_stage_line_in_california_gerald_ahnert_coyright_2013.pdf

Applegate, Jesse. "A Day on the Oregon Trail." *Transactions of the Fourth Annual Re-union of the Oregon Pioneers Association*. Salem, Oregon, 1877, pp. 57–65. (Digitally reprinted under *Annals of American History*.)

Campilio, James John. "A History of the Sacramento Valley Railroad up to 1865." Unpublished thesis, University of Southern California, 1934.

Cockle, Richard, "A Whiskey Bottle Left on the Grave a Toast to the Past." *Seattle Times*, August 27, 2000.

Crews, Tom. "The Ride of Thomas Bedford." National Pony Express Association Website, riders section, www.xphomestation.com.

Department of the Interior, Bureau of Land Management (Nevada State Office). Northern Paiute and Western Shoshone Land Use in Northern Nevada: A Class I Ethnographic/Ethnohistoric Overview, by Ginny Bengston. SWCA Cultural Resources Report No. 02-551, Dec. 16, 2002.

Dunn, Arthur. "Comstock." *Sunset Magazine: The Pacific Monthly* 34 (Jan–June 1915), 1142–1150.

Fike, Richard E. and Headley, John W. "The Pony Express Stations of Utah in Historical Perspective." Washington, DC: Bureau of Land Management. 1979.

Gamble, James. "Wiring A Continent: The Making of the US Transcontinental Telegraph Line." *The Californian*. 1881. Digitized at http://www.telegraph-history.org/transcontinental-telegraph.

Ingram, B. Lynn. "California Megaflood: Lessons from a Forgotten Catastrophe." *Scientific American*, January 1, 2013.

Jackson, W. Turrentine. "A New Look at Wells Fargo, Stage-Coaches and the Pony Express." *California Historical Society Quarterly* 45, no. 4 (1966): 291–324. http://www.jstor.org/stable/25154156.

Lanman, Richard B., et al. "The Historical Range of Beaver in the Sierra Nevada: A Review of the Evidence." *California Fish and Game* 98, no.2 (2012): 65–80.

Long, Clarence D. "Wage Earnings in the United States, 1860–1890," *National Bureau of Economic Research* (1960) http://www.nber.org/chapters/c2500.pdf.

"Lucius Lodosky Hickok: Letter to his wife Pruella Rice Hickok." National Pony Express Association Website, Sacramento section. www.xphomestation.com.

Milgram, James W., M.D. "Pasteup Usage of Western Express Franks." *American Philatelist*, July 2013, pp. 632–644.

Morris, Isaac N. *Abstracted Indian Trust Bond Report* (Main report and supplemental report). Washington, DC: Congressional Printing Office, 1861.

Nevada State Library, "An Outline of Capital Punishment in Nevada." Nevada State Library, Archives and Public Records.

Ott, Jennifer Susan. "Clearing the Country: A history of the Hudson's Bay Company's fur desert policy." Theses, Dissertations, Professional Papers, ScholarWorks at University of Montana. Paper #1809. 1997. (Digitized at scholarworks.umt.edu/etd.)

Root, George A. and Russell K. Hickman. "Pike's Peak Express Companies, Part One: The Solomon and Republican Route." *Kansas Historical Quarterly* 13, no. 3 (August 1944): 163–195. (Digitized through Kansas State Historical Society, Kansas Collection.)

Smith, Grant H. "The History of the Comstock Lode, 1850–1920." *University of Nevada Bulletin* 37 no.3, July 1, 1943, Geology and Mining Series no.37. Mackay School of Mines, University of Nevada State Bureau of Mines, Revised 1966, 1974.

Stanley, Gerald. "Senator William Gwin: Moderate or Racist?" *California Historical Quarterly* 50, no. 3.

Steinacher, Terry L., and Rob Bazell. "Blue River Basin Archaeology." Nebraska State Historical Society. 1997.

"The Pony Express." *Hutching's California Magazine*, July 1860. (Digitized for Annals of American History at http://america.eb.com.)

Trow, J. F. *Trow's New York City Directory*, January 1, 1859. (Digitized on Google Play.)

Turrentine, Jackson W. "A New Look at Wells Fargo, Stage-Coaches and the Pony Express." *California Historical Quarterly* 45, no. 4 (1966): 291–324. (Digitized at http://www.jstor.org/stable/25154156.)

———."Wells Fargo: Symbol of the Wild West?" *The Western Historical Quarterly* 3, no. 2 (1972): 179–196.

Werner, Morris W. "Ghost Towns of Nemaha County." Pioneer Trails section, Kansas Heritage Group (www.kansasheritage.org).

———. "The Pony Express in Nemaha County, and Comparative Table of Distances." Pioneer Trails section, Kansas Heritage Group (www.kansasheritage.org).

U.S. Bureau of the Census, Census of Manufactures: 1905 Agricultural Implements. Bulletin 75, Washington, DC. 1907.

———. Population Schedules of the Eighth Census of the United States. Schedule 1—Free Inhabitants for Virginia City, in the County of Carson, Territory of Utah, 26, August 1860, p. 92.

U.S. Supreme Court. The Floyd Acceptances, Volume 74 U.S. (7 Wall.) 666 (1868). (Summary at Justia U.S. Supreme Court Center: https://supreme.justia.com.)

NEWSPAPER ARTICLES

Daily Alta California, "Fatal Fracas at Virginia City," vol. 12, no. 3917, Nov. 3 1860. (California Digital Newspaper Collection.)

Glascow (Missouri) *Weekly Times*, "President's Message" (President Buchanan's Address) vol. XXL, Thursday, December 13, 1860.

———. "Departure of California Pony Express: Interesting Particulars," vol. XXL, Thursday, April 12,1860.

Lawrence Republican, "Albert D. Richardson's Letters [to the Editor] on the Pike's Peak Gold Region," May 22 to August 25, 1860. (Digitalized on Kansas Collection: Kansas Historical Quarterlies.)

New York Times, "The Robbery of Indian Bonds: Report of the Special Congressional Committee," February 13, 1861.

Sacramento Daily Union, "By the St. Joseph, Placerville and Alta Telegraph Lines. Horrid Massacre by Indians at the Great Bend of the Carson," vol. 19, no. 2845, May 9, 1860.

———. "The Pony Express," vol. 19, no. 2853, May 18, 1860. (California Digital Newspaper Collection.)

———. "By the St. Joseph, Placerville and Alta Telegraph Lines. Arrival of Troops at Virginia City: Shooting Affair," vol. 19, no. 2873, June 11, 1860. (California Digital Newspaper Collection.)

———. "The Roads in Utah," vol. 20, no. 2970, October 3, 1860. (California Digital Newspaper Collection.)

———. "Seven Days Later From St. Louis. Arrival of the Pony Express, Dates to November 7th, inclusive! Lincoln Elected President!!," vol. 20, no. 3007, November 15, 1860. (California Digital Newspaper Collection.)

St. Joseph Daily Gazette, "Amusements: Oscar Wilde," April 19, 1882. (St. Joseph Memory Lane website.)

St. Joseph Morning Herald, "Death of Bean Hamilton," November 22, 1867. (Excerpted in the Riders section of wwwxphomestation.com.)

Wimtier, J. O. "Our Union," *Visalia Weekly Delta*, vol. 1, no. 49, May 26, 1860, p. 5. (California Digital Newspaper Collection.)

———. "The Carson Valley Disaster: Returns of the Killed, Wounded, Missing and Returned," vol. 1, no. 49, May 26, 1860. (California Digital Newspaper Collection.)

WEBSITES AND DIGITAL COLLECTIONS

California Digital Newspaper Collection. Digital Library Consulting, (California newspapers from 1846 to the present) cdnc.ucr.edu.

Joseph Smith Papers, http://www.josephsmithpapers.org.

Kansas History Web Sites, Kansas Heritage Group at www.kansasheritage.org.

Library of Congress: Chronicling America (collection of newspapers online) http://chroniclingamerica.loc.gov.

Missouriana Digital Text Collection, University of Missouri Digital Library. http://digital.library.umsystem.edu/

National Historic Trail, National Parks Service, Auto Tour Route Interpretive Guides (htttp://www.nps.gov). A state-by-state road guide to the highways and side roads that run along or near the original Oregon Trail and Pony Express Route.

The National Pony Express Association (NPEA). A historical organization dedicated to preserving the trail and history of the Pony Express (http://nationalponyexpress.org).

——— Pony Express Homestation website for the NPEA has biographies, letters, and other digitized historical documents (http://www.xphomestation.com).

Newspapers.com: Historical newspapers. Digitized collection of various historical newspapers. https://www.newspapers.com.

Old NYC, New York Public Library. http://www.oldnyc.org. Historical photos, engravings, and other illustrations of New York City streets, architecture, and notable places.

Oscar Wilde in America: A Selected Resource of Oscar Wilde's Visits to America. www.oscarwildeinamerica.org.

Pony Express National Museum online, St. Joseph, MO (digitized at http://ponyexpress.org).

St. Joseph Memory Lane. www.stjosephmemorylane.com.

Virginia Military Institute, Preston Library, Lexington, VA. "Ben Ficklin, Pony Express Pioneer." Digital collection under the VMI.edu website under archives, genealogy-biography-alumni/featured historical biographies.

The William F. Cody Archive. http://codyarchive.org.

SELECT ADDITIONAL WEBSITES AND MISCELLANEOUS RESOURCES

California State Library, Special Collections: Gold Rush
   http://www.library.ca.gov/goldrush/

Calaveras County History
   http://www.calaverashistory.org/

Civil War on the Western Border
   http://www.civilwaronthewesternborder.org/

Death Penalty USA
   http://deathpenaltyusa.org/usa1/date/1860.htm

Encyclopedia Virginia
   http://www.encyclopediavirginia.org/

Expedition Utah: Nevada Pony Express Stations
   http://www.expeditionutah.com/featured-trails/pony-express-trail/
   nevada-pony-express-stations/

Familysearch.org

Forgotten New York: Nassau Street
   http://forgotten-ny.com/2012/11/nassau-street-manhattan/

Forgotten Utah
   http://www.forgottennevada.org/sites/index.html

Ghosts of DC: View of Pennsylvania Avenue in 1860 (near Russell's office)
   http://ghostsofdc.org/2012/06/22/pennsylvania-avenue-1860/

Ghost Towns of Nemaha County (Kansas Heritage)
   http://www.kansasheritage.org/werner/gostnmco.html

Henry County Library, Clinton, MO
   http://henrycolib.org/

Historynet.com
   http://www.historynet.com

House Divided: The Civil War Research Engine at Dickinson College
http://hd.housedivided.dickinson.edu/

The House of Beadle and Adams and its Dime and Nickle Novels by Albert
Johannsen online
http://www.ulib.niu.edu/badndp/bibindex.html

Legends of America
http://www.legendsofamerica.com/

Livingston County Library: County History
http://www.livingstoncountylibrary.org/history_civilwar.htm

Missouri Census Data Center
http://mcdc.missouri.edu/

Missouri Division Sons of Confederate Veterans
http://www.missouridivision-scv.org/

Museum of the Mountain Man: Sublette County Historical Society
http://museumofthemountainman.com/

National Pony Express Association
http://nationalponyexpress.org/

News-Press & Gazette (newspaper covering northwest Missouri, including St.
Joseph)

Online Nevada Encyclopedia, http://www.onlinenevada.org/

True West Magazine
http://www.truewestmagazine.com/

The Pony Express in Nemaha County (Kansas Heritage)
http://www.kansasheritage.org/werner/ponyroad.html

Pony Express National Historic Trail: Historic Resource Study
https://www.nps.gov/parkhistory/online_books/poex/hrs/hrs.htm

Pony Express Territory Nevada
  http://ponyexpressnevada.com/

Pyramid Lake Paiute Tribe
  http://plpt.nsn.us/index.html

University of Missouri Digital Library
  http://digital.library.umsystem.edu/

Utah State University Libraries

Virtual Museum of the City of San Francisco
  http://www.sfmuseum.org/hist6/impact.html

Weston Missouri history page
  http://westonmo.com/?page=history-history

XP Pony Express Home Station
  http://www.xphomestation.com/

SELECT MUSEUMS

With grateful thanks to the many helpful directors, curators, staff, guides and other personnel

Buffalo Bill Ranch, State Historical Park, Nebraska
California Museum, Sacramento
Chimney Rock National Historic Site
Fort Bridger Historic Site
Fort Caspar Museum, Wyoming
Fort Churchill State Historic Park, Nevada
Fort Cody, Nebraska
Fort Collins Museum of Discovery
Fort Kearny State Historical Park, Nebraska
Fort Laramie National Park, Wyoming
Fort Sedgwick Historical Society Depot Museum, Julesburg, Colorado
Fort Sedgwick Museum & Archives, Julesburg, Colorado
Gothenburg Historical Museum, Nebraska
Gothenburg Pony Express Station, Nebraska

Hollenberg Pony Express Station State Historic Park
Lincoln County Historical Museum, North Platte, Nebraska
Marysville Pony Express Home Station #1, Marysville, Kansas
Nevada State Library & Archives, Carson City
Nevada State Museum, Carson City
New York Public Library, Stephen A. Schwarzman Building, Manuscripts
and Archives Division, NYC
Old Sacramento, Sacramento, CA
Patee House Museum, St. Joseph, Missouri
Pony Express National Museum, St. Joseph, Missouri
Rock Creek Station, State Historical Park & Recreation Area, Nebraska
Sacramento History Museum, Sacramento
This Is the Place Heritage Park, Salt Lake City
Wells Fargo History Museum, Sacramento
White Pine Public Museum, Ely, Nevada

Technically not a museum or a place per se, the National Historic Trails Auto Route Tour series provided an excellent guide to landmarks and present-day roads that are on or near the original trail.

INDEX

ABOUT THE AUTHOR

JIM DEFELICE is the coauthor of the #1 *New York Times* bestseller *American Sniper,* the source for Clint Eastwood's Academy Award–winning film; and the *New York Times* bestsellers *American Wife* and *Code Name: Johnny Walker.* DeFelice is the author of *Omar Bradley: General at War,* the first in-depth critical biography of America's last five-star general. He also writes acclaimed military thrillers.

www.jimdefelice.com

ALSO BY JIM DeFELICE

AMERICAN SNIPER
THE AUTOBIOGRAPHY OF THE MOST LETHAL SNIPER IN U.S. MILITARY HISTORY

"Chris Kyle tells his story with the same courage and grit he displayed in life and on the battlefield. *American Sniper* is a compelling read." —Clint Eastwood

The #1 *New York Times* bestselling memoir of U.S. Navy Seal Chris Kyle, and the source for Clint Eastwood's blockbuster movie which was nominated for six Academy Awards, including Best Picture. Gripping and unforgettable, Kyle's masterful account of his extraordinary battlefield experiences ranks as one of the great war memoirs of all time.

AMERICAN WIFE
A MEMOIR OF LOVE, WAR, FAITH, AND RENEWAL

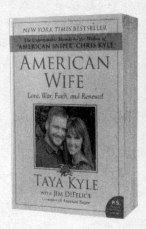

The widow of "American Sniper" Chris Kyle shares their private story: an unforgettable testament to the power of love and faith in the face of war and unimaginable loss—and a moving tribute to a man whose true heroism ran even deeper than the legend. *American Wife* is one of the most remarkable memoirs of the year—a universal chronicle of love and heartbreak, service and sacrifice, faith and purpose that will inspire every reader.

AMERICAN SPIRIT
PROFILES IN RESILIENCE, COURAGE, AND FAITH

Sometimes life leads us through painful and lonely territory. But what happens when you see challenge as an opportunity to discover your purpose—and change the world? Join Taya Kyle and thirty five remarkable Americans on their extraordinary journeys from despair to lives of passion and service. *American Spirit* profiles more than 30 individuals, young and old, rich and not-so-rich, famous and unknown, who have overcome hardship and done extraordinary things for their communities and for the nation at large.